Catering Management

Catering Management

SECOND EDITION

NANCY LOMAN SCANLON

John Wiley & Sons, Inc.

New York • Chichester • Weinheim • Brisbane • Singapore • Toronto

Library of Congress Cataloging-in-Publication Data:

Scanlon, Nancy Loman.
    Catering Management / Nancy Loman Scanlon.—2nd ed.
        p. cm.
    Rev. ed. of: Catering menu management, c1992.
    Includes bibliographical references.
    ISBN 0-471-33327-1 (cloth : alk. paper)
    1. Caterers and catering—Management.   I. Scanlon, Nancy Loman. Catering menu
management. II. Title.
TX921 .S34 2000
642'.4—dc21

                                                00-035201

Printed in the United States of America.

10 9 8 7 6 5 4 3 2 1

Dedication

This edition of Catering Management is dedicated to the future hospitality leaders representative of the "generation 2000" throughout the world. The dynamic spirit, excitement, and energy of this international group will form the future of the hospitality industry as it continues to grow and develop as a major global economic presence. Welcome, all of you, to the world of hospitality and the exciting careers and opportunities that await you.

Contents

Preface

Catering businesses have become the fastest growing segment of the food-service industry internationally. Changing population demographics and lifestyles have been a primary force behind this growth. Two-income families, extended workweeks, and the size of the senior population worldwide are a few of the major influences on this growth trend. The result is an increased demand for professional food preparation and service to both small and large group gatherings in a wide variety of formats and settings, ranging from small delicatessen and specialty take-out food stores to volume catering for thousands of people.

Catering services are incorporated into hotels, restaurants, private clubs, senior living centers, cruise ships, conference and convention centers, large and small businesses, and a wide range of facilities and settings. Independent catering companies provide both on- and off-premise catering services, transporting and servicing group parties in settings as varied as tugboats to aircraft carriers and as traditional as garden weddings. Massive tents now provide temporary and permanent facilities for covered dining and entertainment. "Special Events" have become a significant area of the catering industry requiring special skills in design. Theme parties have evolved into "entertainment happenings," involving guests in activities and interactive venues.

Catering Management has been developed in response to the need by both foodservice professionals and educators for management information that is specifically directed toward catering-related businesses. The variety of settings in which catering services can be offered creates a wide range of opportunities for foodservice businesses to take advantage of this high-growth segment.

In this second edition of *Catering Management,* business development information provides guidelines both for those seeking to establish a new catering operation and for those planning to incorporate catering into an existing foodservice business. Information on market and competition analysis, feasibility studies, and customer profile analysis can enable both new and seasoned professionals to evaluate the future prospects for a catering operation.

Catering business management includes human resources issues such as the hiring and training of both service and food production staff. Equipment management for catering operations details specific information regarding function setups and off-premise equipment specifications.

Catering menu management requires an understanding of menu development and menu pricing. Accurate pricing concepts that reflect customer needs and perceived values for catering menus are necessary for ongoing business development. Catering design and the presentation of menus, special function packages, and conference and convention menu programs contribute to the success of catering businesses. Catering menus should be designed as marketing oriented presentations.

Well-managed beverage programs, both nonalcoholic and alcoholic, can be highly profitable and contribute significantly to the success of a catering business. Customer relations is an important consideration for food-service businesses offering alcoholic beverage service. Both servers and managers must have a thorough understanding of current laws and regulations concerning alcohol service.

The ongoing success of a catering business is dependent on the establishment and continued practice of food and beverage operational controls. Controls are put into place to guarantee that established standards of quality, service, and presentation are met on a daily basis. Cost controls monitor the financial health of the business, providing checkpoints and reports by which management can evaluate operations on a daily and weekly basis. Computer software programs have a significant impact on the successful operations of a catering business. From space availability, to sales contracts, to operating and financial reports, computer generated information can both simplify and maximize these often hard to manage areas of catering businesses.

Marketing is an important aspect of every catering operation. As customer demands increase for catering related services, corresponding marketing efforts will need to be developed. The Internet and company websites provide new and exciting marketing possibilities. The ability of caterers to adapt by developing an extensive product line and a broad range of services will determine how well the changing needs of the general public can be maximized as catering business opportunities.

Nancy Loman Scanlon

Acknowledgments

It would have been impossible to produce this edition of *Catering Management* without the help and cooperation of the managers and catering directors of the many hotels, restaurants and food service businesses whose materials are included here. The rich variety of illustrations that I am privileged to be able to share with you, the reader, is due solely to the generosity of these individuals.

Works such as *Catering Management* take more than a single author to create. To George Conrade at the University of Delaware and Adelaide Friedli at the Swiss School of Hotel and Tourism Management, Chur, Switzerland, my deepest appreciation for your support of this project and help in bringing it together. My colleagues Dr. Lalia Rach, Shar Prohaska, Steven Lambert and Dr. Lori McQueen at New York University's Center for Hospitality, Tourism and Travel Administration, also deserve applause and thanks for their patience and assistance in pulling together the final stages of this manuscript.

Historical Banqueting

CHAPTER ONE

DINNER

Almaden *Pinot Blanc*	*Vol-au-Vent Maryland*
Château *Haut-Brion* *1953*	*Gigot d'Agneau aux flageolets* *Tomates grillé* *Épinards à la crème*
	Mousse aux Concombres
Cuvée Dom *Pérignon Brut* *1952*	*Bombe Glace Caribienne*

The White House
Tuesday, November 7, 1961

The catering profession as we know it in the twenty-first century has a long and intriguing history, the beginnings of which are recorded in the ancient civilizations. The Egyptian nobility sought to supply themselves for the next world by filling their tombs with foodstuffs and cookware; simultaneously they covered the walls with murals recording food preparation styles and table settings. From the records and art of the Greeks and Romans come depictions of banqueting scenes filled with food presentations, table customs, and decorative arts, along with recipes detailing a range of foodstuffs that is startling in its variety.

Written records from the ancient Greek and Roman periods focused primarily on the types of foods eaten rather than on records of the menus for entire meals. There does exist, however, a collection of recipes dating from approximately 42 B.C. to 37 A.D. (Apicius, *Cookery and Dining in Ancient Rome*, 1977). Concentrating on the dining habits of ancient Rome, this collection of recipes includes such familiar dishes as Sole in White Wine and Asparagus, as well as a number of now unknown items such as Sea-Scorpion with Turnips and Dasheens (a root vegetable). The origins of popular twentieth-century food items are found in such recipes as Baian Seafood Stew, in which minced poached oysters, mussels, scallops, and sea nettles are combined with toasted nuts, rue, celery, pepper, coriander, cumin, raisins, wine, broth, reduced wine, and oil. This seafood stew is similar to the basic recipe for bouillabaisse, a staple of the modern cuisine of southern France.

Greek banqueting featured the hors d'oeuvre trolley, on which were served a number of dishes featuring small portions of different food items. Garlic (boiled and roasted), sea urchins, cockles, sturgeon, and sweet wine sop were among the dishes offered. A fifth-century Roman feast elaborated on this concept, beginning:

> *With a drink of heated wine with honey, to be followed by fresh eggs, quarters of beef, mutton, and pork, all highly seasoned with pepper, pickles, caraway, and poppy seeds, saffron, aromatic balsam, honey and salt. There was also boar meat with a garniture of cooked apples, deer, roebuck, hare, and even urus, a wild buffalo.*
>
> *Everything was tasted, from grasshopper to ostrich, from dormouse to wild boar. The whole world was put to gastronomical use, by both soldiers and travellers. Guinea fowl and truffles were brought from Africa, and rabbits from Spain and pheasants from Greece and peacocks from Asia. The number of courses of the banquet gradually rose to twenty and more. A kind of herald announced the merits of such dishes as were worthy of special attention, and prolong the pleasures of the table. There must always be actors, singers, mimes, clowns and everything that could add to the pleasure of people who had gathered for the sole purpose of being amused.[1]*

The Banqueting Hall

The roots of the modern banqueting menu are found in the medieval period of European history. The outline of thirteenth-century meal service followed these instructions for the serving of dishes set down by Bartholomaeus Anglicus, Parisian professor of theology:

> *At feasts, first meat is prepared and arrayed, guests be called in together, forms and stools be set up in the hall, and tables, cloths and towels be ordained, disposed and made ready. Guests be set with the lord in the chief place of the board before the guests wash their hands. First knives, spoons and salt be set on the board, and then bread and drink and many divers messes. The guests are gladdened with lutes and harps. Now wine and messes of meat are brought forth and departed. At the last cometh fruit and spices, and when they have eaten, cloths and relief (trestles) are borne away, and guests wash and wipe their hands again. The grace is said, and guests thank the Lord. Then, for gladness and comfort, drink is brought yet again.[2]*

Food preparation methods included roasting and boiling or stewing.

Elaborate preparations and rituals accompanied banquets of the medieval period. At a feast in honor of Richard II of England in 1387, the head table was placed on a raised platform with long tables set parallel to the main table. The king was provided with an armchair while the other guests sat on backless benches or banquettes. The use of banquettes for seating was the origin of the term banquet.

> *It is two thirty, about half an hour before dinner is to be served. The marshal raises his rod in the sunlit hall and commands the ewerer to set three linen cloths on the high borde. Meanwhile, ushers and grooms arrange subordinate tables with cloths, napkins and surnapes. At each setting the ushers place a trencher, a mazer cup, and a spoon. . . .*
> *Suddenly clarions echo throughout the hall announcing the arrival of the king and honored guests.[3]*

Following the ceremony in which the king's trencher (a plate cut from stale bread) was prepared and drinking water tasted, the meal commenced.

> *As the Latin grace is chanted in unison, a procession of trusted servants emerges from the kitchen, each carrying a resplendent creation prepared by the chefs. Hidden under ornate silver covers are the multitude of delicacies that Richard will sample on this day.[4]*

The three-course menu outline, traditional to the medieval period, could contain as many as 25 dishes per course and became the standard for menu planning used well into the nineteenth century. In Figure 1-1, a three-course banquet menu served in Paris in 1393 details the mixture of sweets, sours, and spices traditionally found in each course.

First Course

MINIATURE PASTRIES FILLED WITH COD LIVER OR BEEF MARROW

CAMELINE MEAT BRERVET
(PIECES OF MEAT IN A THIN CINNAMON SAUCE)

BEEF MARROW FRITTERS

EELS, IN A THICK SPICY PUREE

LOACH, IN A COLD GREEN SAUCE FLAVORED WITH SPICES AND SAGE

LARGE CUTS OF ROAST OR BOILED MEAT

SALTWATER FISH

FRITTERS

ROAST BREAM AND DARIOLES

STURGEON

JELLIES

Second Course

"THE BEST TOAST THAT MAY BE HAD"

FRESHWATER FISH

BROTH WITH BACON

MEAT TILE
(SAUTÉED CHICKEN OR VEAL IN A SPICED SAUCE OF POUNDED CRAYFISH TAILS,
ALMONDS, AND TOASTED BREAD)

CAPON PASTRIES AND CRISPS

BLANK MANGER (BLANCMANGE)

Third Course

FRUMENTRY

VENISON

LAMPREYS WITH HOT SAUCE

SWEETS AND CONFECTIONS

SPICED WINE AND WAFERS

FIGURE 1-1   MEDIEVAL THREE-COURSE MENU, 1393.
(*Source:* Tannahill, *Food in History,* 1973, pp. 185–186.)

Additional documentation of the food customs of the Middle Ages is found in the decorative prayer books called Books of Hours, whose famed colored illustrations record the historical and seasonal events of the period.

The banqueting menu for the marriage of Henry VI of England to Joan of Navarre in 1403 featured a sotelte with each course. Soteltes were food sculptures and show pieces molded or sculpted into animals, figures, or representations of clowns or coats of arms. The elaborate *pièces montées* of the eighteenth and nineteenth centuries were later versions of the sotelte.

RENAISSANCE EUROPE

As part of a sixteenth-century banquet hosted by the Archbishop of Milan in 1529, oranges were the featured food ingredient appearing in the dishes of this three-course menu, seen in Figure 1-2.

IN 1529, THE ARCHBISHOP OF MILAN GAVE A SIXTEEN-COURSE DINNER THAT INCLUDED CAVIAR AND ORANGES FRIED WITH SUGAR AND CINNAMON, BRILL AND SARDINES WITH SLICES OF ORANGE AND LEMON, ONE THOUSAND OYSTERS WITH PEPPER AND ORANGES, LOBSTER SALAD WITH CITRONS, STURGEON IN ASPIC COVERED WITH ORANGE JUICE, FRIED SPARROWS WITH ORANGES, INDIVIDUAL SALADS CONTAINING CITRONS INTO WHICH THE COAT OF ARMS OF THE DINER HAD BEEN CARVED, ORANGE FRITTERS, A SOUFFLÉ FULL OF RAISINS AND PINE NUTS AND COVERED WITH SUGAR AND ORANGE JUICE, FIVE HUNDRED FRIED OYSTERS WITH LEMON SLICES, AND CANDIED PEELS OF CITRONS AND ORANGES.

FIGURE 1-2   DINNER FOR THE ARCHBISHOP OF MILAN, 1529.
(*Source:* McPhee, *Oranges,* New York: Farrar, Straus & Giroux, 1966, p. 69.)

Eighteenth-Century Banqueting

By 1727, the banquet menu had been abridged to two main course settings, with the third course reduced to fruits, nuts, and cheese served with appropriate ports. Menus in the American colonies were mirroring the English menus of the period in the mid-1700s, as seen in Figure 1-3.

First Course

SOUP

RAGOUT OF BREAST OF VEAL

ROAST VENISON

BOILED LEG OF LAMB AND CAULIFLOWER
SERVED WITH SMALLER DISHES OF STEWED EELS

STEWED CARP

A PUREE OF PIGEONS

A ROAST PIG

Second Course

FOUR PARTRIDGES AND TWO QUAILS

LOBSTERS

ALMOND CHEESECAKES AND CUSTARDS
WITH SMALLER DISHES OF FOUR POCKET AND LAMB TESTICLES

APRICOT FRITTERS

STURGEON

FRIED SOLE

GREEN PEAS

POTTED PIGEONS

FIGURE 1-3   COLONIAL AMERICAN MENU, 1727.
(*Source:* Tannahill, *Food in History,* 1973, p. 334.)

First Course

TUREEN OF GARBURE GRATINÉE

PALATE OF BEEF À LA SAINTE-MENEHOULD

KIDNEYS WITH FRIED ONION

TRIPE À LA POULETTE WITH LEMON JUICE

RUMP OF BEEF WITH ROOT VEGETABLES

OXTAIL WITH CHESTNUT PUREE

CIVET OF TONGUE À LA BOURGUIGNONNE

PAUPIETTES OF BEEF À L'ESTOUFFADE WITH PICKLED NASTURTIUM BUDS

FILET OF BEEF BRAISED WITH CELERY

BEEF RISSOLES WITH HAZELNUT PUREE

BEEF MARROW ON TOAST

Second Course

ROAST SIRLOIN

ENDIVE SALAD WITH OX TONGUE

BEEF À LA MODE WITH WHITE JELLY

COLD BEEF GATEAU WITH BLOOD AND FURANCON WINE

GLAZED TURNIPS

BEEF BONE MARROW PIE WITH BREAD CRUMBS AND CANDY SUGAR

BEEF STOCK ASPIC WITH LEMON RIND AND PRALINES

PUREE OF ARTICHOKE HEARTS WITH BEEF STOCK AND ALMOND MILK

BEEF JELLY WITH ALICANTE WINE AND VERDUN MIRABELLES

FIGURE 1-4   DINNER FOR THE DUCE DE RICHELIEU.
(*Source:* From *The New Larousse Gastronomique,* by Montagne.
Copyright © 1977 by the Hamlyn Publishing Group, Inc.
Reprinted by permission of Crown Publishers, a division
of Random House, Inc.)

The eighteenth-century menu underwent a metamorphosis to become the foundation of the twentieth-century banquet menu. The menu in Figure 1-4 details the items served in two courses by the Duce de Richelieu to members of the Hanovarian Court. The duke was limited to serving only meat-based menu items due to a shortage in his food supplies.

Nineteenth-Century Menu Revisions

By 1867 the menu format contained a sharp reduction in the number of menu items offered and a separation of items into distinct menu categories. The menu in Figure 1-5, for example, was served at the Café Anglais in Paris in 1867, and records the evolution of the classical banquet menu into the nine-course format.

Soups

IMPERATICE—FONTANGES

Intermediate Course

SOUFFLÉ À LA REINE

FILET OF SOLE À LA VENITIENNE

CALLOPS OF TUBOT AU GRATIN

SADDLE OF MUTTON WITH BRETON PUREE

Entrées

CHICKENS À LA PORTUGAISE

HOT QUAIL PÂTÉ

LOBSTER À LA PARISIENNE

CHAMPAGNE SORBETS

Rots

DUCKLING À LA ROUENNAISE

CANAPÉS OF BUNTING

Final Course

AUBERGINES À L'ESPAGNOLE

ASPARAGUS

CASSOULETS PRINCESSE

ICED BOMBE

FRUIT

Wines

MADÈRE RETOUR DES INDES 1846

SHERRY 1821

CHATEAU-D'YGUEM 1847

CHAMBERTIN 1847

CHATEAU-MARGAUX 1847

CHATEAU-LATOUR 1847

CHATEAU-LAFITE 1848

FIGURE 1-5 MENU SERVED AT THE CAFÉ ANGLAIS, PARIS, 1867.
(*Source:* From *The New Larousse Gastronomique,* by Montagne. Copyright ©
1977 by the Hamlyn Publishing Group, Inc. Reprinted by permission of
Crown Publishers, a division of Random House, Inc.)

The classical banquet menu in a nine-course format, the end result of this evolution, is seen in Figure 1-6.

An interpretation of this format appears in Figure 1-7, a menu developed by Toulouse-Lautrec for a banquet party in Paris in 1896. It is interesting to note that the third course is imported trout from Lake Michigan in the

FIRST COURSE:	SOUP
SECOND COURSE:	HOT HORS D'OEUVRES
THIRD COURSE:	COLD HORS D'OEUVRES
FOURTH COURSE:	INTERMEDIATE FISH COURSE
FIFTH COURSE:	INTERMEDIATE MEAT, POULTRY, OR GAME COURSE
SIXTH COURSE:	ENTRÉE
SEVENTH COURSE:	ROTIS (POULTRY, GAME, OR BEEF)
EIGHTH COURSE:	SALAD
NINTH COURSE:	ENTREMETS (DESSERT

FIGURE 1-6   NINETEENTH-CENTURY NINE-COURSE MENU FORMAT.

(*Source:* From *The New Larousse Gastronomique,* by Montagne.
Copyright © 1977 by the Hamlyn Publishing Group, Inc.
Reprinted by permission of Crown Publishers, a division of
Random House, Inc.)

United States. Some of the menu items are noted only by course, whereas others are specifically named. The seventh course, sweet, would have been a fruit tart. The eighth course, dessert, would have been fruit. Missing from this menu is the traditional cheese course that, when served, preceded the sweet course.

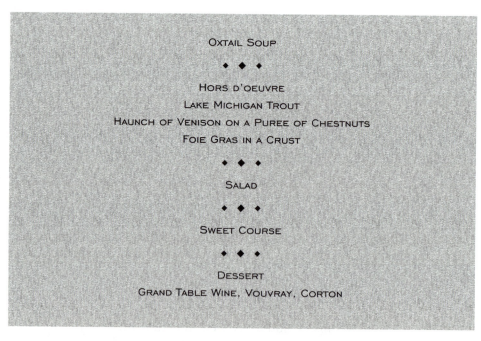

FIGURE 1-7   TOULOUSE-LAUTREC MENU, 1896.

(*Source:* Toulouse-Lautrec and Joyant, *The Art of Cuisine,*
1966, p. 159.)

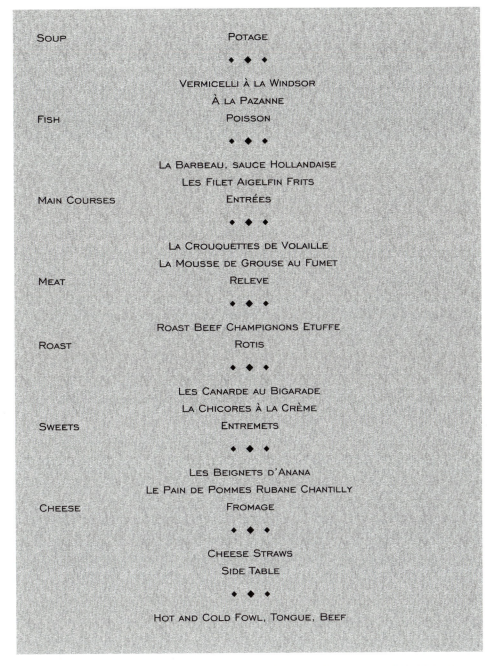

SOUP   POTAGE

◆ ◆ ◆

VERMICELLI À LA WINDSOR
À LA PAZANNE

FISH   POISSON

◆ ◆ ◆

LA BARBEAU, SAUCE HOLLANDAISE
LES FILET AIGELFIN FRITS

MAIN COURSES   ENTRÉES

◆ ◆ ◆

LA CROUQUETTES DE VOLAILLE
LA MOUSSE DE GROUSE AU FUMET

MEAT   RELEVE

◆ ◆ ◆

ROAST BEEF CHAMPIGNONS ETUFFE

ROAST   ROTIS

◆ ◆ ◆

LES CANARDE AU BIGARADE
LA CHICORES À LA CRÈME

SWEETS   ENTREMETS

◆ ◆ ◆

LES BEIGNETS D'ANANA
LE PAIN DE POMMES RUBANE CHANTILLY

CHEESE   FROMAGE

◆ ◆ ◆

CHEESE STRAWS
SIDE TABLE

◆ ◆ ◆

HOT AND COLD FOWL, TONGUE, BEEF

FIGURE 1-8   HER MAJESTY'S DINNER, MONDAY, DECEMBER 17, 1894.
(*Source:* Reprinted with permission of PBC International from Greenstein,
A la Carte: A Tour of Dining History, p. 123. © 1992.)

An additional version of the reduced course adaptation is found in the menu served to Queen Victoria at Windsor Castle, England, on December 17, 1894, seen in Figure 1-8.

European menu presentation continued to influence the United States. Figure 1-9 shows a banquet dinner given in 1866 for President Andrew Johnson at Delmonico's Restaurant in New York City.

WINES   POTAGES
AMONTILLADO   CONSOMMÉ CHATELAINE   BISQUE AUX QUENELLES

◆ ◆ ◆

HORS D'OEUVRES
TIMBALES DE GIBIER À VENITIENNE

◆ ◆ ◆

POISSONS
HECHHEIMERBERG   SAUMON LIVONIEN   PAUPIETTES DE KINGFISH

◆ ◆ ◆

RELEVES
CHAMPAGNE   SELLE D'AGNEAU AUX CONCOMBRES
FILET DE BOEUF À LA POCOHONTAS

◆ ◆ ◆

ENTRÉES
CHATEAUX-MARGAUX   SUPREME DE VOLAILLE DAUPHINE
BALLONTINES DE PIGEON LUCULLUS
FILETS DE CANETON TYROLIENNE
COTELETTES À LA MARECHALE
RIS DE VEAU MONTGOMERY
BOUINS À LA RICHELIEU

◆ ◆ ◆

SORBET À LA DUNDERBERGE

◆ ◆ ◆

ROTS
CLOS DE VOUGEOT   BEBCASSINES BARDEES
ORTOLANS FARCIS
ENTREMETS DE LEGUME
PETITS POIS À L'ANGLAISE   TOMATES FARCIES
AUBERGINES FRITES   ATICHAUTS BARIGOULE

◆ ◆ ◆

ENTREMETS SUCRES
TOKAI IMPERIAL   PECHES À LA NEW YORK MILLE-FEUILLES POMPADOUR
ABRICOTS SICILIENS   GATEAU SOLEIL
MACEDOINE DE FRUITS   MOSCOVITES AUX ORANGES
BAVAROIS AUX FRAISES GELÉE CALIFORNIENNE
CRÈME AUX AMANDES   MERINGUES CHANTILLY
BEAUSEJOUR AU MALAGA   BISCUITS GLACÉS AUX PISTACHES
MADÈRE FAQUAT FRUITS ET DESSERTS
PIÈCES MONTÉES
MONUMENT DE WASHINGTON   FOUNTAINE DES AIGLES
TEMPLE DE LA LIBERTE   TROPHÉE NATIONALE

FIGURE 1-9   DELMONICO'S MENU, 1866.
(*Source:* Cannon and Brooks, *The President's Cookbook,*
1986, p. 263.)

Native American Feasts

Feasting is an American tradition dating back to the social ceremonies of many of the Native American tribes. Early written records of naturalists and explorers such as John Bartram and George Catlin provide a fascinating glimpse of the use of food in ceremonies in Native American societies. A ceremonial feast called a potlatch was held by tribes in the American Northwest to mark important occasions such as marriage or the succession to a chieftainship.

The rules of potlatch required the host to provide, as a sign of conspicuous wealth, the best quality foods available in quantities too great to be eaten by the number of invited guests.

> *He was also expected to give away a fortune in gifts. . . . [A]t a single Kwakiutl potlatch, the guests . . . were gratified with eight canoes, six slaves, fifty-four elk skins, two thousand silver bracelets, seven thousand brass bracelets, and thirty three thousand blankets.*[5]

George Catlin was served the following feast by the Mandan plains tribe:

> *The simple feast which was spread before us consisted of three dishes only, two of which were served in wooden bowls, and the third eaten in an earthen vessel . . . The last contained a quantity of pem-i-can and marrow-fat; and one of the former held a fine brace of buffalo ribs, delightfully roasted; and the other was filled with a kind of paste or pudding, made of the flour of the "pomme blanche," as the French call it, a delicious turnip of the prairie, finely flavored with the buffalo berries which are . . . used with divers dishes in cooking, as we in civilized countries use dried currents, which they very much resemble.*[6]

Prerevolutionary American cuisine and the patterns in which meals were served primarily followed English custom. The menu pattern for formal meals, as shown in Figure 1-10, was offered in two courses, each a complete meal in itself. Figure 1-10 details a banquet meal that would have been served in Providence, Rhode Island at the home of wealthy merchants during the early 1700s.

General Nathanial Greene wrote to General James Varnum of his visit to Philadelphia in 1779:

> *Luxury and dissipation is everywhere prevalent. When I was in Boston last Summer I thought luxury very predominant there: but they were no more to compare with than now prevailing in Philadelphia, than an Infant Babe to a full grown Man. I dine'd at one table where there was a hundred and Sixty dishes: and at several others not far behind.*[7]

In the South during this same period a dinner at Shirley Hall plantation in Virginia was described:

First Course

ASPARAGUS SOUP, REMOVE*

LEG OF GRASS LAMB BOILED WITH CAPERS, CARROTS, AND TURNIPS

BOILED POTATO PUDDING

VENISON PASTIES

RICE PELLAW

FORCED COCK'S COMBS

◆ ◆ ◆

Second Course

WHITE FRICASSEE OF RABBIT

SALAMAGUNDI

RAGOO OF FRENCH BEANS WITH CARROT FORCE

WATER-SOAKEY

PEAR PIE

◆ ◆ ◆

FOLLOWED BY

CHEESE AND GRAPES

*"REMOVE" INDICATES THAT THE SOUP TUREEN WAS REMOVED AFTER THE SOUP
COURSE AND REPLACED BY THE MEAT PLATTERS.

FIGURE 1-10   A DINNER FOR JUNE, 1700s.
(*Source:* The Rhode Island Historical Society,
Providence, Rhode Island.)

His service is all of silver and you drink your porter out of silver goblets. . . . The finest Virginia hams, and the saddle of mutton, Turkey, then canvas back duck, beef, oysters. . . . Then comes the sparkling champagne, after that dessert, plum pudding, tarts, ice cream, peaches preserved in Brandy. . . . then the table is cleared and on comes the figs, almonds and raisins, and the richest Madeira, the best Port and the softest Malmsey wine I ever tasted.[8]

The rich table traditions of the American colonies were continued in menus such as shown in Figure 1-11, served in December of 1884 at the Fifth Annual Ball and Game Supper in East Wallingford, Connecticut. The variety of native American foods and traditional New England cooking is evident in this menu, even as it follows the classical menu format. Although heavy in the dessert section, the influence of the three-course menu is still evident in the presence of the relish course and the fruits and nuts in the dessert course.

Oysters

ESCALLOPED   STEWED   RAW

Game

MALLARD DUCK WITH CURRANT JELLY   SADDLE OF VENISON
ROAST BEAR WITH CRANBERRY SAUCE   RED HEAD DUCK WITH CONFITURE
WILD TURKEY   OYSTER DRESSING   BROILED PARTRIDGE
ROAST WILD GOOSE WITH RASPBERRY JELLY   QUAIL ON TOAST

Entrées

CHICKEN   HAM   CORNED BEEF   LOBSTER   CHICKEN SALAD   LOBSTER SALAD

Relishes

CHOW CHOW   PICKLED CUCUMBERS   MIXED PICKLES   WORCESTERSHIRE SAUCE
SPICED ONIONS   TOMATO CATSUP   FRENCH MUSTARD   OLIVES   CELERY   LETTUCE

Bread

WHEAT BREAD   BROWN BREAD   GRAHAM BREAD

Pastry

APPLE PIE   MEAT PIE   CRANBERRY PIE   LEMON PIE
BLUEBERRY PIE   RASPBERRY PIE

Cakes and Preserves

FRUIT CAKE   SPONGE CAKE   GOLD CAKE   CURRANT CAKE   COCONUT CAKE
JELLY CAKE   DELICATE CAKE   CHOCOLATE CAKE   RIBBON CAKE
CUP CAKE   PEACH PRESERVES   QUINCE PRESERVES   RASPBERRY PRESERVES

Desserts

VANILLA ICE CREAM   LEMON ICE CREAM
GRAPES   APPLES   ORANGES   LAYER RAISINS   FILBERTS
ENGLISH WALNUTS   PECAN NUTS   SOFT SHELL ALMONDS

FIGURE 1-11   BALL AND GAME SUPPER, 1884.

Presidential Banqueting

The presidency of George Washington was America's opportunity to entertain on the world stage. The format for meals followed the three-course menu pattern popular at the time. Figure 1-12 shows the place setting for each of the courses outlined in Figure 1-13. This elaborate setting was repeated for each course.

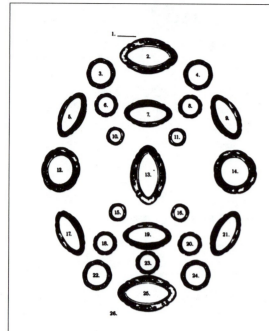

Key to First Course

1. Transparent Soup-remove for
3. Pigeons Comfort
5. French Dip
7. Sauteed Pheasant
9. Torrent of Veal
11. Broccoli
13. Mock Turtle
15. Bottled Peas
17. Sheeps Rumps & Kidneys in Rice
19. House Lamb
21. Sweet Breads A la Royal
23. Beef Olives
25. Hare Soup-remove for

2. fish
4. Fricassee of Chicken
6. Haricot
8. Calf's Sweetbreads
10. Kidney Beans
12. Boilit Turkey
14. Small Ham
16. Sallat
18. Larded Oysters
20. Ox Pallets
22. Florentine of Rabbits
24. Ducks a la Mode
26. Haunch of Venison

FIGURE 1-12   EIGHTEENTH-CENTURY TABLE SETTINGS.

First Course

SMALL CHICKEN PATTIES   SOUP PUREE   PORK CUTLETS
RED CABBAGE STEWED (REPLACED WITH SALMON)   SAUCE ROBERT
BOILED CHICKEN   SHOULDER OF MUTTON IN EPIGRAM   MASHED POTATOES
PLAIN BUTTER   HAM   BOILED TURKEY
SHRIMP SAUCE   BEEF TREMBLONGUE   FRENCH BEANS FRICASEED
DRESSED GREENS   SOUP SANTEA   OYSTER LOAVES
(REPLACED BY STEWED CARP)
SCOTCH COLLOPS

Second Course

MAIDS OF HONOR   TWO WILD DUCKS   RHENISH CREAM
ASPARAGUS À LA PETIT POI   LAMBS TAILS AU BECHAMEL   PRAWNS
SAUCE   HARE ROASTED   SAUCE
TWO TEAL   SWEETBREADS À LA DAUPHIN   PLOVERS
CRAYFISH   THREE PARTRIDGES   SAUCE
SAUCE   CHARDOONS
FRUIT IN JELLY   CUSTARDS   FRICASSED BIRDS

FIGURE 1-13   MARTHA WASHINGTON'S MENU.
(*Source:* Cannon and Brooks, *The President's Cookbook,*
1968, p. 9.)

The menu in Figure 1-13, taken from Martha Washington's cookbook, illustrates the first two courses of dinner. The third course, while not listed here, was offered after the tablecloth had been removed. Decanters of port, cheeses, nuts, and fruit were placed on the table. Menus from this period indicate the diversity and availability of food products in the Mid-Atlantic area as well as Washington's eagerness to present them to his guests.

> *The food served at the President's table from 1789 to the end of Washington's second term in 1797, indicates the new nation's dependence on the land. Game fowl, meats, plantation-grown fruits and vegetables, fish from local rivers or the Atlantic reveal the abundance of the land. Spliced through the menus are the remnants of Washington's English heritage—puddings, cream trifles, a taste for port and wine.[9]*

Thomas Jefferson greatly influenced the development of banqueting styles in America. Following his years as minister plenipotentiary to the court of Louis XVI, Jefferson imported many of the traditions, foods, and wines of the European table to his Virginia home, Monticello. As president of the United States, Jefferson established a pattern of elegant banquets featuring French cuisine and the best available wines.

> *Never before had such dinners been given in the President's house, nor such a variety of the finest and most costly wines. In his entertainments republican simplicity was united with epicurean delicacy; while the absence of splendor, ornament and profusion was more than compensated by the neatness, order and elegant simplicity that pervaded the whole establishment.[10]*

A summary of dinners from November 5, 1804, to February 22, 1805 totals forty dinners, with 564 guests. The banqueting style that Jefferson brought to America was termed cuisine bourgeois, a simplification of the heavy three-course meals held over from the Middle Ages and used throughout Europe through the eighteenth century (see Figure 1-14).

Similar to the twentieth-century modifications to French cuisine, known as la nouvelle cuisine, these changes were a reaction against the rich stocks, sauces, and theatrical *pièces montées* of the eighteenth century. This cuisine appealed to Jefferson's preference for simple elegance.

Jefferson's contributions to American cuisine included ice cream, vanilla, pasta, and tomatoes. Vanilla flavoring was a new ingredient for American cookery, appearing in the recipe for vanilla ice cream written by Jefferson. Pasta appears in Jefferson's notes as macaroni, now known as tubular pasta. Further investigation shows, however, that he was actually referring to the pasta cut known as spaghetti. The tomato, meanwhile, had been taken from Central America and popularized in Southern Europe. Jefferson brought the fruit and its seeds back to Monticello for cultivation.

Jefferson's fascination with French cuisine extended to the equipment used to prepare and serve food; while in Paris he purchased a great deal of

GAZPACHO
TIO PEPE SHERRY
HOT DEVILL'S CRAB
ROAST LEG OF LAMB, CONSERVE OF CURRANTS
CHATEAU LATOUR
SAFFRON RICE GREEN PEAS WITH MINT CORN PUDDING
ASPARAGUS VINAIGRETTE
MONTRACHET
CHEESE MOLD BEATEN BISCUITS
STRAWBERRY MERINGUES CHANTILLY
PEDRO XIMENZ
NUTS AND CANDIED FRUITS
COFFEE BRANDY

FIGURE 1-14 JEFFERSON MENU.
(*Source:* Rysavy and Leighton, *A Treasury of White House Cooking,* 1972, p. 184.)

cooking and baking ware. On his return to Monticello from France the following inventory was added to the plantation books:

Silver service
Pewterware
Dishes for hors d'oeuvres
Porcelain cups
Saucers
Plates
Soup tureens and bowls
Serving platters and casseroles
Crystal goblets
Wine tumblers
Decanters
A tea urn and coffee pot

For the kitchen he included:

28 round saucepans—19 saucepan covers
Frying pans
Food warmers
Chocolate molds
Ice molds
Pie pans
Spoons, ladles
Cleavers, knives
Pair of kitchen scales[11]

By 1825 the John Quincy Adams family occupied the White House. The following describes a levee, or reception, held in 1829:

*Gentlemen and ladies both attend, arrive about eight and leave
about ten. The company is treated with coffee, tea and a variety
of cakes, jellies, ice-cream, and white and red wine, mixed and
unmixed, and sometimes other cordials and liquors, and frequently with West Indian fruit; all of which are carried about
the rooms amongst the guests, upon large trays by servants dressed
in livery.[12]*

Like Thomas Jefferson, John Tyler favored informality blended with
fine cuisine. A gala ball held in the White House in 1845, near the end of
Tyler's presidency, contained:

*[E]normous bouquets of flowers filling the rooms and side tables
loaded with every imaginable delicacy. The atmosphere radiated
luxury and extravagance. The evening was a huge success and
much talked of for years to come. There were many parties given
during the holiday season for Washington officialdom. Always
the tables were laden with substantial and varied foods. Roast
ham, a saddle of venison or some other heavy roast, roast wild
ducks, or other poultry was in evidence. Enormous supplies of
home-made cakes and puddings were on hand. Punch, madeira,
and the ubiquitous champagne were ready. Such galas usually
began around eight o'clock and ended at eleven.[13]*

James Buchanan brought the formal elegance of European society back
to the White House, enlisting a French caterer named Gautuer to reign over
the White House kitchen. Figure 1-15 itemizes the purchasing arrangements
to fill the menu for Buchanan's inaugural ball to which 5000 guests were
invited on March 4, 1857.

SIXTY SADDLE OF MUTTON

EIGHT ROUNDS OF BEEF

SEVENTY-FIVE HAMS

FOURE SADDLES OF VENISON

FOUR HUNDRED GALLONS OF OYSTERS

FIVE HUNDRED QUARTS OF CHICKEN SALAD

ONE HUNDRED TWENTY-FIVE TONGUES

FIVE HUNDRED QUARTS OF JELLIES

TWELVE HUNDRED QUARTS OF ICE CREAM IN ASSORTED FLAVORS

CAKE PYRAMID: FOUR FEET HIGH DECORATED WITH THE FLAGS
OF 31 STATES AND TERRITORIES

FIGURE 1-15 PURCHASING REQUIREMENTS FOR
BUCHANAN'S INAUGURAL BALL MENU.
(*Source:* Cannon and Brooks, *The President's Cookbook,*
1968, p. 221.)

President Lincoln's second inaugural ball in 1865 was not to be over-shadowed by the ongoing Civil War. The menu in Figure 1-16 reflects the diverse cuisine styles of the first one hundred years of the American presidency, combining the nation's bounty of foods so evident at Washington's table with the influences of French cuisine.

At the turn of the nineteenth century the formal seven-course French menu in Figure 1-17 was served on the occasion of a State Dinner.

Stews

Oyster Stew   Terrapin Stew   Pickeled Oysters

Beef

Roast Beef   Filet de Bouef
Beef à la Mode   Beef à l'Anglaise

Veal

Roast Leg of Veal   Fricandeau   Veal Malakoff

Poultry

Roast Turkey   Boned Turkey   Roast Chicken
Grouse   Quail   Venison Pâtés   Pâté of Duck en Gelee
Pâté de Foie Gras   Smoked Hams
Tongue en Gelee   Tongue Plain

Salads

Chicken   Lobster   Ornamental Pyramids

Desserts

Nougat   Orange   Caramel with Fancy Cream   Candy
Coconut   Macaroon   Chocolate   Cakes and Tarts
Almond   Sponge   Belle Alliance   Dame Blanche
Macaroon Tart   Tarte à la Nelson   Tarte à la Orleans
Tarte à la Portugaise   Tarte à la Vienne   Jellies and Creams
Calf's Foot and Wine Jelly   Charlotte Russe
Charlotte à la Vanilla   Ice Cream Vanilla   Lemon White Coffee

Fruit Pies

Strawberry   Orange   Lemon   Grapes   Almonds   Raisins
Coffee and Chocolate

FIGURE 1-16   PRESIDENT LINCOLN'S INAUGURAL BALL MENU, 1865.
(*Source: The President's Cookbook,* 1968, p. 235.)

BLUE POINT OYSTERS

Potages

POTAGE TORTUE À L'ANGLAISE   CONSOMMÉ PRINTANIÈRE ROYALE

Hors d'Oeuvres

CANAPÉ À LA RUSSE   TIMBALES À TALLEYRAND

Poissons

SAUMON, SAUCE HOLLANDAISE   GRENADINES DE BASS
POMMES DE TERRE DUCHESE   CUCUMBER SALADE

Releves

SEILE D'AGNEAU, SAUCE MENTHE   FILET DE BOEUF À LA RICHELIEU

Entrées

RIS DE VEAU À LA PERIGNEUX   COTELETTES D'AGNEAU D'OR MAISON
TERAPIN À LA MARYLAND

Rots

CANVAS BACK DUCK

◆ ◆ ◆

GERMAN ASPARAGUS   PETIT POIS

Entremets

GOLDE AU CHAMPAGNE   FLOMBIERE AUX FRAMBOISE
PUDDING DIPLOMATE
CAFE   FRUITS   FROMAGE

FIGURE 1-17   STATE DINNER AT THE WHITE HOUSE.
(*Source:* Ziemann and Gilette, *The White House Cookbook,*
1906, p. 481.)

Diverse influences in menu planning created changes in the White House kitchen from one administration to another. In 1877 President Grant served the menu in Figure 1-18 to President-elect and Mrs. Rutherford Hayes. A combination of American foods served in the classical French dinner format accompanied by appropriate wines with each course, this menu embodies the marriage of American cuisine and traditional French dining customs.

President Franklin Roosevelt served the informal American cuisine menu in Figure 1-19 to General Charles de Gaulle for a working lunch in 1944.

In marked contrast to the simple style menu in Figure 1-19 is the very formal French menu in Figure 1-20, served by President Nixon to the President of France and Madame Pompidou in 1970.

SHERRY   CONSOMMÉ IMPERIAL

                                BISQUE DE GREVISSE

                                WOODCOCK PATTIES*

                                SALMON

WHITE WINE   ROAST OF BEEF

                                BREAST OF PHEASANT

                                CRAWFISH PUDDING

                                GOOSE LIVERS

ROMAN PUNCH   TURKEY

                                ARTICHOKES

                                CANVASBACK DUCK

RED WINE   SWEET WARM DISH**

 * WOODCOCK IS A SMALL GAME BIRD THAT WAS COMMON TO THE EAST COAST OF THE UNITED STATES.
** A FORM OF DESSERT PUDDING.

FIGURE 1-18   PRESIDENT GRANT'S MENU, 1877.
(*Source:* Cannon and Brooks, *The President's Cookbook,*
1968, p. 279.)

JELLIED BOUILLON

BOILED CHICKEN   CURRANT JELLY

ASPARAGUS   DUCHESS POTATOES

PARSLEYED CARROTS

TOSSED SALAD

VANILLA ICE CREAM   CRUSHED RASPBERRIES

ANGEL FOOD CAKE

COFFEE

FIGURE 1-19   ROOSEVELT–DE GAULLE LUNCHEON MENU, 1944.
(*Source:* Rysavy and Leighton, *A Treasury of White House Cooking,*
1972, p. 140.)

LE SALMON LAFAYETTE

LE CONTRE-FILET DE BOEUF AUX CÈPES

LES POMMES NOUVELLES

LES ASPERGES FRAÎCHES HOLLANDAISE

LE LAITUE DE KENTUCKY

LE FROMAGE DE CAMEMBERT

LE MELON GLACÉ À LA VIGNERONNE

LES PETITS FOURS

FIGURE 1-20   PRESIDENT NIXON'S MENU FOR PRESIDENT POMPIDOU.
(*Source:* Rysavy and Leighton, *A Treasury of White House Cooking,* 1972, p. 107.)

Jacqueline Kennedy was the one individual besides Thomas Jefferson who most influenced the style of banqueting in the White House. Her personal interest in the quality and style of cuisine and service for White House functions changed the patterns that had been carried out by previous presidencies. Mrs. Kennedy, like Jefferson, dramatically changed the menu format, reducing the number of courses from seven to four or a maximum of five, as seen in Figure 1-21. The emphasis on simple elegance that marked Jefferson's banqueting style came full circle in 165 years with the efforts of Jacqueline Kennedy to imbue a similar style to the White House of the early

DINNER

| *Almaden Pinot Blanc* | *Vol-au-Vent Maryland* |

Château Haut-Brion 1953	*Gigot d'Agneau aux flageolets*
	Tomates grillé
	Épinards à la crème

| | *Mousse aux Concombres* |

| *Cuvée Dom Pérignon Brut 1952* | |
| | *Bombe Glace Caribienne* |

**The White House
Tuesday, November 7, 1961**

FIGURE 1-21   KENNEDY WHITE HOUSE MENUS.
(*Source:* Lincoln, *The Kennedy White House Parties,*
1967, p. 11)

DINNER

Inglenook
Pinot
Chardonnay

Boston sole Diplomate

Roast sirloin of beef Chevreuse
String beans with almonds
Braised endive

Château
Corton-Grancey
1959

Galantine of chicken
Green salad

Dom
Pérignon
1955

Charlotte Plombière

The White House
Tuesday, October 1, 1963

FIGURE 1-21   (CONTINUED)

1960s. This change reflected current dining trends and reduced the overall dining time, allowing more time for the evening entertainments that became a hallmark of the Kennedy presidency, as seen in Figure 1-22.

The subsequent administrations of Presidents Johnson, Carter, Reagan, Bush, and Clinton have all brought their particular influences to the format of White House dining, from barbecues, to clam bakes, to formal state dinners. It is Jacqueline Kennedy, however, who made the greatest mark on the traditions of White House dining in the twentieth century.

FIGURE 1-22 KENNEDY WHITE HOUSE ENTERTAINMENT.
(*Source:* Lincoln, *The Kennedy White House Parties*, 1967,
pp. 154–155.)

Summary

Modern banqueting has its roots in the traditions of the Greeks and Romans. The Greeks introduced the hors d'oeuvre course, to which the Romans added up to twenty courses as they furthered the development of the banquet feast. From this twenty-course format evolved the three-course medieval menu offering as many as 25 menu items with each course.

The menu format revisions of the late eighteenth and nineteenth centuries transformed the three primary courses with multiple dishes into a series of nine courses, each featuring an individual menu item. These revisions were incorporated into menus throughout Europe and America in a variety of formats.

The history of American banqueting begins with the feasts of the Native Americans. The menu formats of early colonial American feasts were primarily influenced by England. French cuisine and menu formats initially threaded their way through the colonies via English recipes and customs. The emigration of the French royalists during the French Revolution accelerated the assimilation of both French cuisine and menus into American banqueting customs. Thomas Jefferson greatly aided the development of American banqueting during his years in the White House. His simplification of the menu and emphasis on wines were major elements in the development of a style of banqueting that would continually appear during the next 165 years of

White House functions. During the presidency of John Kennedy, banquets were enhanced by the contributions of Jacqueline Kennedy. Like Jefferson, she preferred menus emphasizing a style of simple elegance and concentrating on a high quality of food and service.

The records tracing the development of the banquet menu throughout the centuries provide a rich and exciting chronicle of food items, recipes, and traditions. Many of these food items and recipes have endured as part of our contemporary food customs.

Endnotes

1. Apicius, Cookery and Dining in Imperial Rome. Edited by Joseph Dommers Vehling, New York: Dover, 1977, p. 6.
2. Brillat-Savarin, Jean Anthelme. The Physiology of Taste. Edited by M. F. K. Fisher. San Francisco: North Point Press, 1986, pp. 287–290.
3. Sass, Lorna J. To The King's Taste. New York: Metropolitan Museum of Art, 1975, pp. 29–30.
4. Sass, Lorna J. To The King's Taste. New York: Metropolitan Museum of Art, 1975, p. 31.
5. Root, Waverly and Richard de Rouchemont. Eating in America. New York: William Morrow & Co., 1976, p. 36.
6. Root, Waverly and Richard de Rouchemont. Eating in America. New York: William Morrow & Co., 1976, p. 37.
7. Showman, Richard K. The Papers of General Nathanael Greene, 1983, p. 223.
8. Root, Waverly and Richard de Rouchemont. Eating in America. New York: William Morrow & Co., 1976, p. 95.
9. Cannon, Poppy and Patricia Brooks. The President's Cookbook, 1968, p. 112.
10. Kimball, Marie. Thomas Jefferson's Cookbook, 1972, p. 184.
11. McLaughlin, Jack. Jefferson and Monticello, 1988, p. 230.
12. Cannon, Poppy and Patricia Brooks. The President's Cookbook, 1968, p. 112.
13. Cannon, Poppy and Patricia Brooks. The President's Cookbook, 1968, p. 170.

Styles of Catering Operations

Catering operations, as either a stand-alone facility or as part of a larger hospitality-related business, exist in a wide variety of formats, or styles. Most common are those that are readily identifiable as private rooms in restaurant operations, hotel facilities, and independent catering facilities. The increased demand by the international public for private function space outside of their own homes and businesses has led the catering segment of the foodservice sector of the hospitality industry to be a leader in the continued growth of both facilities and revenue.

Forward thinking foodservice businesses from fine dining restaurants to delicatessens are incorporating catering services into their operations in recognition of the expanding market for preprepared foodservices. Off-premise catering and take-out services offer an excellent avenue for increasing revenue with minimal costs.

This chapter summarizes the ways in which catering services have been incorporated into foodservice operational styles, providing operators with techniques and methods for expanding the profit making potential of their businesses. The categories of foodservice operations offering catering reviewed in this chapter are:

1. Full-service restaurants
2. Hotel food and beverage facilities
3. Catering halls
4. Independent caterers
5. Private clubs
6. Contract feeding
7. Charcuteries and delicatessens

"Services" in the context of a foodservice operation refer to the opportunities management makes available to the customer to purchase food, beverage, entertainment, and ancillary services. Services include:

1. Table foodservices
2. Packaged take-out foodservices
3. Beverage services
4. Entertainment services
5. Business meeting services
6. Conference and convention services
7. Contract feeding services
8. Off-premise foodservices
9. Home-replacement foodservices

Full-Service Restaurants

Full-service restaurants have the opportunity to offer a variety of catering services to their customers. Before any decision is made to offer these services, however, six important factors should be considered:

1. Location
2. Customer profile
3. Restaurant style or concept
4. Staffing capabilities
5. Restaurant physical layout
6. Cuisine and menu offerings

Additional material on identifying and developing these factors is discussed in Chapter Three, Catering Foodservice Development.

LOCATION

The proximity of the restaurant to office complexes and centralized business areas will help to establish whether its catering service will be focused on business or social marketing efforts.

Businesses in the twenty-first century are spread from urban centers to suburban locations in office parks. Central urban locations offer a concentrated market for both office delivery and take-out. A significant factor in developing the market for business catering is that service is generally required during the business week, leaving weekend periods free to service social business. In addition, locations such as museums, concert halls, and historical sites offer interesting venues to catered functions for both local businesses and conventions.

Both urban and suburban restaurants can successfully develop social catering business. Suburban locations are generally more appropriate for social catering to private homes, clubs, churches, and other facilities. Delivery to urban locations can pose security and logistical problems, creating additional costs for transportation and service labor.

Population density also affects the volume of anticipated catering business. Restaurants situated in rural areas with low population density cannot expect immediate high volumes of catering business. Areas of high-density population yield a variety of catering opportunities that steadily increase in volume through referrals and reputation.

The location of the physical restaurant building plays a role in the type of catering services to be offered. Storage facilities, expansion possibilities, and access to major transportation routes are factors important to catering service production.

CUSTOMER PROFILE

Restaurants have the advantage of a built-in customer pool to whom they can market in-house and off-premise catering services. In addition, the attraction of being associated with a restaurant's reputation will help to expand the possible market to include new business and social clients.

The market profile should classify customers as business or social catering clients, designated by income bracket. In addition the range of activities for which each customer pool will need catering services should be researched as thoroughly as possible. This will help in developing package programs along with potential menu programs and accompanying pricing concepts.

STYLE OR CONCEPT

The style, concept, and/or theme of the restaurant should be taken into consideration when planning potential catering services. Off-premise catering services do not necessarily have to blend with the facilities offered by the restaurant. On-premise catering services should, however, be designed to function within the restaurant facilities.

FACILITIES

Restaurants facilities are a major factor in providing on-premise catering. The ratio of catering functions to restaurant services that can be handled at a given time is dependent on the size and flexibility of the physical plant. Small private parties are often incorporated into the general dining room setting. Large parties must, however, be given facilities that are separated from the general public. The restaurant floor plan in Figure 2-1 outlines flexible catering space for a full-service restaurant operation. This restaurant has a private dining room and bar facility with a dance floor that can also be used for additional restaurant seating during busy time periods and holidays. Flexible facilities such as these allow a restaurant to maximize revenues.

Many restaurants that offer in-house catering schedule large parties, such as weddings, anniversaries, luncheons, and dinners, on days and times when the restaurant is not otherwise open. Often catering business must be refused because sufficient on-premise facilities are not available. When management is continually turning away catering business, a decision will need to be made as to how the restaurant will balance is future development of catering versus full-service dining services.

Kitchen facilities play a major part in determining when and how catering service demands can be met. Kitchen equipment must be flexible, allowing for volume production to take place simultaneously with à la carte restaurant service. The kitchen cooking load and holding capacity of ovens and auxiliary equipment is important to determine if a kitchen is to be used to its full capacity during busy times.

Storage and refrigeration facilities determine the amount of food products available at any given time. The cost of waste from food spoilage due to lack of refrigeration and freezer space could dilute the profit from additional catering business. A further discussion of equipment capability for catering service is found in Chapter Twelve.

CUISINE AND MENU

The primary cuisine and menu offerings of a restaurant constitute one of the most important considerations for on-premise catering. As discussed earlier, off-premise catering services do not necessarily need to be the same as those offered at the restaurant for full-service dining.

Purchasing and production requirements are crucial to the successful development of catering services. On-premise catering should offer menu items that duplicate the established menu as closely as possible in order to enhance production capabilities. Surrounding items, such as vegetables and starches, are the most effective area of the menu to duplicate. Kitchen production is more efficient when the number of surrounding menu items is

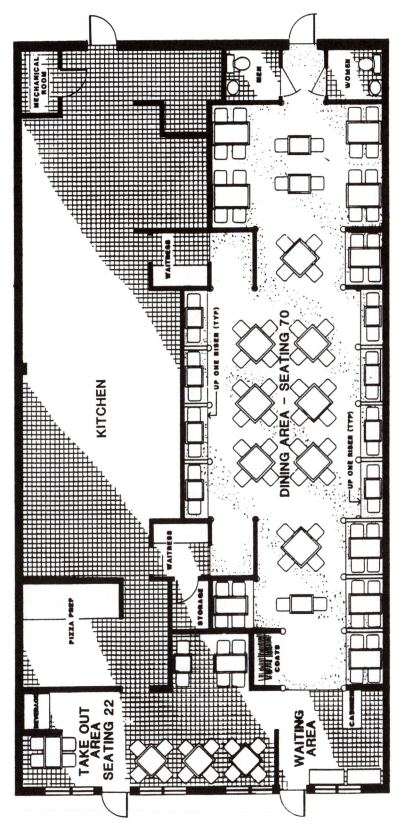

FIGURE 2-1 RESTAURANT FLOOR PLAN.

limited. Profitable and effective purchasing for catering functions requires that the ingredients for menu items be the same or similar to those on the restaurant menu. This allows the purchasing agent to place orders for maximum volume pricing and quality.

OFF-PREMISE CATERING

The decision to participate in off-premise catering requires a thorough review of a restaurant's resources. A successful in-house catering program can lead management into perceiving that taking on the challenge of off-premise catering will not cause operational difficulties.

Several problems must be anticipated regarding the off-premise facilities in which the final production and service for functions takes place. During in-house catering functions, service staff can often work between private parties and the dining room, filling in where needed, while the kitchen staff functions as usual, having planned ahead to handle the increased production load. In order to service off-premise functions, however, a separate waitstaff needs to be scheduled. In addition, at least one member of the kitchen production staff will be assigned to the function and therefore will be unavailable to the restaurant kitchen for the time period involved for the off-premise function.

Equipment as well as food will need to be transported both to and from the off-premise function location. Hot food and cold food must be kept at specific temperatures to prevent food spoilage. A refrigerator truck may be necessary at certain times of the year. Transportation routes and problems involving traffic congestion need to be considered in the timing of deliveries.

Subcontractors may be necessary for equipment such as tables, chairs, dishes, glassware, linens, dance floors, and tents. The extent to which a restaurant commits to a full-service catering business determines the amount of extra effort required to handle the increased business. Planning for off-premise catering requires attention to detail. Contingency plans for bad weather, delays in food transportation, and the failure of on-site equipment to function properly should be established in advance so that problems can be dealt with expediently as they arise. Additional costs are incurred when solutions to these situations are not planned for in advance. Contract prices must include these contingencies or management will find that overall costs are higher than the fees charged to the customer for food and services. The off-premise catering organizational guide in Figure 2-2 offers an outline of the areas of operational concern.

TAKE-OUT

Take-out service is the most profitable way for restaurants and catering services to increase revenues without increasing costs. Because take-out service does not require extra seating, it generally will not require an operation to expand its facilities beyond accommodating takeout customers with a pickup and waiting area. Kitchen production can plan and schedule to handle large increases in volume for short time periods. In addition, take-out does not require the additional expenses incurred by table service for glassware,

Client: _____

Date/Time: _____

Function/Theme: _____

_____

_____

FACILITY:

Address:

Contact Name:

Phone: Fax:

E-Mail: Cell Phone:

Routing Directions:

Travel Time:

_____

LOCATION:

Indoor _____ Outdoor_____

Loading Area _____

Challenges _____

_____

_____

Square Footage _____

Energy Sources

Gas/Electric _____

_____

Water Sources: Hot_____

Cold _____

Lighting Availability _____

_____

_____

Staging on Premise _____

_____

_____

FIGURE 2-2   OFF-PREMISE CATERING ORGANIZATIONAL GUIDE.

Equipment on Premise

Kitchen _____

Prep Area _____

_____

Sinks _____

Refrigeration _____

_____

_____

Freezer Space _____

_____

Range Tops _____

_____

Ovens _____

_____

_____

Microwave _____

Grills _____

Indoor _____Outdoor_____

Other _____

_____

Dishwasher Availability _____

_____

Dishwasher Location _____

Loading for Kitchen _____

_____

Service Area

Banquet Boxes _____

_____

Service Station Areas _____

_____

Equipment on Property _____

_____

_____

FIGURE 2-2   (CONTINUED)

Equipment Needs Kitchen

Item	Source	Delivery	Cost
_____	_____	_____	_____
_____	_____	_____	_____
_____	_____	_____	_____
_____	_____	_____	_____
_____	_____	_____	_____

Equipment Needs Service

Item	Source	Delivery	Cost
_____	_____	_____	_____
_____	_____	_____	_____
_____	_____	_____	_____
_____	_____	_____	_____
_____	_____	_____	_____

Tenting

Size _____

Floor _____

Heaters/Fans _____

Decor/Theme Accessories

_____

_____

_____

_____

Floor Plans/Layout

_____

_____

Audiovisual

Protection Equipment_____

Screens _____

Sound _____

_____

FIGURE 2-2 (CONTINUED)

Energy and Power Needs

_____

_____

_____

Entertainment

Number of Performers _____

Rehearsal Time _____

Performance Time_____

Backstage Space Requirements_____

_____

Contact Name _____

Phone _____ Fax_____

Food & Beverage

Menu _____

Service Setup _____

Staff Requirements

Captains _____

Servers _____

Bartenders _____

Permits/Licenses

Food Sanitation _____

Off-Premise Beverage License_____

Special Effect/Sound Permits_____

Parking Permit_____

Event Permit _____

Occupancy Permit _____

Insurance

Proof of Workman's Compensation

Proof of Liability Insurance

Proof of Liquor Liability

FIGURE 2-2   (CONTINUED)

Parking

Guest Parking: Number of Spaces _____

     Location _____

     Restrictions_____

Valet Service Company _____

Phone _____

Staff & Equipment Parking: Number of Spaces_____

     Location _____

     Restrictions_____

Signage_____

Contracted to_____

Phone _____ Fax_____

Restroom Facilities

Type and Number: Male _____ Female _____

Handicapped Location _____

Signage_____

Emergency/Security Management

Ambulance on Site _____

First Aid Location _____

Security Management Contact_____

Phone _____ Fax_____

Number of Security Staff _____

Emergency Evacuation Plan _____

Fire Exit Locations _____

_____

Signage & Lighting _____

Trash Removal

On Site _____

Contract Removal Contact _____

Phone _____ Fax_____

FIGURE 2-2   (CONTINUED)

Special Conditions_____

_____

_____

Weather Contingency Plans_____

_____

_____

Figure 2-2   (Continued)

linens, flowers, menus, and entertainment. Disposable dishes, plastic flatware, and a carrying container are the basic requirements for take-out service. Successful take-out service does, however, require planning to assure that customers receive menu items in satisfactory condition. As with the catering menu, the selection of take-out menu items should be drawn from the restaurant menu in order to maximize purchasing and production efforts.

Hotel Food and Beverage Facilities

The hotel food and beverage department provides food-related guest services throughout a hotel, conference, or resort property. Outlets for food and beverage services can include the following:

1. Full-service restaurant
2. Coffee shop
3. Catering facilities
4. Room service
5. Recreational areas
6. Lobby area bars
7. Food market or delicatessen

Food items for these combined foodservice areas are provided from a central kitchen, with the exception of large hotel facilities where satellite kitchens provide auxiliary production and service areas. An executive chef supervises production for all areas, consulting with the manager of each foodservice area.

Of the seven food service areas, catering affords the possibility for the greatest profit, in addition to providing much-needed cash flow during periods when room sales are slow. Hotel catering services are usually classified as:

1. Business
2. Convention/conference
3. Social

The volume of catering service available to a hotel is based on the size and number of facilities that can be used for private functions as well as the availability of production and service staff and related equipment.

The primary catering market for a hotel is based on three factors:

1. Location
2. Hotel facilities
3. Customer profile

LOCATION

The location of a hotel determines the demand for in-house catering. In-house catering is defined as guest-related foodservice functions associated with business meetings, conferences, conventions, and social concerns.

A hotel with a remote location focuses its catering efforts on the business booked into the hotel. Resort locations often provide additional opportunities for catering services at sports facilities and landscape venues throughout the property.

A hotel with a suburban or downtown location can expect to develop a large volume of outside catering business, both business-related and social in addition to conferences and conventions. The Chicago Hilton, for example, located in downtown Chicago, breaks down its annual catering business into the following percentages:

65% conference/convention
35% outside social

The amount of combined catering business that can be handled at any one time in a hotel is based primarily on the number and size of the facilities available. The major function rooms are usually referred to as the ballroom areas. These are complemented by a series of meeting rooms, some adjacent to the main ballroom area and some located in other areas of the hotel.

The diagram in Figure 2-3 shows the variety of catering and meeting room facilities available at The Flamingo Hilton in Las Vegas, Nevada. The main facility is a ballroom that seats 1620 guests for banquets and 2400 for theater style meetings. Adjacent to the ballroom is a series of connecting function rooms. These lead to another series of rooms that begin with an open reception foyer and lead to a second ballroom area seating 600 for dinner. An open terrace area is adjacent to these rooms, offering an outdoor reception, dining, and entertainment area. Private meeting rooms are available in other locations throughout the hotel.

CUSTOMER PROFILE

The customer profile for hotel catering services is made up of both business and social clientele. Customers who use the hotel as a location for a two- or three-day meeting consider meal functions as part of the total meeting

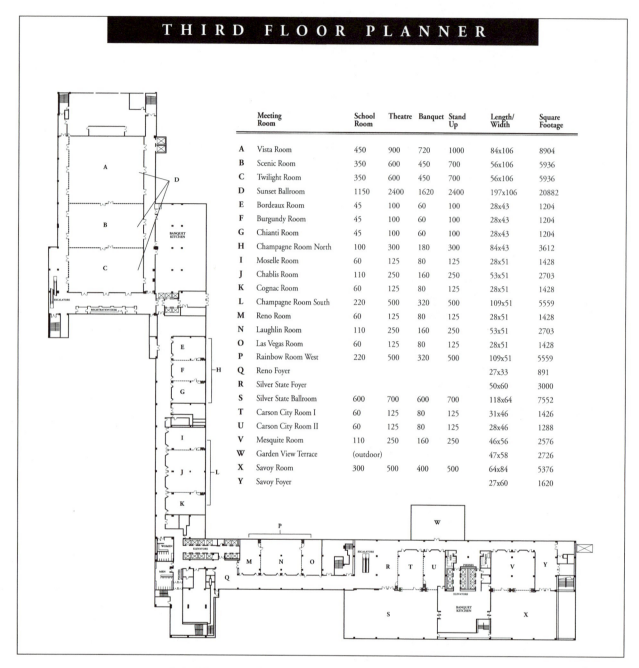

THIRD FLOOR PLANNER

	Meeting Room	School Room	Theatre	Banquet	Stand Up	Length/Width	Square Footage
A	Vista Room	450	900	720	1000	84x106	8904
B	Scenic Room	350	600	450	700	56x106	5936
C	Twilight Room	350	600	450	700	56x106	5936
D	Sunset Ballroom	1150	2400	1620	2400	197x106	20882
E	Bordeaux Room	45	100	60	100	28x43	1204
F	Burgundy Room	45	100	60	100	28x43	1204
G	Chianti Room	45	100	60	100	28x43	1204
H	Champagne Room North	100	300	180	300	84x43	3612
I	Moselle Room	60	125	80	125	28x51	1428
J	Chablis Room	110	250	160	250	53x51	2703
K	Cognac Room	60	125	80	125	28x51	1428
L	Champagne Room South	220	500	320	500	109x51	5559
M	Reno Room	60	125	80	125	28x51	1428
N	Laughlin Room	110	250	160	250	53x51	2703
O	Las Vegas Room	60	125	80	125	28x51	1428
P	Rainbow Room West	220	500	320	500	109x51	5559
Q	Reno Foyer					27x33	891
R	Silver State Foyer					50x60	3000
S	Silver State Ballroom	600	700	600	700	118x64	7552
T	Carson City Room I	60	125	80	125	31x46	1426
U	Carson City Room II	60	125	80	125	28x46	1288
V	Mesquite Room	110	250	160	250	46x56	2576
W	Garden View Terrace	(outdoor)				47x58	2726
X	Savoy Room	300	500	400	500	64x84	5376
Y	Savoy Foyer					27x60	1620

FIGURE 2-3   THE FLAMINGO HILTON'S FLOOR PLAN.
(Courtesy of the Flamingo Hilton, Las Vegas, Nevada.)

package. This arrangement not only enables customers to work within a budget that covers the entire project, but also fits with an approach to planning catering functions that considers the success of the overall meeting rather than each individual function. The catering manager is generally given the responsibility of creating a menu plan for the entire program along with theme functions and special events.

The target market for hotel catering functions is a customer who reflects the social, business, and economic profile of the community. Hotel catering services attract a wide base of customers with a broad range of requests. Customers who plan business functions on a regular basis are familiar with the catering staff and services of the hotel. Their needs are often quickly identified and provided for. Customers who plan social functions on a one-time basis, however, need more personal guidance throughout much of the planning stage. Pricing is a primary concern of this customer group.

OFF-PREMISE SERVICE

Hotel food and beverage departments are often requested to handle the arrangements for functions to be held away from the hotel property. If a company wants to retain as much revenue as possible from business, convention, and social customers, an off-premise catering policy should be developed.

Using the off-premise catering organizational guide in Figure 2-2, hotel catering departments can easily develop an off-premise catering program. Often, a hotel will have the facilities in place to offer a limited menu of take-out items. Figure 2-4 shows the take-out menu from the Baur au Lac Hotel in Zurich, Switzerland. Items have been selected from the hotel dining room menu to offer to the general public on a take-away basis. Hotels have the advantage over many private catering companies of being able to use their own equipment. In addition, kitchen and storage facilities are available to handle large volumes of both food and beverage as well as equipment. If the volume of on-property business requires the use of hotel equipment, rentals can cover the additional needs, with costs being charged back to the customer.

Catering Halls

A catering hall is a facility dedicated to private parties with an on-site production kitchen and staff. These facilities can offer a wide range of both in-house and off-premise catering services. The major factors that influence the market for a catering hall are:

1. Style or concept
2. Facilities
3. Customer profile

Catering halls offer customers a self-contained private function space independent of a hotel or restaurant. Many catering halls specialize in social functions such as weddings and plan the design of the landscaping and building to accent such functions. This design is also often aimed at a particular segment of the customer market, depending on location of the hall and the density and ethnic background of the surrounding population.

Catering halls can also specialize in large functions, providing space for groups that cannot normally be accommodated in other facilities. Such halls are generally designed to host a wide range of social and business functions and a variety of special event themes.

Entrées froides

	p.p.
Viande séchée des Grisons	Fr. 26.00
Régal des Grisons (viande séchée, jambon cru, salsiz)	Fr. 20.00
Foie gras de Strasbourg	Fr. 34.00
Mousse de foie gras	Fr. 25.00
Melon (selon saison)	Prix du jour
Salade de poulet	Fr. 21.00
Viandes froides assorties	Fr. 24.00
Salade niçoise	Fr. 19.00
Salade composée	Fr. 11.00
Tartare de saumon crû ou et fumé	Fr. 25.00
Salade de fruits de mer vietnamienne	Fr. 23.00
Vitello tonnato	Fr. 25.00
Roastbeef froid jardinière	Fr. 28.00

Barbecue et buffet de salades   à partir de 30 personne

Sélections de salades de saison et sa garniture, sauce et salades
Grillades, sauces et beurre à votre désir   **Prix selon votre choix**

Spécialités asiatiques   (minimum 6 personnes)   p.p.

Rouleaux de sushi japonais et californien   Fr. 45.00

Rouleaux de langoustines aux vermicelles de riz vietnamien
Sauce cacahuètes et soja aux piments rouges

Rouleaux de printemps aux légumes et pousses de soja
Sauce aigre-doux

Entrées froides

		p.p.
Caviar Osciètre Malossol	100g	Fr. 125.00
Cocktail de crevettes (préparé avec sauce gourmet)		Fr. 19.00
Cocktail de homard (préparé avec sauce gourmet)		Fr. 51.00
Aiguillette de saumon moderne (garnie oeuf fourré, pointes d'asperges, concombres farci, sauce verte)		Fr. 27.00
Saumon fumé Frédéric (garni: oignons, câpres, olives, citron, raifort Chantilly)		Fr. 25.00
Truite fumée (garnie: oignons, câpres, olives, citron, raifort Chantilly)		Fr. 19.00
Anguille fumée (garnie: oignons, câpres, olives, citron, raifort Chantilly)		Fr. 19.00
Langouste montée parisienne (garnie: demi oeuf au caviar, pointes d'asperges, fond d'artichaut) minimum 10 médaillons		Prix du jour

Potages et consommés

	p.p.
Crème d'asperges	Fr. 12.00
Bisque d'homard à l'estragon	Fr. 17.00
Consommé aux ravioli de ricotta à l'épinard	Fr. 12.00
Essence de queue de boeuf au sherry	Fr. 13.00
Potage Mulligatawny	Fr. 12.00
Gazpacho ou Vichyssoise (en été seulement)	Fr. 12.00

Buffet Campagnard

à Fr. 70.-- par personne, à partir de 20 personnes

Bouillon aux dés de moelle, croûtons

Saucisson en brioche

Jambon en pâte à pain

Carré de veau rôti primeurs

Boeuf bouilli vinaigrette

Plateau de fromages

Salades de pommes de terre, tomates,
concombre et haricots verts

Raifort Chantilly et sauce tartare

Tartes aux fruits de la saison

Meringue et crème double

Buffet chaud et froid

à Fr. 80.00 par personne, à partir de 20 personnes

Froid:

Crevettes en sauce gourmet
Mousse de foie gras
Panaché des Grisons
Truite, anguille, saumon fumés
Roastbeef froid
Cornet de jambon à la mousse de volaille
Terrine de poisson

Chaud:

Ragoût de fruits de mer au Pernod
Célestine de volaille Devonshire
Train de côte de porc rôti
Filet goulache Stroganoff
Riz, nouilles

Entremets:

Crème caramel
Mousse au chocolat
Tarte aux fruits de la saison
Glace vanille
Salade de fruits
Mignardises

FIGURE 2-4   THE BAUR AU LAC HOTEL'S TAKE-OUT MENU.
(Courtesy of The Baur au Lac Hotel, Zurich, Switzerland.)

FACILITIES

The flexibility, and often the originality, of function spaces are important to the success of a catering hall. Customers will travel considerable distances to social functions held in facilities that offer a unique setting or experience. Wedding receptions are often planned in locations over an hour away from the site of the ceremony so that the bride and groom can have a specific setting for their reception. The Del Coronado Hotel ballroom, seen in Figure 3-2, offers not only a beautiful and historic interior but a view of the Pacific Ocean as well. Annual social functions are constantly looking for new or different themes to draw attendees. Catering halls can provide the setting for special event themes ranging from futuristic to country western, offering menu and entertainment packages to match.

CUSTOMER PROFILE

The customer target market for catering halls, like hotels, is based on the social, business, and economic profile of the community. Catering halls, also like hotels, are available in a variety of price venues, generally appealing to customers who are looking for menu and function packages within a specific range of prices. Identifying a customer group toward which to target marketing efforts includes surveying the competition, establishing a price range, and determining specific geographic areas of the community in which potential customers live based on demographic information such as annual income, family size, and age. Chapter Three suggests methods of conducting market surveys and identifying customer profiles.

OFF-PREMISE CATERING

Catering halls have a great deal of flexibility regarding the type of business that they can solicit. The amount of off-premise catering that can be handled by an operation is limited only by the ability to service it. Location, transportation routes, and population density play a major role in determining this segment of the business. The ability to transport food and equipment and provide service and production staff are other limiting factors. Figure 2-2 outlines a checklist for organizing off-premise events.

Independent Caterers

Independent caterers are private businesses offering catering services to the general public. These businesses operate with or without permanent facilities of their own in which to hold functions. Those caterers who operate without a formal facility must arrange for kitchen production and storage space. Kitchen space can be rented from schools, churches, senior citizen centers, and other institutional facilities with commercial refrigeration and production space. Storage space can be arranged for in self-storage warehouse rental facilities that combine short-term leases with flexible storage space and 24-hour access. Some catering companies have their own production facilities and enough warehouse space to handle large volumes of business.

Chairs, floor covering, tables, and the table setup necessary for large functions are either sourced from a catering company's own warehouse or contracted through a local rental supplier. Many independent caterers focus on off-premise catering, maintaining only a small catering hall with limited facilities to house their production and storage needs. Their focus is on both business and social functions within a wide geographical area. In order to successfully cater to as many functions as possible simultaneously, a catering company has to be extremely well organized. Although equipment needs, staffing, and transportation are major concerns, the primary product, food, is the most important issue.

MENU DUPLICATION

The key to successfully providing catering services to a number of functions simultaneously is the duplication of as many of the menu items as possible in order to minimize kitchen production. All surrounding items, salads, and desserts can be standardized. The main course selection should be limited to three or four items on any given day if possible. Menu items should be chosen for their ability to be precooked for completion in another location. Foods should have excellent holding properties and retain heat. An example of an independent caterer's menu selection for a busy Sunday is shown in Figure 2-5.

This menu offers one appetizer, one salad and two choices of dessert. Dessert #2 is a chocolate dessert shell filled with frozen yogurt that can be preassembled or purchased frozen and transported to function locations within reasonable proximity to the main function kitchen. The gateau chocolate is contracted from an outside baking source, as are the breads. Whipped cream is served with the cake using a high-quality product from aerosol containers.

The main course offers a choice of two meats, one poultry, and one fish. All four of these items fulfill the requirements for preproduction and holding properties. Two vegetables selections are offered, one appropriate for the meat dishes and one better-suited for the poultry and fish, but acceptable for any of the main course selections. Standardization procedures such as these minimize the problems of serving multiple parties in off-premise settings and ensure that food presentation is of the best possible quality.

Private Clubs

Private clubs offer a self-contained facility that operates both full-service dining rooms and private function space along with a variety of food and beverage outlets. Private clubs are generally dependent on their membership for both dining room and catering business. Functioning as nonprofit organizations, clubs are, in many areas, prohibited by law from accepting or soliciting business from nonmembers. If such is the case private clubs may, however, cater functions that are sponsored by members and attended by nonmembers, allowing them to service both social and business activities.

SUNDAY MARCH 9, 1999

Appetizer

FRESH FRUIT BOAT

◆ ◆ ◆

Salad

MIXED SEASONAL GREENS

◆ ◆ ◆

Breads

AN ASSORTMENT OF FRESH BAKED ROLLS

◆ ◆ ◆

Main Course Items

FILET OF BEEF

LAMB CHOPS

BREAST OF CAPON

ROLLED FILET OF FISH

◆ ◆ ◆

Vegetables & Starches

1. VICHY CARROTS

ROASTED RED POTATOES

2. WHOLE GREEN BEANS

WILD RICE PILAF

◆ ◆ ◆

1. GATEAU CHOCOLATE

2. CHOCOLATE YOGURT DESSERT SHELL

FIGURE 2-5   OFF-PREMISE MENU SELECTION FOR A BUSY SUNDAY.

Factors that influence the success of restaurant and hotel catering services, such as location, facilities, and customer profile, also affect private clubs. Off-premise catering services can also be offered to private club members.

Private clubs may also contract out their foodservice operation to a contract foodservice operator. An example of this type of arrangement is The Colonial Inn, Concord, Massachusetts, and the local country club. The management of The Colonial Inn turned to the local country club as a source of both kitchen production space and private function rooms. The Inn itself, a historic property located in the middle of a crowded town, has no available adjacent property on which to develop additional catering facilities.

As a vehicle to increase their food and beverage revenues without incurring capital expenditures, the catering management team had identified a market for off-premise catering in the suburban Boston area adjacent to Concord. Without additional kitchen production space, however, the project could not go forward. In addition, during heavy business periods throughout the year, the Inn could not accommodate all of the requests that they received for private functions on property.

Through an arrangement with the local country club, management now not only has a satellite kitchen in a nearby facility but can also lease function space from the club on an as available/as needed basis. This alliance creates revenues and capitalizes on the needs of The Colonial Inn and the facilities of the club. A sample of the menu from The Colonial Inn is seen in Figure 2-6.

LOCATION

Clubs are broken down into two general classifications: private clubs and country clubs. Private clubs are generally situated in the downtown areas of larger towns and cities. The club facility is used primarily as a location for meetings, private dining, social and business functions. Country clubs require a suburban location and usually promote a combination of golf, tennis, and/or boating as their primary recreational facilities. Private dining and catering facilities are located in the clubhouse.

Acceptability of location is based primarily on general location and accessibility to major transportation routes. Downtown city locations can create problems regarding parking and security for people traveling into the city.

FACILITIES

Club facilities can greatly influence the volume of catering business. Clubs offering spectacular settings, access to garden areas for outdoor functions, or well designed interiors, such as seen in Figure 2-7, will easily attract social business.

OFF-PREMISE CATERING

A club's ability to accept off-premise catering function business is controlled by the same laws and regulations as the solicitation of nonmember business. Beyond these restrictions, the same considerations for restaurants and hotels concerning transportation, staffing, production, and service apply. The outline in Figure 2-2 suggests the operational considerations for off-premise catering for the majority of food and beverage operations. While the general specifications apply to almost everyone, each business will need to create specifications in each operational area according to its individual needs, availability of services, and budgets.

We cordially invite you to share your wedding day with us

Cocktail Reception
White Glove Service

Open bar with attendants throughout your function for three hours
serving name brand liquors, our house wines, champagne and beer

A Fancy Selection of Hot Hors d'Ouevres
(Choice of Three)
Caviar with Toast Points
Scallops wrapped in Bacon
Smoked Salmon Canapes
Teriyaki Sesame Beef Brochettes
Water Chestnuts and Snow Peas wrapped in Bacon
Chicken Satay with Peanut Ginger Sauce
Crab and Spinach Stuffed Mushroom Caps
Vegetable Egg Rolls
Chesapeake Crab Cakes
Goat Cheese Croustade
Petit Quiches
Spanakopita

Presented From a Skirted Table
Deluxe International Cheese Display on a Mirrored Platter
complemented with Crackers and Fruit
Fancy Crudite Diplay with House Dip

Chafing Dish Selections
Choice of one:
Swedish Meatballs
Chicken Marsala
Stir Fry Vegetables
Ratatouille Crepes
Chicken Etouffee
Stew of Wild Mushrooms with Fresh Thyme and Polenta

Pasta Station
Choose two pastas prepared in the room by a pasta chef

FIGURE 2-6   SAMPLE OF THE COLONIAL INN'S CATERING MENU.
(Courtesy of The Colonial Inn, Concord, Massachusetts.)

Appetizers

New England Clam Chowder

Beef Minestrone

Fresh Fruit Compote with Maple Yogurt Dressing

Rainbow Tortellini with Peas and Prosciutto

(Available at an Additional Cost)

Presentation of Chilled Shrimps with Cocktail Sauce	$7.25 pp
Seafood Vol Au Vent	$6.75 pp
Smoked Salmon with Champagne Salad & Toast Points	$7.25 pp

Salads

Traditional Caesar Salad

Mixed Field of Greens with Raspberry Walnut Vinaigrette

Arugula Salad with Goat Cheese

Intermezzo

Fresh Lemon Sorbet in a Lemon Shell

Entrees

Roast Breast of Chicken with choice of one Sauce: $95.00 pp

- Green Peppercorn & Brandy Sauce   • Teriyaki Sesame Glaze
- Fresh Herb & Zinfandel Cream   • Green Grape Chardonnay Cream
- Tarragon Asparagus Cream   • Three Citrus Glaze

Duet Plate: Roast Tenderloin of Beef with Brandied Mushroom Sauce,

   served with one of the following: $105.00 pp

- Half Chicken Breast with One of the Above Sauces
- Broiled Salmon with Lobster Caviar Cream
- Seafood Mousse Stuffed Shrimp

Roast Tenderloin of Beef with Brandied Mushroom Sauce	$110.00 pp
Oven Poached Salmon with Snowcrab, Asparagus and Bernaise Sauce	$108.00 pp
Roast Prime Rib of Beef with Cracked Pepper Jus	$110.00 pp
Sauteed Medallions of Veal with Raspberry Cream	$110.00 pp

All entrees are accompanied by Rolls and Butter, Potato

or Rice, and the Freshest Vegetable of the Season

Coffee, Tea, Decaffeinated Coffee

Dessert

Fruit Tarts

Chocolate Dipped Fruit Kabobs

Selection of Miniature Pastries

Vanilla Ice Cream and Strawberry Sauce

Dark Chocolate or Fruit Mousse

Please note: Above price per person includes entire package.

Above prices do not include 5% Massachusetts sales tax and 19% Service Charges

12/97

FIGURE 2-6   (CONTINUED)

FIGURE 2-7   CLUB FACILITIES.
(Courtesy of The Chicago Club, Chicago, Illinois.)

Contract Feeding

Contract feeding companies provide institutions such as hospitals and schools, as well as businesses, with in-house meal programs designed to meet specific needs. Food production and service is contracted for long-term periods with designated budget restrictions.

The contract feeding segment of the foodservice industry has been steadily growing since the late 1980s. Major corporations such as Marriott International created large contract feeding companies to service a wide range of customers. In the late 1990s a separate company, Host Marriott, was created and now operates independently of Marriott International, serving institutional customers internationally.

As food costs have increased and available labor decreased, institutions and businesses have turned to outside contractors to operate their food-service programs. In most cases, these programs function as a service to either patients, clients, or employees; they are subsidized benefits, not profit making operations. By using a professional contract foodservice operator to handle this area of operations, businesses find that the quality of service increases significantly along with client and employee satisfaction.

The major factors that can influence the success of catering services within a contract feeding location are:

1. Facilities
2. Customer profile

FACILITIES

Contract feeding can be offered in a wide variety of dining room and catering facilities. The type and number of facilities that can be used for function spaces within a business or institutional setting will help to determine the volume of in-house catering. Catering functions in these settings are usually business related, but open area spaces can be used by private groups for social functions.

CUSTOMER PROFILE

Identifying the customer profile for large and diverse groups of people in a business situation is initially done by job classification level. Private dining room service and business meeting menu selections should be based on the expectations associated with the job levels of the people who attend these functions.

The types of food products that will be popular in a cafeteria area depend on the profile of the employee population group. The proximity of the business to an urban center and the general education level of the customer group, along with local and regional food preferences and subsidy budgets, determine the range of food products offered.

OFF-PREMISE CATERING

Contract feeding companies working for a business or institution are often called upon to produce foodservice functions in off-premise locations. The organizational principles outlined in Figure 2-2 apply as equally to contract feeding operations as to restaurants and catering companies.

Charcuteries and Delicatessens

Charcuteries are food stores that offer take-out foodservice along with gourmet food products. Many of these products are used as ingredients in the preparation of the food line. In some cases a small seating area will be offered for eat-in customers. The trend for home-replacement food is significant to this type of operation. When customers want something beyond fast food for a take-home meal, they turn to establishments that can provide meals that they would like to have prepared for themselves. Home-replacement food is being provided in a number of types of foodservice facilities, including upscale supermarkets.

This type of foodservice operation usually specializes in a regional or national cuisine. Menu items range from salads and sandwiches to fully prepared meals. The success of a charcuterie depends on two major factors: location and customer profile.

LOCATION

Charcuteries should be located where the customer profile supports the level of cuisine offered. Pricing for this type of foodservice operation is generally higher than that of delicatessens and supermarket preprepared and packaged food items; hence it requires a customer base willing to pay for gourmet food products. Smaller independent caterers often operate out of this type of retail outlet, using the facility for both production and storage in addition to a means of advertising and promotion. Delicatessens are food stores that provide a variety of food products and offer both eat-in and take-out food service. The location should be reasonably close to the targeted customer base. Menu item offerings range from sandwiches, salads, and pizza to preprepared meals-to-go. Take-out foodservice of preprepared foods is a major business segment for this type of foodservice operation.

CUSTOMER PROFILE

The profile of customers for a charcuterie/delicatessen operation is drawn largely from the demographics of the population in the immediate area of the business. Primary customers can be identified as either employees of adjacent businesses or local area residents. A customer profile is determined for each of the two primary customer groups. For example, the twice a week business customer, with an average check of five to six dollars, could be in the mid-20s to 40s age group and low to middle income bracket. The local resident profile, with an average check of twelve dollars or more two times a week, may be in the mid-30s to 50s age group, middle to upper income bracket. Further investigation may show that the business employee is a morning coffee and lunch customer while the local resident is an evening customer for home-replacement meals.

OFF-PREMISE CATERING

Delivery of in-office and at-home preprepared food items can be a profitable extension of a delicatessen's business. From packaged lunches to party trays and platters, delicatessens often provide off-premise food items on a daily basis to a wide range of customers. The off-premise menu for Einstein Bagels is shown in Figure 2-8. This menu capitalizes on the restaurant's bagel bakery while also promoting salads, sandwiches, and desserts. Seating for these restaurants is generally limited due to their location in high rent districts. Marketing take-out and delivery services creates revenues without significantly increasing costs.

Summary

The opportunities for foodservice operations to offer catering services are many and varied. Catering management in the 2000s will continue to expand in both volume and diversity as the demand for ready-to-serve preprepared foods increases.

The ability of a foodservice operation to successfully offer catering services will be affected by a variety of factors. Location, customer profile, facilities, and menu offerings, along with style or concept, are some of the factors that must be considered before deciding which catering services to offer.

BOX LUNCHES

EACH BOX LUNCH INCLUDES UTENSILS, NAPKINS & CONDIMENTS. ALL SANDWICHES SERVED WITH CHIPS, KOSHER PICKLE SPEAR AND ONE HUGE COOKIE.

Add a side salad of our Broccoli Poppyseed Coleslaw or Potato Salad for $1.00.

SPECIALTY BAGEL SANDWICHES

TRADITIONAL DELI
Your choice of 99% Fat Free Turkey Pastrami, Smoked Turkey, Ham, Tuna or Chicken Salad with Cheese, Lettuce & Tomato...$6.95
with a side salad $7.95

"HOLEY" COW
Medium Rare Shaved Top Round of Beef, Cheddar Cheese, Zesty Horseradish Sauce, Lettuce & Tomato...$7.50
with a side salad $8.50

THE TASTY TURKEY
Smoked Turkey, Onion & Chive Cream Cheese, Lettuce, Tomato, Sprouts & Cucumber...$7.95
with a side salad $8.95

THE VEG OUT Vegetarian
Reduced Fat Garden Veggie Cream Cheese Shmear, Feta Pine Nut Spread, Sprouts, Lettuce, Cucumber, Tomato & Marinated Onions...$6.50
with a side salad $7.50

MEDITERRANEAN Vegetarian
HUMMUS & FETA
Hummus and Feta Pine Nut Spread, Roasted Red Peppers, Tomatoes, Red Onion & Cucumber...$6.50
with a side salad $7.50

NY LOX & BAGELS
Smoked Salmon on a Bagel with Plain Cream Cheese, Tomato, Sweet Onion & Capers...$8.50
with a side salad $9.50

CHALLAH SANDWICHES

THE COBBIE
Smoked Turkey & Peppered Bacon with Avocado Spread, Lettuce, Red Onion Tomato & Gorgonzola Mayo...$7.95
with a side salad $8.95

CLUB MEX
Traditional Club with Peppered Bacon, Pepper Jack Cheese, Tomato, Lettuce, Red Onion and a Zesty Ancho Lime Mayo...$7.95
with a side salad $8.95

BAGUETTE SANDWICHES

HAM & SMOKED GOUDA
Ham, Smoked Gouda, Tomatoes, Mind Bageling Greens and Raspberry Grain Mustard...$7.95 with a side salad $8.95

ROASTED CHICKEN & SMOKED GOUDA
All White Meat Chicken Breast, Smoked Gouda, Tomatoes, and Mind Bageling Greens served with Raspberry Grain Mustard...$7.95 with a side salad $8.95

OUR BIG HERO
Smoked Turkey, Ham & Pepperoni, Provolone Cheese, Mind Bageling Greens, Tomato, Marinated Red Onions and Roasted Red Pepper with Balsamic Vinaigrette...$7.95 with a side salad $8.95

SALAD BOX LUNCHES
SERVED WITH OUR FLATBREADS

CHICKEN CAESAR SALAD
with bagel croutons
Chicken Caesar served with our asiago & rosemary flatbread and one huge cookie. $7.50 Without Chicken $6.50

BROS BISTRO
Mind Bageling Greens tossed with our raspberry vinaigrette, candied walnuts & gorgonzola cheese served with our asiago & rosemary flatbread and one huge cookie. $6.95

ASIAN CHICKEN
All white meat chicken breast, rice noodles, mind bageling greens, asian veggies, peanut & chow mein noodles with low fat asian sesame dressing served with our peanut sesame flatbread and one huge cookie. $7.95

MAKE IT A MEAL

A LITTLE SWEET
COOKIE VARIETY BOX
A dozen assortment of our huge cookies packed in a neat little box. Serves 10-12 $14.99

HALF-DOZEN SWEETS
Your choice of any combination of 6 Brownies, Rice Crispy Treats or Poundcake slices. $9.99

SIDE SALADS FOR GROUPS
Our fan BROCCOLI POPPYSEED COLESLAW or POTATO SALAD
Your choice of Side Salad served family style. Serves 8-10 $17.50

"Coca-Cola" is a registered trademark of the Coca-Cola Company.

fancy schmancy catering

CASUAL CATERING FOR MEETINGS AND GET-TOGETHERS

www.einsteinbros.com

FIGURE 2-8 OFF-PREMISE MENU FOR EINSTEIN BAGELS. (Courtesy of The Einstein Bagel Corp.)

Off-premise catering can be very successful for independent caterers and problematic for full-service restaurants. Equipment and resources are the factors that will often determine how well an operation can conduct off-premise catering.

The availability of catering services is limited only by the ability of foodservice operations to provide them. Whether in the executive dining room of a large corporation or at a garden wedding, it is possible for food-service operators from five star hotels to delicatessens to provide quality food and service.

Catering Foodservice Development

CHAPTER THREE

Developing a Catering Business

The successful development of any business rests on a foundation of information identifying the market for the products or services offered for sale. The population group that represents the people who are intended to be the primary customer group is known as the target market. Information regarding the target market is gathered through market survey research conducted in the community.

The market survey analyzes the community in which a business is being developed, concentrating on four major segments of the market:

- Customer
- Competition
- Community
- Labor pool

Each of these four market segments contributes to the success of a foodservice operation. It is important to analyze these segments individually in terms of the type of product/service that is being offered. In order for a business to be successful the following information must be determined.

1. Who is the target market that needs the product/service in the community?
2. Will the target market perceive a value for the product service equal to the selling price?
3. Is the target market willing to pay for the product/service?
4. Will the business be competitive with others identified as offering a similar price/product/service to the target market?
5. Are sufficient skilled foodservice production and service personnel available within the community to fulfill the requirements of the business?

Market Survey Information

In order to provide complete information with which to analyze the market, an effective market survey will include the following information:

A. Customer:
1. Population breakdown by age
2. Percent population growth forecasted for next five years
   Percent population growth forecasted for next ten years
3. Number of households
   Number of two-income households
4. Average family income for 35- to 60-year-old population group
5. Average family size for 35- to 60-year-old population group
6. Average education level for 35- to 60-year-old population group

B. Competition:
1. Number of foodservice operations offering catering services

    2. Number of independent catering businesses
    3. Number of competitive catering businesses

C. Community:
    1. Number of overall businesses
    2. Percent growth in past five years
    3. Percent growth in past ten years
    4. Percent of retail food and beverage sales to total retail sales
    5. Anticipated growth of community for the next ten-year period
    6. Community organizations:

    _____
    _____
    _____
    _____
    _____

    7. Community businesses:

    _____
    _____
    _____
    _____
    _____

    8. Percent growth of group meeting and conference business in last five years
    9. Percent growth of travel tourism business in last five years

D. Labor:
    1. Availability of trained foodservice production personnel
    2. Availability of trained restaurant service personnel
    3. Projected increase/decrease in overall labor pool in next five years
    4. Availability of vocational and/or community college foodservice programs
    5. Community unemployment rate

The market survey results are analyzed according to the needs of the prospective business. The information from the market survey that will be most valuable to foodservice businesses offering catering services will be that which indicates the primary influences on prospective customers to patronize a catering foodservice business. A discussion of the significance of the primary influences follows to help in understanding how to analyze the market survey information.

1. The availability of expendable income to pay for "extra" food services

Unit of Analysis: Average family income for 35- to 60-year-old population group (Customer item #4)

Due to its work patterns, social and business obligations, and family patterns, the 35- to 60-year-old population group constitutes the segment of the population group that is most likely to use catering services. Family income should range upward of $50,000 per year to be eligible for target market designation.

2. Lack of time for food preparation

Unit of Analysis: Number of two-income households (Customer item #3)

The number of two-income family households indicates the possibility of a shortage of time for food preparation and a need for preprepared food products.

Community demographics and trends also influence the patronage of catering businesses. In addition to economic trends, social, religious, and cultural movements within the community will affect the volume and scale of catering functions.

3. A population growth within the age groups that require catering services

Unit of Analysis: Percent of population growth over five- and ten-year periods (Customer item #2)

Catering services are required by each population group identified. The 18- to 25-year-old group will need graduation parties, proms, and weddings; the 25- to 35-year-old group, weddings and social functions; and the 35- to 70-year-old group, social, business, and family-related functions. An anticipated population growth in this 35- to 70-year-old age range indicates a healthy demand for catering services over a ten-year period.

4. The availability of funds for community development and marketing

Unit of Analysis: Percent of growth of community and businesses (Community items #2, 3, and 5)

Growth in the business community indicates the possibility of the availability of funds for community development, charitable as well as industry-oriented, and increased marketing efforts. Both of these factors are favorable signs for an increased demand for catering services for private business and social functions.

5. Strong presence of charitable organizations

Unit of Analysis: Community organizations (Community item #6)

A survey of community organizations that sponsor fund-raising functions for charitable programs allows prospective caterers to assess the need for catering services for private parties.

6. Strong interest from outside sources in holding meetings and conferences within the community

Unit of Analysis: Community businesses (Community item #8)

A survey of hotels, conference and convention centers, and the chamber of commerce identifies the level of group meetings and conference business. Meetings lasting two days or longer often need outside sources for entertainment and function planning. A growth in this business segment indicates an increased demand for catering services.

Market survey information outlines the target market profile and begins to identify characteristics and trends that are important to the success of a business. Using these percentages and statistics as a foundation, management can form a complete picture of the customer, competition, and community. Additional research into the history of local business can also help in forecasting for the future.

Customer

Determining a customer profile for catering services is difficult, due to the range of ages that participate in catered functions. Teenagers attend proms and banquets held in a variety of locations from school gymnasiums to hotel ballrooms. Weddings are popular in the 20- to 25-year-old market. The 25- to 30-year-old group plans both business functions and weddings. The 35- to 70-year-old bracket uses catering services in a variety of settings, from tennis tournaments to hospital picnics. Social and business occasions are increasingly serviced by caterers. The increased demand for "home meal replacement," in addition to at-home functions, ranges from party trays to full-course dinners. The shortage of time to prepare food causes many single- and two-income families to turn to catering services.

The following customer profile emerges from the market survey and additional observations:

CUSTOMER PROFILE

- AGE: 35 TO 50
- AVERAGE INCOME: $70,000 ANNUAL
- OCCUPATION: PROFESSIONAL
- FAMILY PROFILE: FOUR MEMBERS, TWO INCOMES

This information can now be used to target direct marketing efforts toward the customer group that matches this profile.

Competition

Competitive businesses can often provide valuable information to new and developing operations. Catering services that have opened as independent businesses or recently been added to existing foodservice operations indicate the presence of customer and community need. Current trends in take-out meals and home meal delivery reflect both the need and receptiveness of local customers to catering services. The ongoing use of restaurant, charcuterie, and delicatessen services for home meal replacement indicates the customers' perceived value of the time required for home food preparation. Such customers are likely to take advantage of catering services.

A complete analysis of the competition requires a comparison of the variety of catering services, the menu items offered, and the pricing structure.

Catering services often use a package format for pricing to include food and beverage services along with entertainment or theme programs. It is important to identify the numbers and types of services contained in the packages of each competitive catering business in order to accurately compare prices.

The competition survey in Figure 3-1 outlines the information that is needed for each catering operation and foodservice facility offering catering services.

Style of Catering Operation

Full-service restaurant   _____
Hotel food and beverage facility _____
Catering hall   _____
Independent caterer, delivery only _____
Country club   _____
Contract foodservice   _____
Charcuterie   _____
Delicatessen   _____
Other   _____

Location

Address _____

_____

Access to major roads _____

_____

Available parking _____
Problems in locating _____

_____

Services

Catering services in-house_____
Outside caterer allowed_____
Meal services available: breakfast _____ lunch_____
dinner _____ coffee service _____ other_____
Full or limited liquor license_____
Table service styles_____
Entertainment _____
Business meeting services _____
Conference and convention services _____

_____

Concept and theme party services_____

_____

Cuisine specialty_____

FIGURE 3-1   SURVEY OF COMPETITIVE CATERING OPERATIONS.

Facilities

    Number of function rooms _____

    Total available seating _____

    Breakdown of seating by function room_____

    _____

    _____

    _____

    _____

    Decorative theme _____

    Condition of exterior facilities_____

    Condition of interior facilities _____

    Dance floors: portable _____ built-in _____ size _____

    Bars: portable _____ built-in_____

    Floor plans available _____

Availability

    Heavily booked _____ Some dates available _____

    Many dates available _____

    Heaviest booking period _____

Service Reputation

    Food service: good _____ average _____ poor _____

    Party planning service: good _____ average _____ poor _____

    Theme parties: good _____ average _____ poor _____

    Entertainment: good _____ average _____ poor _____

    Meeting services: good _____ average _____ poor _____

    Overall follow-through: good _____ average _____ poor_____

    Invoicing and billing: good _____ average _____ poor _____

    Pricing: competitive _____ high _____ low_____

Marketing Materials

    Menus _____

    Presentation cover _____

    Theme brochures _____

    _____

    Floor plans _____

    Maps to location _____

    Other _____

    Copies of attached _____

    Completed by:_____

    Date:_____

FIGURE 3-1   (CONTINUED)

Analyzing the Competition

A comparison of competitive catering services reveals trends in private party formats, cuisine menus, theme and entertainment concepts. The introduction of new theme and menu ideas into the catering market can create increased customer interest. Customers who use catering services on an ongoing basis are constantly looking for original and different ideas to highlight both business and social functions. The window of opportunity for new and ongoing catering businesses exists in the identification of unique cuisine, entertainment, and theme concepts that result in quality food and service at a reasonable price.

Prospective caterers can use the information on the competition survey form to identify the direct competition and determine how their catering services can compete in the established marketplace. An understanding of why customers choose a certain caterer and facility is important in identifying which services and/or facilities are needed by both customers and the community. Price is the primary determinant in the decision making process for most customers. When, however, the pricing structure for similar services is reasonably close, customers will consider four additional major factors:

- Availability
- Location
- Facilities
- Service

AVAILABILITY

Customers have generally identified a specific date when they begin to plan a private function. Although they may have taken the precaution of choosing two or three alternate dates, one date is clearly preferable. The catering service that can offer both price and availability of the primary date will receive first consideration.

LOCATION

As most guests drive to private parties in the United States, access of the location to major transportation routes, personal security, and availability of parking influence the selection of the final location. Outstanding facilities or locations will often be a primary factor in the customer's decision. The ballroom of the Hotel Del Coronado, near San Diego, California, shown in Figure 3-2, is a historical structure and overlooks the Pacific Ocean. The ballroom offers a spectacular view of the ocean and the interior of the room itself is an elegant setting. While the location of the property requires traveling to a remote setting, customers are more than willing to accept the inconvenience in exchange for the facilities and the ocean view.

FACILITIES

The specific needs of a private party can be the determining factor in the final selection of a facility. Social functions often need reception areas for

FIGURE 3-2   HOTEL DEL CORONADO BALLROOM.
(Courtesy of The Hotel Del Coronado, Coronado, California.)

cocktail parties; customers may want outdoor settings. A variety of function areas, dance floors, seating capacities, audiovisual equipment availability, and special functions planning are just some of the other facility demands that customers may consider necessary to the success of their functions. The tent facility, like the one shown in Figure 3-3, has become a popular alternative function area for catering events. Whether permanently attached to a hotel facility or set up temporarily for a specific function, tenting has significantly widened the scope of available space for private functions. Tenting is used for sports events in open areas or to create a function space adjacent to private homes, museums, and other facilities.

SERVICE

The reputation of a catering service for providing quality product, timely delivery, special customer attention, and creative eventing abilities also influences the final customer decision to contract a specific catering business. Customers consider all of these combined factors when making their decision, as seen in the following two examples:

Catering Service A: This business can provide service and facilities to match customer needs but does not have the preferable date available. If the date is flexible, service and facilities will generally be the persuading factor in the decision.

FIGURE 3-3   TENT FACILITY.
(Courtesy of Aztec Tents and Events,
Torrance, California.)

Catering Service B: They have an excellent location with availability of the preferable date. The facilities, however, are not exactly what is needed but can be adjusted to the function. In this case, location and availability should sway the decision, regardless of the compromise on facilities.

Community

Economic health of the community is the single most important community factor that can affect the success of a new catering operation. While fast-food and casual family restaurants are considered necessary expenses by many people, full-service restaurants and catering services are not. These last two are supported by expendable income availability that, in times of economic recession and uncertainty, becomes unavailable.

Communities, as well as individuals, adjust their dining and social activities according to the current economic situation. The U.S. economy flourished in the last part of the 1990s. As a result both personal and community incomes rose with expendable income available for increased social activity.

In the early 1990s, however, many state and local governments experienced budgetary problems, forcing them to make significant cutbacks in both services and employees. It would have been ill-advised for these governments to support activities such as awards dinners, employee picnics, or business-related functions at a time when the job stability of many of their employees was questionable. Economic difficulties, however, can create the need for alternative funding for many community services, offering a potential market for catering operations with creative and unique special event and fund-raising ideas.

Labor

The availability of labor that is both skilled and able to work the flexible hours required by catering services is essential to the success of a catering business. Restaurants have full-time staff on call to work at catered functions. Independent catering businesses, however, operate with a skeleton staff of full-time employees supplemented by part-time help as needed. While this practice reduces the cost of employees significantly, a ready source of labor is always questionable. The two major classifications of labor that fulfill catering service needs are kitchen personnel and service staff. Chapter Ten discusses hiring and personnel concerns at greater length.

Labor will be one of the most critical supply areas in the foodservice industry for the first part of the twenty-first century. Trained waitstaff is difficult to find and retain. Labor turnover is often high, depending on the type of foodservice operation, geographical location, and average age of the staff.

The benefit of flexible hours and the guaranteed earnings offered by catering work is valued by every age group in the labor pool. Employees who work on a continual part-time basis generally know in advance when functions will be held. Work can be accepted according to personal schedule needs for families, education, and other jobs. Wages paid for catering service are based on federally mandated guidelines. Gratuities are charged as a percentage of the price of the food and beverages being served and are divided equally among the servers.

Applying Market Survey Information

Market survey information can be applied to catering menu management in a number of areas of a menu program and is particularly helpful in menu pricing. Competitive catering menu pricing requires a thorough analysis of the competition's pricing. In order to develop a successful pricing structure, management should review the following questions for each menu in their menu program:

Menu Pricing Questions

- What is the competition charging for a similar catering menu? Are portion sizes and quality of food items similar to the competition's?
- How important is this menu to the total menu program? Will a lower selling price and the resulting higher food cost of this menu cause the overall food cost to be too high? Will volume sales of this menu create the desired profit at the lower menu price?
- Will the average catering customer accept this price as meeting his or her perceived value of all of the menu items included in the menu?
- Will this menu price blend into the pricing range for the total menu program?

The responses to these questions will determine how the menu is finally priced. If the original price calculation is higher than that of the competition, management must carefully weigh the benefits and drawbacks of offering a lower price. Unless the average catering customer accepts the price as valid, the menu will not be selected. Management often determines price acceptability by using its competitor's efforts as an indication of the probable success of promoting the item for volume sales. The final menu price must blend with the other prices in the menu program to create a range from which customers can choose. Large discrepancies, or too many similarities, in the range of menu prices can frustrate customers.

Summary

Market survey research is essential to the success of every catering service. The four major interest segments that a market survey must investigate are the customer, the competition, the community, and the availability of a labor pool.

Statistics and data from the market survey provide information that can be used to assemble a profile of the average customer. The customer profile becomes a major means of identifying the target market on which to focus the marketing efforts for the sales of the product service provided by the business.

Customers base the decision on which catering service to use for a private function on four major factors: availability, location, facilities, and service. A thorough survey of the competition regarding these factors identifies those restaurants and catering services that are directly competing for the same target market.

The availability of trained foodservice personnel is a critical concern of every catering business. Catering service does, however offer prospective employees the benefits of flexible hours and guaranteed income. Both of these factors have a significant perceived value within the part-time labor pool. Caterers who can create a core of reliable part-time employees, both production and service, will be secure in their ability to service customers.

The application of market survey information throughout the menu program can increase sales as well as customer volume. Menu pricing is one area in which this information can have a significant effect. By thoroughly analyzing the menu prices of the catering businesses that have been identified as direct competition, a pricing structure can be developed to reflect current acceptable menu prices and customer needs.

Catering Menu Program

CHAPTER FOUR

DINNER ENTREES & BUFFETS

LUNCH ENTREES & BUFFETS

BREAKFAST ENTREES & BUFFETS

COFFEE BREAKS & SNACKS

ALA CARTE

Assorted Pastries
(Danish, Muffins, Cinnamon Rolls)
Donuts
Strudels
Cinnamon Rolls
Turnovers (Apple or Cherry)
Bagels with Cream Cheese & Assorted Jams

Assorted Muffins
(Banana, Chocolate Chip, Bran, Blueberry)
Cookies
Brownies
Assorted 8 oz. Flavored Yogurt
Assorted Ice Cream Bars (Haagen Daz)
Soft Pretzels with Mustard

BEVERAGES

Soft Drinks – Pepsi Products
IBC Root Beer
IBC Cream Soda

Lemonade
Fruit Punch
Individual Fruit Juices

Mineral Water
Assorted Herbal Teas
Fresh Brewed Coffee (Regular or Decaf)

EARLY RISER
Fresh Brewed Coffee, Tea or Decaf

HOLIDAY INN CONTINENTAL
Assorted Pastries (Danish, Muffins, Cinnamon Rolls)
Array of Fresh Fruit
Assorted Juices, Assorted Teas, Coffee

SWEET TOOTH
Assorted Cookies
Fudge
Soda
Milk
(Minimum 30 people)

HEALTH NUT
Bran Muffins
Assorted Fresh Fruit Slices
Fresh Squeezed Juice

PIZZA TIME
Assorted Pizza & Sodas
(Minimum 30 people)

All items add 17% gratuity & applicable tax.

The catering menu program in any foodservice operation includes all of the menus for the range of meal services offered for private functions. This includes menus for receptions as well as theme functions. The basic menus included in a catering program are:

- Breakfast, lunch, and dinner menus
- Hors d'oeuvre menus
- Receptions menus
- Special function menus
- À la carte menus (dessert or salad menus)
- Beverage menus (wine, liquor, cordial, and specialty)

Each menu in the program represents a selection of menu items presented in the sequence of the menu format identified for a specific meal service. The identification of specific menu items is based on six major factors regarding the catering operation:

1. **Style of Service:** Style of service determines equipment, staffing, and food production needs.
2. **Price Range:** Price range determines both the forecasted catering sales volumes on a month-by-month basis and the anticipated annual profit.
3. **Menu Item Selection:** The selection of menu items is based on the skill levels of the kitchen production personnel along with management's goals and objectives for the overall catering operation.
4. **Cuisine:** Cuisine orientation helps to determine the pricing structure of the menu program.
5. **Food Production Capabilities:** Food production capabilities identify menu items within the cuisine that can be successfully produced for catering services based on the available equipment and the skill level of the production personnel.
6. **Awareness of Customer Needs:** Management's awareness of customer needs is reflected in a knowledge of current trends in dining and eating patterns.

A creative and flexible menu program requires that catering specifications be developed for every item in the catering menu file. These specifications provide a basis for prepricing individual menu portions of catering menu items, a process that allows management to adjust the menu content and price according to customer needs.

Creativity and flexibility also involve the ability of the entire operation to react to new and unique concepts and ideas in catering menu development, theme, and entertainment packaging. This ability will set a catering service apart from the competition within the market segment in which it has become established.

Menu Formats

The basic menu formats used to develop catering menus are based on the classical French menu plans for dinner, luncheon, and breakfast. Laid down by Auguste Escoffier in the early 1900s, these are used, either in whole or in part, to present a series of menu items for a preplanned meal program in both institutional and commercial settings.

The classical dinner format for catering service, as shown in Figure 4-1, offers eight courses. Including both a fish and meat course, it places the salad course after the main meat course. American versions of this menu will often place the salad course between the soup and fish course. A sorbet (frozen ice) is offered between the fish and meat course as a palate cleanser. The use of this menu format in its entirety is usually reserved for formal occasions. The accompanying beverage program for this menu format offers appropriate wines with the appetizer, fish, meat, dessert and cheese courses. After-dinner cordials are generally offered at the completion of the entire menu service.

The commercial adaptation of the classical dinner menu format most commonly used by catering services is shown in Figure 4-2. The first course is either a soup or appetizer selection. Only one main course selection is offered, and the salad course precedes the entrée selection for American

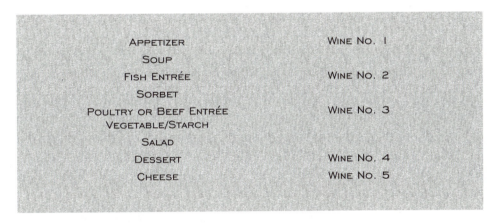

FIGURE 4-1   CLASSICAL DINNER FORMAT.

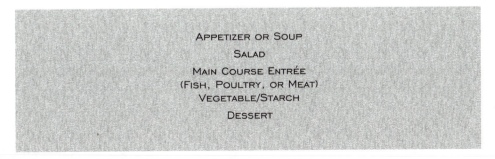

FIGURE 4-2   COMMERCIAL CATERING ADAPTATION OF
THE CLASSICAL DINNER MENU.

Appetizer

OYSTERS ROCKEFELLER

Salad

FRESH SALAD GREENS

Entrée

ROASTED TENDERLOIN OF BEEF
SAUCE CHASSEUR
SAUTÉED MUSHROOMS EN BEURRE
POMMES TOMATE
PETITE FRENCH ROLLS
AND BUTTER

Dessert

BANANAS FOSTER FLAMBÉ
CAFÉ AND TEA

FIGURE 4-3   COMMERCIAL CATERING MENU FOLLOWING
THE CLASSICAL DINNER MENU FORMAT.

service. Cheeses are eliminated from the menu. A sample commercial catering menu using this menu is shown in Figure 4-3.

The catering luncheon menu format is governed by the type of function for which it is being served. Business luncheons need to be brief to accommodate either speaker programs or afternoon meeting schedules. Menus for social luncheons are designed around the theme of the occasion. The classical format from which luncheon menus are adapted is shown in Figure 4-4.

Breakfast is not a formal part of the tradition of French cuisine. Many Europeans prefer a breakfast that offers a fruit, cheese, and meat, while other cultures include spicy foods, tofu, or Kaisó (seaweed). The English have a formal breakfast format that includes fish and/or meat, breads, jams, and butter, and often begins with a hot porridge.

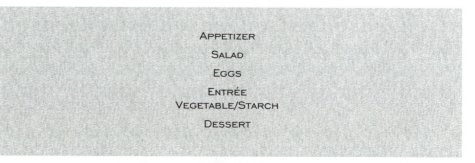

APPETIZER

SALAD

EGGS

ENTRÉE
VEGETABLE/STARCH

DESSERT

FIGURE 4-4   CLASSICAL LUNCHEON FORMAT.

LOBSTER CUTLETS	DROPPED CODFISH BALLS
BEEF HEART SAUTÉ	BROILED OYSTERS
FRIED SMELT	VEAL SOUFFLÉ
FRICASSEE OF RABBIT	TRIPE À LA LYONNAISE
MINCED VEAL MOLDED	BROILED PIG'S FEET
SCRAMBLED MUTTON	DEVILED CLAMS
SPAGHETTI AND HAM TIMBALES	STEWED SQUABS
LAMB CHOPS AND HOMINY HEARTS	MINCED CALF'S LIVER

FIGURE 4-5 MAIN COURSE BREAKFAST DISHES, 1901.
(*Source: 365 Breakfast Dishes, 1901.*)

JUICE
FRUIT
CEREAL/GRAIN
EGGS
MEAT
VEGETABLE/STARCH
BREADS
BEVERAGES

FIGURE 4-6 CATERING BREAKFAST FORMAT.

The nineteenth-century American breakfast was built around the English menu with the primary objective of providing a full meal prior to a day of heavy agricultural labor. The assortment of breakfast dishes listed in Figure 4-5 is selected from a cookery collection published in 1901 by George W. Jacobs & Co. in Philadelphia titled *365 Breakfast Dishes*. In the year 2000, this grouping of hearty dishes would be more appropriate for the main course item on catering luncheon and dinner menus than breakfast. The comparison between this listing of breakfast items and the reality of the average American breakfast is an indication of the major changes that have taken place in diet and eating patterns since the late nineteenth century.

The catering breakfast menu in the year 2000 reflects both current trends in meal planning and healthy eating concerns. The general catering breakfast menu outline is given in Figure 4-6.

Styles of Service

Establishing the level and type of table service that a catering service will offer as a daily standard of operation is necessary to the menu development process. The selection of service style is influenced by the following factors:

1. Skill level of available waitstaff
2. The cuisine being served
3. Available equipment
4. Menu price range
5. Customer profile

The styles of table service that are adaptable for banquet service are:

- French service
- Russian service
- American service
- Buffet service

FRENCH SERVICE

French service in American foodservice operations is often combined with various aspects of Russian service. Classical French service requires a *brigade de service,* or six-member dining room staff, and is inappropriate for catering service due to high labor demands. However, aspects of table side preparation, such as a Caesar salad preparation, the slicing of a whole filet of beef, and completing a flambé dessert preparation, are easily incorporated into formal catering menu presentations. These table side preparations require that table captains be properly trained so that these menu items match the quality of the balance of the menu as it is served from the kitchen. An extra per person charge is generally added to the total bill for each additional service activity.

RUSSIAN SERVICE

The most appropriate and popular style of table service used for more formal catering service is Russian service. This service style is ideally adapted to table seatings of six to twelve guests. All food items are arranged on platters and serving dishes. Servers portion and serve the food directly to the guest at the table as seen in Figure 4-7. Previously discussed aspects of French service are often incorporated with Russian service techniques. Labor requirements for this type of service include skill training in Russian and French service. In addition, a high ratio of servers to guests increases labor costs. The number of waitstaff required to successfully accomplish this service style is higher than for other service styles.

AMERICAN SERVICE

American service is the style of table service most commonly used in catering service in the United States. All food is prepared and served onto plates in the kitchen. The main course item, surrounding vegetables, and starches are served on one plate. A plate cover is fitted tightly over the main plate, keeping the meal warm and allowing plates to be stacked by servers onto large banquet trays. Once in the dining room, the waitstaff can serve large numbers of guests quickly. This style of table service employs a minimum number of servers and requires basic table service skills.

FIGURE 4-7   RUSSIAN STYLE TABLE SERVICE.
(Courtesy of and © by Johnson and Wales University,
Providence, Rhode Island.)

BUFFET SERVICE

Buffet service is a popular style of service for private functions and is often combined with American service. Appetizer, beverage, and dessert may be served to the table with salads, vegetables, and main course items featured on the buffet. The service style does, however, require more time for the overall meal. Guests must wait by table until they are directed to approach the buffet. To expedite buffet service, sections of the buffet table are often set up around the room, as pictured in Figure 4-8. Iced shellfish displays,

FIGURE 4-8   PEABODY HOTEL BUFFET STYLE SERVICE.
(Courtesy of The Peabody Hotel, Orlando, Florida.)

SPECIALTY STATIONS

Italiano

SHRIMP, SQUID & MUSSELS IN A MEDITERRANEAN HERB MARINADE

PROSCIUTTO WITH SWEET MELON

SHRIMP FLAMBÉED WITH BRANDY AND A PIQUANT TOMATO SAUCE

MILK-FED VEAL RACK WITH A MUSHROOM RAGOUT

GRILLED SWORDFISH TIDBITS WITH HERB BUTTER

FETTUCCINI ALFREDO

CLASSICAL CAESAR SALAD

Low Lands Cajun

LOUISIANA CRAYFISH TAILS IN A SAFFRON TOMATO SAUCE

CARVED ROAST BREAST OF WILD DUCK
ORANGE AND MADEIRA SAUCE

GRILLED MEDALLIONS OF BEEF TENDERLOIN
VIDALLIA ONION RAGOUT

AVERY ISLAND TOBASCO GUMBO

GREENS AND RED BEANS WITH RICE

RACK OF LAMB DIJONNAISE
MUSTARD CRUSTED WITH RED ONIONS

FIGURE 4-9   SPECIALTY CUISINE STATIONS MENU FOR BUFFET PRESENTATION.

salad bar presentations, and dessert tables complement a main course buffet that can include vegetables, starches, entrée items, and often a carving station with a chef slicing meat to order. An example of a buffet menu offering a variety of table stations is seen in Figure 4-9.

Buffet service requires the least amount of labor, both kitchen and service. A busy catering operation can increase its flexibility by applying this style of table service to one large function while simultaneously serving another party with American service. Once the buffet food items have left the kitchen, the kitchen staff can plate-up the second party's main course items for service.

Price Range

The pricing structure for catering menus established by management to meet both customer needs and profit goals controls three major aspects of the menu program:

- The level of cuisine
- The menu items selected
- The quality of food product

The selection of menu items offered to the customer for any given meal service or function should represent a range of prices that has been identified as acceptable to the average customer of the foodservice operation. In order for a menu program to be successful, the customer's perceived value of the total menu and its assigned price must match. This marketing pricing theory applies to all of the catering menus, including beverage. The pricing methods for a menu program are covered in detail in Chapter Five.

Menu Item Selection

Serving numbers of the same menu items within a given time period in a private function setting, for an established price per person, is the basic objective to be considered in the selection of menu items for catering menus. Catering menu items should be chosen according to how they fulfill three basic purchasing requirements:

1. Can the required quality of this item be purchased in large volumes?
2. Is this item available for purchase through normal distribution channels on a year-round basis?
3. Is this item available for purchase at a price that, when combined with other menu items, results in an overall food cost that yields an acceptable food cost percentage?

Cuisine

Catering operations can offer a wide variety of cuisine offerings priced according to the target market's customer needs. Ethnic and regional menu item specialties can easily be incorporated into menus for business and social functions as well as special event themes. The per person price of the menu will determine the cuisine level of the actual menu items to be included.

The menu in Figure 4-10, for example, would generally be used for a wedding when the customer has requested an emphasis on Italian cuisine. This catering menu can be priced to meet the demands of middle-income families while providing a level of cuisine items that are perceived as acceptable for a wedding dinner. The Southwest holiday buffet menu in Figure 4-11 would be appropriate for a wide range of social and business functions. The main course item can be changed according to customer budget and requirements.

Food Production

The capability of a foodservice operation to carry out the preparation and service of a menu is based on the production capacities of both equipment and labor.

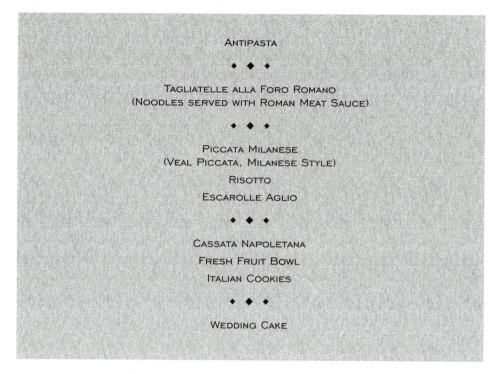

FIGURE 4-10   ITALIAN CUISINE WEDDING DINNER.

The ability of kitchen staff to produce menu items in the volumes required for catering menus is a major management concern. Before offering a customer the availability of menu items, catering management should consult with the executive chef to ensure that skilled staff is available to produce the menu item at the established level of quality in the volumes required to satisfy customer needs.

Not all prospective menu items can be produced in large volumes to the standard of presentation and taste that the customer might expect. A good example of this type of menu item is Eggs Benedict. Hollandaise sauce, a major ingredient for this item, requires very specific temperature and time controls in order to be served properly. Hollandaise sauce will separate if cooked too long or held above certain temperatures. In addition, the dish must be served immediately after the sauce has been poured over the eggs or it will thicken and form a tough outer skin. Attempting to serve Eggs Benedict with American service for 250 guests simultaneously poses major production and equipment challenges. Stainless steel plate covers stacked one on top of each other form condensation on the inside top of the cover that, in turn, drips down onto the sauce, breaking through the outer skin and causing the sauce to separate. Timing must be extremely well coordinated between the maître d' and the kitchen in order to plate up the menu item and get it to the guest as quickly as possible while it is still hot.

Equipment becomes a major concern in the production of large-volume catering functions. Table service equipment is often supplemented by rental equipment for large parties. Kitchen production equipment, on the other hand, cannot easily be adapted or added to. Expensive rentals pose the

SOUTHWEST HOLIDAY BUFFET
(Minimum of 100 People)

Hearty Posole
With Pork and New Mexico Red Chile

Grilled Jalapeño Caesar Salad

Jicama and Orange Salad
With Peanuts and Cilantro

Black Bean, Cucumber and Red Onion
With Chipotle Vinaigrette

(Select Three Entrees)
Chile Rellenos
With Green Chile Sauce and Sour Cream

Pork Tamales
Smothered with Monterey Jack Cheese
and Red Chili

Beef Enchiladas
Layered with Red and Green Chiles

Blue-Corn Crusted Trout
With Roasted Corn and Tomatillo Salsa

Calabacitas Con Queso

Spanish Rice with Tomatoes and Garbanzos

Fresh Tortillas

Display of Fresh Baked Biscochitos and Empanaditas

Warm Bread Pudding with Rum Sauce

Mountain Berry Flan

Fresh Brewed Coffee, Decafe and Tea Selection

33.00++

Prices Do Not Include 19% Service Charge and New Mexico State Sales Tax
Buffet Charge of $50.00 will be charged for groups under 100 people

FIGURE 4-11   SOUTHWEST HOLIDAY BUFFET.
(Courtesy, Hyatt Regency Albuquerque, New Mexico.)

MENU SELECTION   SPEISE KARTE

♦ ♦ ♦

AUSTERN KAISER WILHELM
(BROILED OYSTERS IN HERB SAUCE)

PILZA SUPPE
(CREAM OF MUSHROOM SOUP)

BOHEN SALAT
(GREEN BEAN SALAD)

POSCHIERTES SERZUNGE
(POACHED FILET OF SOLE)

SORBET WEIS
(CHAMPAGNE SORBET)

ROULADEN KRAUTNUSSE
(ROLLED BEEF WITH BRUSSEL SPROUTS AND NUTS)

ROTKOHL
(RED CABBAGE)

DEUTSCHES KARTOFFELSALAT
(GERMAN POTATO SALAD)

SCHWARTZBROT
(BLACK BREAD)

SCHWARTZWALDER KIRSH TORTE
(BLACK FOREST CAKE)

KAFFE
(COFFEE)

FIGURE 4-12   SIX COURSE GERMAN CUISINE MENU FOR 1000 GUESTS.

problem of finding both space and an energy source. An accurate assessment of the ability of existing equipment to produce a complicated menu should be made before committing to the customer.

The dinner menu in Figure 4-12 is designed to serve 1000 guests. The production schedule in Figure 4-13 identifies each menu item in the order in which it is served along with the preparation and holding areas of the kitchen required. In addition, prepreparation as well as service preparation times are noted. The combination of food production methods used to prepare menu items and the ability of existing equipment to hold courses at specified temperature levels prior to service will determine the final menu selection. The menu in Figure 4-11 can be served in volumes of this size precisely because catering management identified a selection of items that can be preprepared or purchased from outside vendors to complement those items that must be prepared at the time of service. In addition, enough equipment is available to hold preprepared food items successfully. The service strategy for this menu requires split-second timing and a great deal of cooperation between the kitchen and service staff.

MENU ITEM	NUMBER OF PORTIONS	PREPARATION STATION	HOLDING AREA	PREPARATION TIME
OYSTERS, HERB BUTTER	1000	LINE: BROILER	BANQUET BOX	AT SERVICE
MUSHROOM SOUP	1000	RANGE TOP	BANQUET KITCHEN	DAY BEFORE OR FROZEN, REHEAT PRIOR TO SERVICE
GREEN BEAN SALAD	1000	PREP KITCHEN	WALK-IN BOX	SALAD: DAY BEFORE SET-UP: AFTERNOON
FILET OF SOLE	1000	BANQUET OVEN	BANQUET BOX	AT SERVICE
CHAMPAGNE SHERBET	1000	PREP KITCHEN	PANTRY FREEZER	TWO DAYS BEFORE
ROLLED BEEF	1000	BANQUET KITCHEN	WALK-IN BOX/ BANQUET OVEN	DAY BEFORE, REHEAT FOR SERVICE
RED CABBAGE	1000	CANNED/ BANQUET KITCHEN	BANQUET RANGE	AT SERVICE
GERMAN POTATO SALAD	1000	BANQUET KITCHEN	WALK-IN BOX/ FRONT LINE OVENS	TWO DAYS BEFORE, REHEAT FOR SERVICE
BLACK BREAD	1000	VENDOR/ PANTRY AREA	PANTRY AREA	DAY OF DELIVERY
BLACK FOREST CAKE	1000	VENDOR/ PANTRY AREA	TRAY RACKS PORTION SLICED	DAY OF DELIVERY TRAY UP: AFTERNOON

FIGURE 4-13   PRODUCTION SCHEDULE FOR A DINNER FOR 1000.

Awareness of Customer Needs

Understanding the impact of current trends in both dining customs and eating patterns in today's society is an important skill for every catering manager to develop. The catering service market is highly competitive and requires an ability on the part of management to respond to customer needs, often before they are indicated.

Major trends in today's society center around healthy dining. Catering services need to recognize this by offering menus that are both interesting and healthy. Fried foods, heavy sauces, high levels of salt, and rich desserts are discouraged by healthy dining programs. Menus that concentrate on broiled or grilled foods, salads, fruits, and low-fat food items respond to current customer demands. The healthy catering menu in Figure 4-14 features such choices.

MINESTRA PRIMAVERA

MESCLUN SALAD, BALSAMIC DRESSING

POACHED FILET OF ATLANTIC SOLE
LEMON SAUCE
RISOTTO TOMATE
BROCCOLI FLORETTES

RYE AND WHEAT BREADS

FRESH SEASONAL BERRIES
STRAWBERRIES, BLUEBERRIES, RASPBERRIES

DECAFFINATED COFFEE, TEA, AND HERBAL TEAS

FIGURE 4-14   HEALTHY DINING MENU.

The flexibility of the menu program determines management's ability to respond to customer needs and change overall menu pricing. Each item is reviewed by both catering management and the kitchen for content, quality, and ability to be used interchangeably with other menu items. The portion size, garniture, and cost for each item are listed on a printed format called a banquet specification form, as shown in Figure 4-15.

Banquet specifications outline each menu item on an individual basis so that the selection of menu items on any given menu can be changed in order to adjust the price up or down. The use of banquet specifications assures management that the actual food cost of the total menu will reflect the desired food cost and produce a quality product for the guest. The application of banquet specifications to customized menu item pricing is discussed in Chapter Five.

Creativity and flexibility are attitudes and skills that encourage caterers to adapt to new and unique ideas for catering functions. Catering menu specifications, flexible kitchen formats, creative menu planning, and the ability to communicate with both staff and customers can provide a catering operation with a leading edge in today's highly competitive market.

Summary

The catering menu program includes a series of menus to be offered for a variety of catering services and meals. Factors that influence the success of the menu program are table service style, price range, cuisine orientation, food production capabilities, customer awareness, and the ability to be creative and flexible with function planning as well as menu development and pricing.

Basic menu formats for dinner, luncheon, and breakfast outline the course presentation of menu items for catering service. Each format is adaptable to the needs of individual customers. The actual number of menu items to be offered in a menu format will depend on the style and service of the catering operation.

MENU ITEM	PORTION SIZE	COST PER
APPETIZERS		
FRUIT CUP	6 OZ MIXED FRESH AND CANNED FRUIT	.93
MELON	1/2 FRESH SEASONAL MELON	1.02
MARINATED SHRIMP	6 OZ BABY SHRIMP PAPAYA SLICE	1.10
CONSOMME EN TASSE	6 OZ CONSOMME 2 CHEESE STRAWS	.51
CLAM CHOWDER	6 OZ NEW ENGLAND	.37
SALAD		
CAESAR SALAD	6 OZ GREENS WITH DRESSING	.59
MARSAILLES SALAD	6 OZ MIXED GREENS WITH DRESSING	.72
MARINATED VEGETABLE	7 OZ MIXED VEGETABLE	.90
ENTREES		
STUFFED BREAST OF CHICKEN/BOURSIN	8 OZ BREAST STUFFED	3.75
POACHED SALMON	6 OZ FRESH	3.20
PRIME RIB	12 OZ PRIME RIB	5.28
ROAST SIRLOIN OF BEEF SLICED	8 OZ SIRLOIN WILD MUSHROOM SAUCE	3.60
DESSERT		
CHOCOLATE MOUSSE	3 OZ CHOCOLATE MOUSSE WHIPPED CREAM	.55
KEY LIME PIE	1/6 SLICE OF PIE	.80
BOMBE MARIE LOUISE	FROZEN BOMBE	.83

FIGURE 4-15 BANQUET SPECIFICATION FORM.

The style of table service selected by a catering service reflects staff capabilities and the level of cuisine being served. The styles of table service most appropriate for catered functions are Russian service and American service. Buffet service combines aspects of different methods of table service, food production, and presentation.

Menu item selection is based on the need to provide quality food products in large volumes. These items should be available for purchase on a year-round basis at a price that allows the caterer to meet the desired overall food cost percentage for the menu.

The ability to offer a variety of cuisines offers caterers the capability to respond to customer needs. Ethnic and regional items, as well as diet and health-related foods, can easily be incorporated into menus.

The ability of both service and kitchen personnel to produce required menu items is basic to the success of the menu program. It is important that management accurately access the production capabilities of both labor and equipment when selecting menu items.

A successful menu program must be flexible and open to new and unique ideas in menu development. The competition for catering service business in the 2000s requires that operators be able to adjust their pricing structure and production capabilities to meet the demands of both business and social customers.

CHAPTER FIVE

Catering Menu Pricing and Controls

Catering Menu Cost Form

Menu Item	Cost	Selling Price
		$20.00
Consommé	$ .51	
Salad	.59	
Entrée (chicken)	3.75	
Vegetable	.50	
Starch	.35	
Roll and butter	.30	
Dessert	.55	
Beverage	.35	
Total food costs	$ 6.87	
Selling price	$20.00	
Actual food cost %	34%	

Menu pricing is an important management control that is directly related to the overall profitability of a foodservice operation. Effective and accurate menu pricing requires a thorough knowledge of a foodservice operation's costs and profit goals. Successful menu pricing also requires a knowledge of what customers will find acceptable and the prices being charged for similar menus and packages by competitive foodservice operators.

Costs and Profit

Prior to calculating menu prices it is necessary to determine how much profit a foodservice operation will need to generate in order to cover operating costs. Profit is that portion of revenue that remains after *all* operating costs are paid. Costs are all expenses required to conduct business. They include rent or mortgage, taxes, licensing fees, and contracts such as laundry, pest control, equipment service, and trash removal in addition to food, labor, supplies, telephone, heat, electricity, water, advertising, and printing, to name a few. Costs are broken down into three major categories:

Food and Beverage Costs: The cost of all food-related purchases required to produce completed menu items.

Labor Costs: The costs associated with all labor, including benefits, taxes, wages, meals, uniforms, and so on.

Overhead Costs: The costs of operating the business.

To these three costs is added profit:

Profit: Funds remaining after all costs have been paid from revenues.

In the average foodservice operation these four factors generally are allocated the percentages shown in Table 5-1.

TABLE 5-1   PIE CHART OF COSTS AND PROFIT

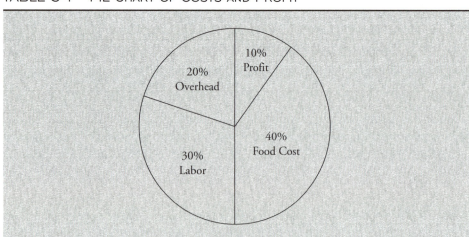

Breakeven Analysis

A method of identifying how much revenue needs to be generated before an operation begins to make a profit is called a breakeven analysis. In this analysis costs are distributed into two categories: fixed costs and variable costs. Fixed costs are those costs that remain constant regardless of the volume of business. Variable costs are those costs that are associated with the volume of business and that are therefore flexible. These two categories are combined as total costs. The breakeven chart in Table 5-2 posts costs of sales on the vertical axis and revenue from sales on the horizontal axis. Fixed costs are established and posted as a solid horizontal line across the graph. Variable costs are posted as a line that begins at the fixed costs point. This line is plotted to rise across the graph on an angle to the point that represents total variable costs for the period being calculated. This now combines both fixed and variable costs as the total cost line. Revenues are then posted on the graph. The point at which the revenue line crosses the total costs line is the breakeven point. This is the point at which revenue has covered costs and can become profit. Note that costs are still being incurred in order to continue producing catering services and products.

Once an operator knows how much revenue is required to cover costs and make a profit, the volume of business that will be needed to create a successful business can be established.

TABLE 5-2   BREAKEVEN GRAPH

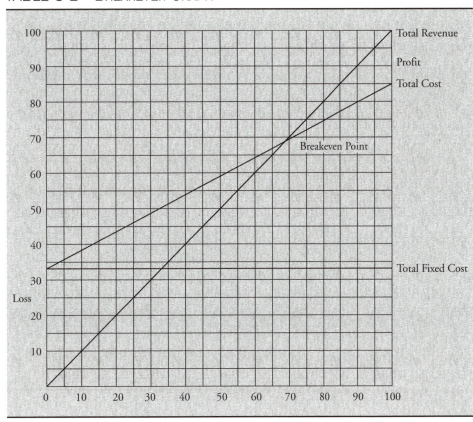

Menu Pricing

Menu pricing for catering menus is based on two primary costing formats or on a third which combines them. These formats are:

Menu Pricing Formats

> Fixed Price or Table d'hôte
> Mixed Pricing or Semi à la Carte
> Individual Course Pricing or à la Carte

FIXED PRICE OR TABLE D'HÔTE

Fixed price, or table d'hôte, presents a catering menu with a price that includes all food and beverage items posted as in Figure 5-1. This menu offers five lunch buffet menus priced per person for the total menus. A service note at the bottom of the menu page advises guests of an optional location setup fee and that gratuities and taxes are not included in the per person price. The menu in Figure 5-2 lists five breakfast menus at an inclusive per person price and offers an upsell option for each menu for the first course. Figure 5-3 presents six lunch and dinner menus priced per person. Prices are posted on a separate sheet coded to the menu number.

MIXED PRICING OR SEMI À LA CARTE

With this menu pricing format, the customer is offered a set price menu with the option of changing different courses on the menu, for an additional charge per person. Figure 5-4 outlines the à la carte menu offerings for the appetizer, salad, and dessert courses that may replace those on the established menu. In this way, customers may individualize their menus, adjusting the per person price as it suits their budget.

INDIVIDUAL COURSE PRICING OR À LA CARTE

À la carte menu pricing offers every course item on the menu for a separate per person price. Figure 5-5 displays the à la carte luncheon menu program for the Bellagio Hotel in Las Vegas, Nevada. Customers have the ability to build their own menus according to individual taste and budgets. Rolls and butter along with the coffee and tea service are included in the per person price. The program stipulates that there is a minimum of three courses and that gratuity and tax is additional.

The à la carte menu program in Figure 5-6, from the Opryland Hotel in Nashville, Tennessee, allows guests to design their own menus by first choosing an entrée item from the appropriate lunch or dinner menu and then selecting appetizers, salads, and desserts from a separate listing. Items that are not priced are included in the base menu price for every entrée item.

This concept requires guidance from the catering sales staff to help guests develop menus that are acceptable combinations of food items as well as workable in terms of production.

Theme Lunch Buffets

(20 PERSON MINIMUM)

Country Western

ICEBERG SALAD WITH 2 DRESSINGS

3 BEAN SALAD

WESTERN FRIES

CHUCK WAGON BEANS

CORN ON THE COB

BARBEQUE CHICKEN BREAST

CORN BREAD WITH BUTTER

PEACH COBBLER

COFFEE, TEA AND DECAF

$24.00++

Mexican Fiesta

ENSALADA TOPPOPO WITH AVOCADO, GRILLED
CHICKEN, JICAMA, TOMATO AND CORN CHIPS

REFRIED BEANS

SPANISH RICE

CREAMY CHICKEN ENCHILADAS WITH SOUR
CREAM, TOMATO AND CILANTRO

BEEF FAJITA BAR, WITH SWEET PEPPERS
AND ONIONS

FLOUR TORTILLAS, PICO DE GALLO

SOPAIPILLAS WITH HONEY BUTTER

MEXICAN FLAN

COFFEE, TEA AND DECAF

$27.00++

Pasta Buffet

MISTA VERDE SALAD—THE GIORGIO'S
HOUSE SALAD

ASSORTED ANTIPASTOS

CHEF'S SELECTION OF TWO HOT PASTAS—
ONE VEGETARIAN AND ONE WITH MEAT

ITALIAN BREAD AND BUTTER

NEW YORK STYLE CHEESECAKE

COFFEE, TEA AND DECAF

$20.95++

Italian Buffet

MISTA VERDE SALAD—THE GIORGIO'S HOUSE
SALAD

POMODORO SALAD—OF HOMEMADE
MOZZARELLA, VINE RIPENED TOMATOES AND
BERMUDA ONIONS

GRILLED CHICKEN BREAST—WITH SAUCE
RUSTICA, ROASTED PEPPERS, OLIVES AND
HOMEMADE MOZZARELLA

SAFFRON ORZO

FRESH VEGETABLES

ITALIAN BREAD & BUTTER

CANOLIS & PETIT FOURS

COFFEE, TEA AND DECAF

$23.95++

Tokyo Luncheon Buffet

CALIFORNIA ROLL

ORIENTAL SPINACH SALAD

CHICKEN TERIYAKI WITH VEGETABLE SPRING ROLL

STEAMED RICE

SESAME BUTTERFLY NOODLES

FRESH MELON SALAD

COFFEE, TEA AND DECAF

$26.00++

*IF DONE OUTSIDE ON THE PATIO AN ADDITIONAL $2.00++ PER PERSON WILL BE ADDED.

ALL PRICES SUBJECT TO 18% GRATUITY AND 7.3% SALES TAX

FIGURE 5-1   BELLAGIO HOTEL FIXED PRICE THEME LUNCH BUFFET.
(Courtesy of Mirage Resorts, Incorporated.)

Plated Breakfasts

Poached Eggs Florentine

WITH CRISP BACON
AND HOLLANDAISE SAUCE
BASKET OF WARM SOURDOUGH BREAD
COFFEE, TEA AND DECAF
$14.50++

FRESH FRUIT PLATE WITH BERRIES
AS THE 1ST COURSE
$18.00++

Italian Scrambled Eggs

WITH TOMATOES AND FRESH HERBS
BACON, HAM OR TURKEY SAUSAGE
ROASTED RED POTATOES
BASKET OF TOASTED PANETTONE
COFFEE, TEA AND DECAF
$13.50++

FRESH FRUIT PLATE AS THE 1ST COURSE
$16.50++

French Toast Italiano

WITH A CORN FLAKE CRUST, MAPLE SYRUP,
WHIPPED CREAM, AND STRAWBERRIES
CRISP BACON
COFFEE, TEA AND DECAF

$16.75++
FRESH FRUIT PLATE AS THE 1ST COURSE
$19.75++

Eggs Benedict

WITH CANADIAN BACON AND HOLLANDAISE
HASH BROWN POTATOES WITH
PEPPERS AND ONION
ASSORTED BREAKFAST BREADS
COFFEE, TEA AND DECAF

$14.50++
PAPAYA AND BANANA ON CINNAMON CREAM
$17.00++

Belgian Waffles

WITH CINNAMON WHIPPED CREAM, STRAWBERRIES AND MAPLE SYRUP
$11.75++
WITH PAPAYA AND WILD BERRIES
$15.75++
(20 PERSON MAXIMUM)

*ALL INCLUDE YOUR CHOICE OF JUICE: FRESH SQUEEZED ORANGE, APPLE, CRANBERRY OR TOMATO
ALL PRICES ARE SUBJECT TO A 18% GRATUITY AND 7.3% SALES TAX

FIGURE 5-2   BREAKFAST MENUS AT AN INCLUSIVE PER PERSON PRICE.
(Courtesy of The Peabody Hotel, Orlando, Florida.)

CAYLABNE BAY RESORT

Set Lunch or Dinner Menus

SEAFOOD MENUS

Menu #17

MIXED SEAFOOD MINESTRONE
ICEBERG LETTUCE w/THOUSAND ISLAND
DRESSING
GRILLED MEDALLION OF TUNA FILLET
PARSLEY POTATOES, STEAMED RICE
BUTTERED VEGETABLES, GARLIC/CHILI SAUCE
MIXED TROPICAL FRUITS
BREAD AND BUTTER
COFFEE OR TEA

Menu #18

SPICY PRAWN SOUP
HAWAIIAN SALAD
STEAMED BABY LAPU-LAPU WITH SOY SAUCE
WHITE RICE
BOILED VEGETABLES
MANGO ALA MODE
BREAD AND BUTTER
COFFEE OR TEA

Menu #19

SHRIMP BISQUE
EXOTIC SALAD
OVEN-BAKE LAPU-LAPU IN
CREAMY WHITE SAUCE
CREME CARAMEL
BREAD AND BUTTER
COFFEE OR TEA

Menu #20

MIXED SEAFOOD CHOWDER
AVOCADO SHRIMP SALAD
CRISPY SIDED KINGFISH WITH
TRIO COLOR PASTA
BUKO PIE
BREAD AND BUTTER
COFFEE OR TEA

Menu #21

MUSSEL AND GINGER
ROLLED FISH FILLET
PANACHE OF SEAFOON EN CROUTE
CREME CARAMEL
BREAD AND BUTTER
COFFEE OR TEA

Menu #22

CORN AND PRAWN SOUP
FISH TERRINE
GRILLED FILLET OF LAPU-LAPU MEUNIERRE
BUTTERED VEGETABLES
STEAMED RICE
TIRAMISU WITH FRESH FRUITS
BREAD AND BUTTER
COFFEE OR TEA

FIGURE 5-3   CAYLABNE BAY RESORT LUNCH AND DINNER MENUS PRICED PER PERSON.
(Courtesy of The Caylabne Bay Resort, the Philippines.)

TO ADD AN UPSCALE TOUCH TO YOUR DINNER WE OFFER THE FOLLOWING:

Appetizers

PLEASE ADD $2.50 PER GUEST

SCALLOP AND SPINACH SAUTE WITH A PERNOD CREAM SAUCE

TOMATO RAVIOLI STUFFED WITH CHICKEN AND MUSHROOMS SAUCED WITH MARINARA

COLD POACHED JUMBO SHRIMP BEDDED ON SHREDDED RED CABBAGE SLAW
WITH BALSAMIC VINAIGRETTE

GRILLED CHICKEN BREAST AND TOMATO FETTUCCINI WITH
A MILD DRIED ANCHO PEPPER CREAM SAUCE

Salads

PLEASE ADD $1.75 PER GUEST

CAESAR SALAD

THIS CLASSIC FEATURES IN-ROOM PRESENTATION

WARM RATATOUILLE SERVED ON OUR OWN CHEESE BRUSCHETTA

WILD FIELD GREENS WITH RASPBERRY VINAIGRETTE AND TOASTED WALNUTS
TOSSED IN ROOM

Desserts

PLEASE ADD $1.75 PER GUEST

CRANBERRY ITALIAN ICE

ELI'S CHICAGO CHEESECAKE WITH FRESH STRAWBERRIES

PRALINE ICE CREAM BOMBE

WHITE CHOCOLATE MOUSSE WITH RASPBERRY SAUCE SERVED IN
A DARK CHOCOLATE CUP

FRESH BERRIES WITHIN GRAND MARNIER CREAM

BANANA CHOCOLATE GELATO

FIGURE 5-4   À LA CARTE MENU OFFERINGS FOR THE APPETIZER,
SALAD, AND DESSERT COURSES.
(Courtesy of The Peabody Hotel, Orlando, Florida.)

A menu pricing program can use both primary formats and variations simultaneously, or elect to focus on only one. The decision on which format to use is directly tied to the style of catering operation and the target market.

Package Pricing

Package prices can combine reception, dinner, beverage, flowers, entertainment, and theme costs as one per person price. The pricing structure of the menu is often controlled by the overall package price. Any number of services can be included in the per person price; the costs for flowers and entertainment are broken down on a per person basis and added into the total

LUNCHEON A LA CARTE SELECTIONS
Three Course Minimum

Your Luncheon will Include Freshly Baked Bellagio Hearth Breads
Coffee and Tea Service

APPETIZERS

Smoked Scottish Salmon with Simmered Fingerling Potatoes and Cucumber Slaw @ $9.50
French Couscous Salad with Assorted Grilled Vegetables
and a Light Sherry Vinaigrette @ $7.00
Buffalo Mozzarella and Ripe Tomatoes with Basil, Extra Virgin Olive Oil
and Balsamic Vinegar @ $6.50
Fresh Rock Shrimp Cocktail with Avocado, Tomato, Shaved Fennel
and a Light Lime Dressing @ $9.50
Grilled Asparagus with Canadian Bay Shrimp in a Vinaigrette @ $8.00

SOUPS

Wild Mushroom Cappuccino @ $4.50
Chicken-Lime Soup with Cilantro and Crispy Tortilla Chips @ $4.50
Lobster Bisque with Aged Armagnac @ $8.50
Chicken Consommé with Orzo Pasta Printaniere @ $4.50
Cream of Asparagus Soup with Chervil @ $5.00
Tomato Soup with Basil and Garlic Croutons @ $4.50
Chilled Melon Soup with Berries and Mint @ $5.00

SALADS

Spinach Salad with Crispy Pancetta, Chopped Eggs and Caramelized Onion
with a Grain Mustard Vinaigrette @ $5.50
Romaine with Shaved Romano, Garlic Croutons and Caesar Dressing @ $5.75
Baby Greens and Teardrop Tomatoes with a Red Wine Garlic Vinaigrette @ $5.00
Radicchio, Bibb, Watercress and Frisée with
Toasted Pecans and Raspberry Vinaigrette @ $5.50
Romaine, English Cucumber, Peppers, Feta Cheese and Greek Olives
with Oregano Vinaigrette @ $6.00
California Greens, Tomatoes, Carrots with Honey Mustard Dressing @ $5.00

Japanese Chopped Vegetable Salad with Fried Wontons
and Miso Dressing in Radicchio Cup @ $6.50
Mixed Greens with Goat Cheese Crouton, Vine-Ripened Tomatoes
and Aged Sherry Vinaigrette @ $6.00
Frisée and Lollarosa with Grilled Vegetables with a Balsamic Vinaigrette @ $6.50

Prices are subject to 7% tax and 18% gratuity

10/98

FIGURE 5-5   BELLAGIO HOTEL À LA CARTE MENU PRICING.
(Courtesy of Mirage Resorts, Incorporated.)

LUNCHEON A LA CARTE SELECTIONS
Continued

COLD ENTRÉES

Smoked Breast of Chicken with Pear, Toasted Walnuts,
Gorgonzola Cheese on a Zesty Orzo Pasta Salad @ $16.50

Scallops, Shrimp and Lobster in a Lemon Shallot Vinaigrette
with Chilled Vegetables @ $22.50

Lightly Cured Smoked Salmon Medallion with a
Horseradish Crème Fraîche and French Lentil Salad @ $16.00

Peppered Beef Tenderloin Roasted with Yukon Gold Potato Salad and
Grilled Vegetables in a Herb Aïoli @ $18.50

Poached Salmon with Artichokes, Asparagus, White Beans
and a Roasted Red Pepper Coulis @ $16.50

Seared Ahi Tuna on Sushi Rice with Wasabi Cream, Ginger
and Pickled Cucumber @ $20.00

Shrimp and Roasted Vegetables on Fusilli, Champagne Vinaigrette @ $16.50

Prices are subject to 7% tax and 18% gratuity

10/98

FIGURE 5-5   (CONTINUED.)

LUNCHEON A LA CARTE SELECTIONS
Continued

HOT ENTRÉES

Filet of Chilean Sea Bass with Lemon and Caper Beurre Blanc @ $18.00

Norwegian Salmon Medallion Coated with Chinese Mustard @ $16.00

Ahi Tuna Steak Charred Rare with Thai Spiced Lentils and Mango Chutney @ $20.00

Orange Roughy Grilled with Bananas and Macadamia Nuts @ $16.00

Grilled Swordfish Steak with Roasted Chili Salsa @ $18.50

Breast of Chicken Saltimbocca with Madeira Jus Lie @ $14.00

Breaded Breast of Chicken Paillard with Lemons and Herb Butter @ $14.00

Grilled Double Lamb Chop with Dijon Mustard Sauce @ $25.00

Herb Crusted Veal Rib Eye with Sun-dried Tomatoes and Roasted Shallots @ $24.00

Petite Filet Mignon with Red Wine and Tarragon Sauce @ $22.00

Sicilian Grilled Beefsteak with Peperonata @ $20.00

Our Chef's Choice of Fresh Seasonal Vegetables and
Appropriate Starch will Complement Your Hot Entrée Selection

Prices are subject to 7% tax and 18% gratuity

10/98

FIGURE 5-5 (CONTINUED.)

LUNCHEON A LA CARTE SELECTIONS
Continued

DESSERTS

Triple Chocolate Terrine with Praline, White and Dark Chocolate Mousse,
Fresh Raspberries @ $6.00

Oreo Cookie and Cream in Chocolate Bird's Nest @ $5.50

Lemon Meringue Torte with Blackberry Sauce @ $5.00

Espresso Tiramisu with Kahlúa Sauce @ $6.50

Pecan Fudge Decadence with Bourbon Ice Cream @ $5.50

White Chocolate Mousse in a Chocolate Tulip with a Shortbread Cookie @ $6.00

Baked Chocolate Flan with Orange Sauce and Whipped Cream @ $5.00

Georgian Peach Cobbler with Vanilla Sauce @ $5.00

Spiced Pear Torte, Caramel Sauce and Whipped Cream @ $5.00

Choice of Gelato, Ice Cream or Fruit Sherbet Served with a
Gingersnap Wafer and Seasonal Berries @ $5.00

Warm Chocolate Cake Pudding with Banana Macadamia Ice Cream @ $7.00
500 Person Maximum

Prices are subject to 7% tax and 18% gratuity

10/98

FIGURE 5-5   (CONTINUED.)

COLD APPETIZERS

JUMBO SHRIMP COCKTAIL
with Tangy Cocktail Sauce $9.50

RIPE CANTALOUPE MELON WEDGE
with Thinly Sliced Italian Prosciutto and
Cracked Pepper/Mayonnaise Dressing ... $5.50

HOT APPETIZERS

MARYLAND STYLE LUMP CRAB CAKES
with a Citrus Beurre Blanc.................... $10.50

WILD MUSHROOM AND CHICKEN STRUDEL
Enhanced with Chef's Garnish $6.75

SALADS

RAINBOW
Tossed Garden Greens Garnished with
Carrots, Beets and Daikon Vinaigrette
Dressing - Tossed Tableside

CUMBERLAND RIVER
Crisp Garden Greens with Artichoke Hearts,
Radishes, Mushrooms, Cherry Tomatoes
and Alfalfa Sprouts House Vinaigrette -
Tossed Tableside

Appetizers, Salads and Desserts

TRADITIONAL CAESAR SALAD
Grated Parmesan and Croutons, Creamy
Caesar Dressing - Tossed Tableside

SPINACH SALAD OPRYLAND
Spinach Leaves with Orange and Grapefruit
Sections, Enoki Mushrooms Chilled Sweet
and Sour Dressing........................... $2.00

ROCKWELL'S COLORATION
Bibb, Radicchio, Belgian Endive and Sprouts,
Choice of Dressing $2.00

MARINATED SLICED TOMATOES
Tomatoes, Buffalo Mozzarella, Basil Vinaigrette
Dressing $2.00

CHOPPED ICEBERG
Iceberg and Radicchio with Dilled Cucumbers,
Creamy Basil Dressing $2.00

HEARTS OF PALM
Hearts of Palm on Tender Greens, Choice of
Dressing $3.00

*(Prices indicate an additional charge to the
meal price)*

10/98   All prices listed in our menus are subject to 19% service charge and applicable sales tax.

FIGURE 5-6   OPRYLAND HOTEL À LA CARTE MENU PROGRAM.
(Courtesy of The Opryland Hotel, Nashville, Tennessee.)

package price. This marketing approach often creates a perceived value for the customer and the assumption that the overall function price is less expensive than if each item were charged for at a flat fee. Package pricing methods are discussed in detail in Chapter Thirteen.

Price Range

Catering menus should be established within a range of no more than $12 to $15. A range with a high of $45.00 per person and a low of $18.00 per person, for example, is too wide. Customers have to make a value judgment as to whether to spend a greater or lesser amount on a catering menu. When

COLD ENTREES

(Price is based on a three course meal. Please refer to the Price List.)

TRIO OF SALADS
Chicken, Bay Shrimp and Tri-Color Corkscrew Pasta Salad on a Bed of Lettuce Garnished with Sliced Seasonal Fruit

CANTALOUPE MELON CROWN
Cantaloupe Filled with all White Meat Chicken Salad Garnished with Fresh Fruit and Walnut Bread

CROISSANT SANDWICH
Choice of Giant Roast Beef, Turkey Croissant, or Vegetarian Sandwich Served with Cold German Potato Salad, Crisp Vegetable Garnish with Appropriate Condiments

SHRIMP CAESAR
Traditional Caesar Salad with Jumbo Grilled Shrimp, Romaine Lettuce, Croutons and Parmesan Cheese
Creamy Caesar Dressing

HOT ENTREES

LEMON PEPPER CATFISH

BAKED SALMON FILET
With Sauce Maltaise

SEA BASS
With a Red Onion Confit

Luncheon

APPLEGROVE CHICKEN
A Boneless Breast stuffed with Cinnamon Apples and Topped with a Tangy Calvados Sauce

CHICKEN PARMIGIANA
A Tender Baked Chicken Breast Topped with Tomato Sauce, Mozzarella Cheese and served with Orzo Pasta

CHICKEN PICCATA
Sauteed in Butter with Lemon Capers

STUFFED PORK CHOP
With Cornbread Dressing

MEDALLIONS OF PORK TENDERLOIN
Sauteed with a Light Cajun Sauce

FILET MIGNON
Grilled Petite Filet Mignon San Francisco Topped with Sautéed Artichoke Hearts, Mushrooms and Sun-Dried Tomatoes

ROAST SIRLOIN
Sliced Roast Sirloin of Beef, Topped with Chasseur Sauce Blended with Shallots and Mushrooms

PASTA PRIMAVERA
Featuring al Dente Linguine served with Crisp Seasonal Vegetables in a Creamy Garlic Parmesan Sauce

LASAGNA AL FORNO
A Multi-Layer of Lasagna Noodles Baked with Cheese and Topped with a Meat and Tomato Sauce

10/98   All prices listed in our menus are subject to 19% service charge and applicable sales tax.

FIGURE 5-6   (CONTINUED.)

provided with a limited range they can feel comfortable about their decision without being forced to feel either extravagant or "cheap."

Catering Pricing Methods

Catering menu prices must reflect the total costs of the operation as well as the desired profit. As discussed earlier in this chapter, costs and profits must both be considered in order to achieve catering menu prices that will generate enough revenue to cover costs as well as profit. The selling price is equal to the sum of costs and profit. Methods of menu pricing and pricing

PLATED DINNERS

BROILED FILET OF SALMON
With Sauce Mousseline

SEA BASS
Filet of Sea Bass Baked Provencal

MAHI MAHI
Grilled Mahi Mahi with a Mixed Fruit Chutney

GRILLED CHICKEN
Grilled Boneless Chicken Breast Served with a
Side of Green Tomato-Pineapple Relish

CHICKEN BREAST ORIENTAL
Tender Grilled Chicken, Topped with a Plum-
Ginger Sauce, Shiitake Mushrooms,
Garnished with a Crab Claw

BREAST OF CHICKEN WELLINGTON
Wrapped in a Flaky Pastry Crust with Mushroom Duxelle, Served with Madeira Sauce

CHICKEN CALYPSO
Chicken Breast Stuffed with Shrimp, Andouille
Sausage and Spinach, Topped with
Chicken Lie

PRIME RIB
Roast Prime Rib of Beef Au Jus

Dinner

NEW YORK STRIP
New York Strip Steak Madagascar Topped with
an Herb Green Peppercorn Butter

FILET
Roquefort Crusted Filet of Beef with Burgundy
Sauce

VEAL ROSEMARY
Roast Loin of Veal Rosemary Served with a
Julienne of Bacon, Diced Tomatoes and
Pearl Onions

VEAL CHOP
Grilled Veal Chop Served with a Creamy Morel
Sauce

PORK LOIN
Center Cut Roast Pork Loin with Sauteed
Apples and Fried Onions

10/98   All prices listed in our menus are subject to 19% service charge and applicable sales tax.

FIGURE 5-6   (CONTINUED.)

formulas are used to determine the selling price depending on which factors and costs are already known and which need to be calculated.

Only a few of the methods used by the foodservice industry to calculate food costs are applicable to catering due to its limited menu formats. These methods are:

- Actual cost method
- Food cost percentage method
- Factor pricing
- Contribution to profit method

TABLE 5-3   ACTUAL COST METHOD

COST	PERCENT OF SELLING PRICE
TOTAL	100%
OVERHEAD	−25%
LABOR	−30%
PROFIT	−10%
AVAILABLE FOR FOOD COST:	35%

ACTUAL COST METHOD

The actual cost method is applied in situations when the selling price is established before the cost of food has been calculated. Once the cost of food has been determined, management can refer to the catering menu cost form, as we shall see in Table 5-4, to find appropriate menu items that can be combined to match the available food cost.

Let's examine how the actual cost method determines the percentage that each of the four price components should represent, based on costs currently incurred by the foodservice business and a preestablished profit percentage goal, as shown in Table 5-3.

In this example the customer has expressed a need for a menu priced at $20.00 per person. The amount of money available for food cost is calculated as follows:

COST	PERCENT OF SELLING PRICE	SELLING PRICE
TOTAL	100%	$20.00
OVERHEAD	−25%	−5.00
LABOR	−30%	−6.00
PROFIT	−10%	−2.00
AVAILABLE FOR FOOD COST:	35%	$ 7.00

From the catering menu cost form in Table 5-4, management now selects appropriate menu items to total a selling price of $20.00.

FOOD COST PERCENTAGE METHOD

The food cost percentage method of menu pricing is the method used more frequently in restaurant operations to price individual menu items. Its application as a method of pricing catering menus determines what the selling price should be, based on a known food cost percentage. This method also allows management to identify how much money is available for food cost once the selling price and food cost percentage have been established.

Two of the following three factors must be known in order to apply the food cost percentage to menu pricing:

- Food cost percentage
- Cost of food
- Selling price

TABLE 5-4   CATERING MENU COST FORM

MENU ITEM	COST	SELLING PRICE
		$20.00
CONSOMMÉ	$ .51	
SALAD	.59	
ENTRÉE (CHICKEN)	3.75	
VEGETABLE	.50	
STARCH	.35	
ROLL AND BUTTER	.30	
DESSERT	.55	
BEVERAGE	.35	
TOTAL FOOD COSTS	$ 6.87	
SELLING PRICE	$20.00	
ACTUAL FOOD COST %	34%	

The food cost percentage method consists of three pricing formulas, one for determining each unknown factor. The formulas and their abbreviations are:

1. Food cost ÷ Food cost % = Selling price

$$FC \div FC\% = SP$$

2. Food cost ÷ Selling price = Food cost %

$$FC \div SP = FC\%$$

3. Selling price × Food cost % = Food cost

$$SP \times FC\% = FC$$

The formulas can be applied to catering menu pricing in the following ways:

1. Management is conducting a periodic review of the catering menus in order to evaluate the cost of food and current selling prices. If food costs have increased, it will be necessary to raise menu prices. Management would like to maintain a 30 percent food cost percentage for this selection of menus. By dividing the food cost by the food cost percentage, the new selling price can be calculated.

$$(FC)\ \$9.75 \div (FC\%)\ 30\% = (SP)\ \$32.50$$

2. Management wants to maintain the current selling price for a catering menu. The current food cost is known. If the current food cost percentage based on these two factors is not acceptable, then the food cost

will have to be decreased. By dividing the food cost by the selling price, the food cost percentage can be calculated.

$$(FC) \$3.85 \div (SP) \$12.00 = (FC)\ 32\%$$

3. The customer has asked for a catering menu priced at $20 per person. Management knows that the selling price must result in a 35 percent food cost. In order to develop a menu it is necessary to know the amount of money available for the cost of food. By multiplying the selling price by the food cost percentage the food cost can be calculated.*

$$(SP) \$20.00 \times (FC\%)\ 35\% = (FC)\ \$7.00$$

FACTOR PRICING

The factor pricing method establishes a factor that represents the food cost percentage. The factor is based on the number of times that the percentage can be divided into 100:

$$100\% \div 40\ (\text{percentage}) = 2.5\ (\text{factor})$$

The factor is multiplied by the food cost to calculate the selling price:

$$\$3.35\ (\text{food cost}) \times 2.5\ (\text{factor}) = \$8.37$$

Management can apply the factors for the food cost percentages that are most commonly used in their operation to quickly calculate selling prices. The chart in Table 5-5 identifies the factors for a range of food cost percentages.

Maintaining Food Cost Percentages

The foodservice industry in the 2000s is highly competitive. Market pressures grow daily from increased participation in the catering sector. Restaurants, in an effort to expand their revenue share, are participating in home delivery programs in addition to offering their customers the opportunity for private parties and outside catering services.

Shrinking profit margins require managers to be constantly aware of the percentage of the selling price that cost is representing. When the percentage of cost is above that necessary to maintain a desired profit, either the selling price must be increased or costs must be adjusted. As customers usually react to price increases by turning to the competition, management should raise prices only when necessary and at predetermined times in the operations planning schedule.

---

*This formula was used to calculate the food cost by the actual food cost method.

TABLE 5-5   FACTOR/FOOD COST PERCENTAGE TABLE

FOOD COST %	FACTOR	FOOD COST %	FACTOR	FOOD COST %	FACTOR
20	5.00	30	3.33	40	2.50
21	4.76	31	3.23	41	2.43
22	4.55	32	3.13	42	2.38
23	4.35	33	3.00	43	2.32
24	4.17	34	2.94	44	2.27
25	4.00	35	2.85	45	2.22
26	3.85	36	2.78	46	2.17
27	3.70	37	2.70	47	2.12
28	3.57	38	2.63	48	2.08
29	3.45	39	2.56	49	2.04

Source: Lendel H. Kotschevar, *Management by Menu*, 3rd ed., 1994.

Note: Decide what percentage of food cost you wish and then multiply actual food cost by the desired percentage factor to arrive at the desired selling cost. Example: If an item has a food cost of $1.50 and you want a 28% food cost, look up the factor opposite 28 (3.57) and multiply this by $1.50:

$$1.50 \times 3.57 = \$5.35$$

The base selling price is $5.35.

Developing selling prices for catering menus that accurately meet the needs of both the caterer and the customer requires a thorough analysis of both the business and the customer profile. As discussed in Chapter 4, management must set a range of prices that meet its established goals and objectives regarding catering revenue and profit. It is important to maintain this range as menu prices and menu items change. By increasing prices on an individual menu basis, management can lose track of the range of menu prices. Suddenly the original $12 to $15 spread between prices slips to $20 to $22, resulting in customer confusion as to which end of the price range they should choose, high or low.

Management recognition of the value perceived for menus is critical to the maintenance of a successful menu pricing program. A menu price of $28.00 per person for a 12 ounce strip sirloin steak may yield an acceptable food cost percentage for management, but meet with resistance from customers. If customers do not perceive that the price represents the true value of the menu item, then they will hesitate to select it. In some cases, prices may need to be lowered in order to increase sales. In such cases management should review the entire menu to determine which surrounding items can be replaced to reduce the overall food cost of the menu.

FOOD COST REVIEW

In order to maintain successful menu prices, caterers must listen to customer reactions to menu item content and menu prices. In addition they must also periodically evaluate the competition's menu prices for similar items and content in addition to monitoring daily, weekly, and monthly food costs to maintain desired food cost percentages and profit margins.

Daily and weekly reviews of purchasing prices help management to identify price increases on food products that significantly affect the overall food cost. Items that are sold in large volume should be watched diligently for price increases.

For example, prime rib of beef is a popular catering menu entrée. If 40 to 50 percent of the catering menus for the week require prime rib and the cost of beef has risen, the food cost percentage on this item could increase, thus reducing overall profits. A daily price review keeps management aware of possible problems. The food cost on the new menu can be lowered by changing surrounding items on the menu, such as vegetables, or adjusting the portion size of the prime rib serving. Catering menus that specify "chef's vegetable choice" can be flexible.

Weekly reviews compare total food purchases and inventory requisitions against sales for the week. This information can be posted daily or reviewed on a weekly and monthly basis as shown in Table 5-6.

SALES MIX AND CONTRIBUTION TO PROFIT

The sales mix is a means of ranking menu items according to their contribution to the overall volume of sales. Actively used in restaurant management as a means of tracking the popularity of individual menu items, the sales mix has limited use in a catering menu program. It is important, however, to periodically evaluate sales to identify those menu items that are creating the highest volume sales.

It is also necessary to access the contribution that each menu item makes to overall profit in order to ensure that the menu price is actually generating the desired profit margin. For example, a catering menu for prime rib of beef that has been priced below cost for competitive reasons may result in an increased volume of sales, but at the same time be draining the overall profit margin. In order to restore the profit margin, management may need to change some of the surrounding menu items or identify another entrée item to promote.

The contribution to profit method is based on the selection of menu prices according to what the customer will pay for an item and the contribution that the sales of the menu item will make to the gross profit of the operation.

Each menu item is evaluated according to customer acceptability and projected sales volume. The initial selling price for each menu item is based

TABLE 5-6   WEEKLY REVIEW FOR SIX DAY PERIOD

INVENTORY REQUISITIONS	$3450.00
FOOD PURCHASES	900.00
TOTAL COSTS	$4350.00
TOTAL SALES	$15,000.00
(FC) $4350.00 ÷ (SP) $15,000 = (FC%) 29%	

TABLE 5-7   CONTRIBUTION TO PROFIT METHOD

ITEM	FOOD COST	FC%	SELLING PRICE	MENU PRICE	GROSS PROFIT
A	$2.29	35	$ 6.54	$ 9.25	$6.96
B	$5.18	40	$12.95	$ 8.95	$3.77
C	$4.55	33	$13.67	$13.95	$9.40

on a desired food cost percentage as in the contribution to profit method chart in Table 5-7. The final selling price is determined by management's estimation of what the customer will perceive as an acceptable selling price for that item, as in the following example:

Contribution to Profit Example

An 8-ounce preprepared stuffed chicken breast and surrounding vegetable and starch items will have an actual food cost of $2.85. This item, when calculated at a 35 percent food cost, has a selling price of $8.00. Management feels that customers will accept a higher selling price of $10.50. At $10.50 the contribution to gross profit on this item is $7.65.

$$\text{(SP) Selling price} - \text{(FC) Food cost} = \text{Contribution to profit}$$
$$\$10.50 - \$2.85 = \$7.65$$

The differential between the menu price of an item and its food cost is called the contribution to gross profit. Gross profit refers to all monies left after the food cost is deducted from the selling price. Remaining costs must then be deducted in order to calculate the net profit.

In order to answer customer needs, a well balanced menu program includes items that represent high, medium, and low contributions to profit. An item may have a low contribution to profit and a low sales volume, but its presence on the menu satisfies a certain percentage of the customers. The profit from items with a high contribution to profit and high volume sales balance the loss of profit on the less profitable menu items.

Control systems that monitor production, purchasing, and costing on a daily, weekly, and monthly basis are instrumental in achieving revenue and profit goals.

Summary

Menu pricing is important to the ongoing success of every catering operation and service. Established food cost percentages that accurately reflect the needs of the operation yield profits. Catering menu prices are calculated based on the amount of revenue needed to cover the four pricing components: overhead cost, labor cost, food cost, and profit. The four pricing methods most adaptable to catering menus are the actual cost method, the food cost percentage method, the factor pricing method, and the contribution to profit method.

Maintaining successful pricing requires daily and weekly monitoring of food costs to ensure desired food cost percentages and profit margins. Control systems such as food cost reviews, the sales mix, and contribution to profit analysis are used to achieve successful menu prices.

A successful menu program must meet management goals and objectives for revenues and profits. Properly applied menu pricing techniques and the application of control systems are necessary for any catering operation to be profitable.

CHAPTER SIX

Catering Menu Design

LUNCHEON MENU

◆◇◆◇◆◇◆◇◆

APPETIZER

Asparagus Bouquet with cottage cheese

MAIN COURSE

Grilled Shark with ginger scallion butter

Seven Grain Rice Pilaff

Braised Spinach with Nutmeg

❖❖❖

Rolls and Butter

DESSERT

Apple Souffle
with Warm Vanilla Cream

COFFEE and TEA

A variety of sales and marketing techniques are applied to create the physical design of catering menus and promotional packages. The presentation of menus influences which catering service, restaurant, hotel, or club customers choose. In many instances, catering menus are reviewed by customers in their homes or offices without the assistance of a catering sales representative who might guide their selections. By the time catering management reaches the customer, initial decisions have often been made.

The presentation of catering menus in an effective marketing format can lead customers to purchase the most profitable menus and services. The sales presentation folder includes a number of design elements:

1. Package cover
2. Design format
3. Layout
4. Typeface
5. Paper and color
6. Illustration and graphic design
7. Copy

Unlike restaurant menus, in which the selection of menu items is an impulse purchase, the choice of catering menus is given considerable thought and is often conducted by a committee. Because catering functions involve anywhere from 10 to 10,000 guests and represent important business and social occasions and sizeable financial investments, at least two people are usually involved in the menu selection process. A catering menu that effectively incorporates marketing techniques into its overall presentation and design will be more persuasive to group decision-makers.

Sales Presentation Covers

The design format of catering menus and services is often shaped by the presentation cover. The sales presentation cover is an optional design piece used as a folder in which to present contracts, correspondence, menus, and other information. The design format of the package cover determines the shape and size of insert pages.

The most common format is a two-panel 9-by-12 inch cover. This size fits easily into business mailing envelopes and is standard in the U.S. printing industry. (The paper and envelope sizes considered standard will vary from country to country outside of the United States.) There are usually pocket flaps on the inside of the cover, which serve to hold materials in place. Figure 6-1 shows an alternative format using curved panel flaps to hold materials in place on the two side panels with a small flap at the bottom of the center panel. Both side panels are also designed so that additional materials can be inserted on the front of each panel. This design, from the MGM Grand Hotel in Las Vegas, Nevada, opens in the center of the front panel and is held shut with an interlocking tab extended from the raised golf embossed logo of the MGM lion in the center of the cover, as seen in Figure 6-2.

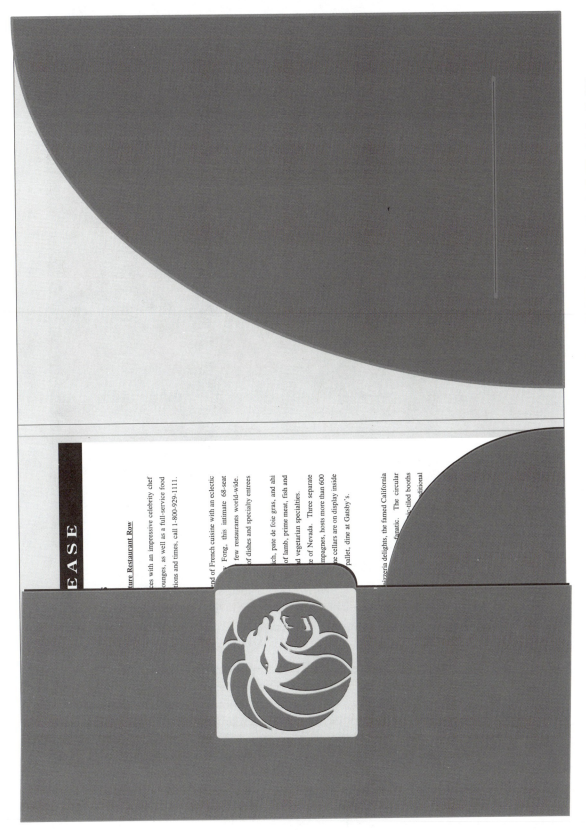

FIGURE 6-1 MGM GRAND HOTEL'S ALTERNATIVE SALES PRESENTATION FOLDER DESIGN WITH CURVED PANEL FLAPS.
(Courtesy of The MGM Grand Hotel, Las Vegas, Nevada.)

FIGURE 6-2   MGM GRAND HOTEL'S SALES PRESENTATION FOLDER
WITH GOLD EMBOSSED LOGO.
(Courtesy of The MGM Grand Hotel, Las Vegas, Nevada.)

Another variation on this design is shown in Figure 6-3, from the Hyatt Regency in Scottsdale, Arizona. The inside design features a side pocket to hold banquet menus as well as the bottom flap pocket. The visual space on the face of the side pocket is used to feature a color photograph of a catering function set up against the backdrop of mountains and an elaborate swimming pool complex. Figure 6-4 shows an envelope design for the presentation folder. The center panel opens from the center front to reveal the menu selection held in place by two flaps, top and bottom.

Yet another variation on the two-panel fold is shown in Figure 6-5. Using the same overall dimensions of 9 by 12, the cover opens on the horizontal rather than the vertical fold. The cover art is a striking photograph of

The Catering Staff at Hyatt Regency Scottsdale proudly presents these carefully selected menus for your enjoyment. A variety have been selected to complement your special events. If a particular favorite is desired, but not found, please consult your catering manager.

FIGURE 6-3   THE HYATT REGENCY'S SALES PRESENTATION FOLDER COVER. (Courtesy of The Hyatt Regency, Scottsdale, Arizona.)

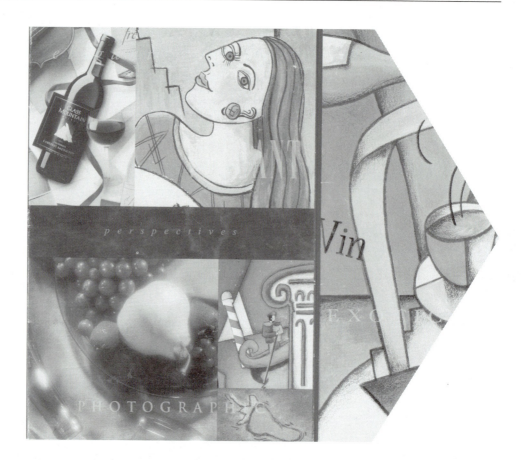

FIGURE 6-4
ENVELOPE DESIGN
FOR A SALES
PRESENTATION
FOLDER.
(Courtesy of
Associates Design.)

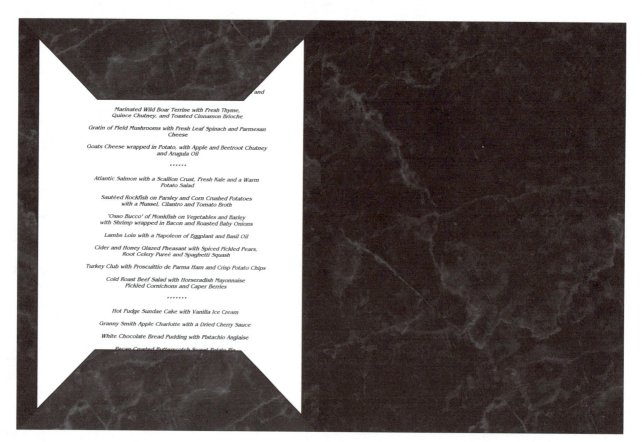

and

Marinated Wild Boar Terrine with Fresh Thyme,
Quince Chutney, and Toasted Cinnamon Brioche

Gratin of Field Mushrooms with Fresh Leaf Spinach and Parmesan
Cheese

Goats Cheese wrapped in Potato, with Apple and Beetroot Chutney
and Arugula Oil

• • • • • •

Atlantic Salmon with a Scallion Crust, Fresh Kale and a Warm
Potato Salad

Sautéed Rockfish on Parsley and Corn Crushed Potatoes
with a Mussel, Cilantro and Tomato Broth

'Osso Bucco' of Monkfish on Vegetables and Barley
with Shrimp wrapped in Bacon and Roasted Baby Onions

Lambs Loin with a Napoleon of Eggplant and Basil Oil

Cider and Honey Glazed Pheasant with Spiced Pickled Pears,
Root Celery Pureé and Spaghetti Squash

Turkey Club with Proscuittio de Parma Ham and Crisp Potato Chips

Cold Roast Beef Salad with Horseradish Mayonnaise
Pickled Cornichons and Caper Berries

• • • • • • •

Hot Fudge Sundae Cake with Vanilla Ice Cream

Granny Smith Apple Charlotte with a Dried Cherry Sauce

White Chocolate Bread Pudding with Pistachio Anglaise

Pecan Crusted Butterscotch Sweet Potato Pie

FIGURE 6-5   THE INN AT MORROW BAY'S HORIZONTAL OPENING SALES PRESENTATION FOLDER.
(Courtesy of The Inn at Morrow Bay, Morrow Bay, California.)

the view from the terrace of The Inn at Morrow Bay in Morrow Bay, California. The inside of the cover uses the back panel only, with a bottom fold panel, to hold the menu presentation.

Even when the standard format of two panels with pockets, the most common type of presentation folder, is used, the wide variety of cover graphic designs available still provides an exciting selection of folder styles. Figure 6-6 shows a design border in browns and peach tones with the hotel's insignia embossed in the center panel just above the name. The front panel of the folder in Figure 6-7 focuses on an inset watercolor of the hotel's front facade done in gold, yellow, and blue tones to highlight the brown-gold color of the folder. Figure 6-8 is a very classical cover interpretation from The Greenbrier in White Sulpher Spring, West Virginia. The simple design takes advantage of a contemporary paper design in muted shades of gray, beige, and yellow to highlight the hotel's name. The overall effect is at once classical and contemporary.

For Keswick Hall in Keswick, Virginia, near Thomas Jefferson's home, Monticello, a two-panel presentation folder is designed with panels cut to create a curving line across the open folder. This package cover, shown in

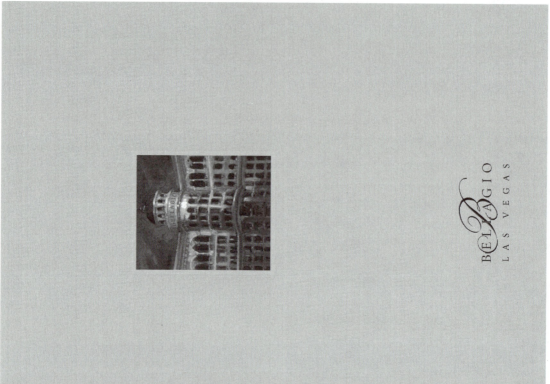

FIGURE 6-7 THE BELLAGIO HOTEL'S SALES
PRESENTATION FOLDER COVER DESIGN.
(Courtesy of Mirage Resorts, Incorporated.)

FIGURE 6-6 HOTEL DU PONT'S SALES PRESENTATION
FOLDER COVER DESIGN.
(Courtesy of The Hotel Du Pont, Wilmington, Delaware.)

FIGURE 6-8   THE GREENBRIER'S CLASSICAL FOLDER COVER DESIGN.
(Courtesy of The Greenbrier, White Sulpher Spring, West Virginia.)

Figure 6-9, is used to cross-market the three Ashley Hotels. The presentation folder in Figure 6-10, for Llangoled Hall in Wales, U.K., is a book format that showcases the public rooms of the hotel.

A two-panel cover design is shown with the wedding package for the Flamingo Hilton in Figure 6-11a. The two front panels open in the center to reveal a center pocket that holds menus and wedding details, as seen in Figure 6-11b. The two interior side panels are printed with marketing information. Graphics illustrate the hotel's concept of a flamingo garden.

FIGURE 6-9   SALES PRESENTATION FOLDER FOR THE THREE ASHLEY HOTELS.
(Courtesy of Ashley Hotels.)

FIGURE 6-10 SALES PRESENTATION FOLDER FOR LLANGOED HALL IN WALES, U.K.
(Courtesy of Ashley Hotels.)

(A)

FIGURE 6-11   THE FLAMINGO HILTON'S
WEDDING PACKAGE FOLDER. (A) COVER WHEN
CLOSED. (B) OPEN, SHOWING THE CENTER
POCKET AND TWO SIDE PANELS.
(Courtesy of The Flamingo Hilton, Las Vegas,
Nevada.)

(B)

Package cover sizes and shapes that use die cuts in their design are generally limited to conference and convention centers and hotels, due to their cost. Individual catering businesses do not often invest in the design and printing expense required for these presentations. The simpler cover format in Figure 6-12 is an effective sales presentation that fits within stricter budget requirements.

FIGURE 6-12   THE HYATT REGENCY ALBUQUERQUE'S SIMPLER
SALES PRESENTATION FOLDER COVER FORMAT.
(Courtesy of The Hyatt Regency Albuquerque, New Mexico.)

Menu Design Format

A wide range of design formats is available on which to present catering menus. The most traditional is the basic single-panel page. The single panel may incorporate a number of different menus, as in Figure 6-13, from the Inn at Morrow Bay, or only one menu, as in Figure 6-14, from the Plaza Hotel in New York City.

A variation on the single panel is an index format seen in Figure 6-15. This format provides an easy reference guide from which to select menus. This index in Figure 6-16, from the Garden of the Gods, in Colorado Springs, Colorado, clearly identifies menu sections along with beverage lists, catering policies, and menu prices. A variation on this design is shown in Figure 6-17 from the Flamingo Hilton in Las Vegas, Nevada. By cutting the upper right-hand corner of the menu pages on the diagonal, an index is created identifying the types of menu available along with receptions, theme menus, and beverage lists. This format allows for a full 8½ by 11 sheet of paper to be used for menu layout. The design of this paper incorporates the theme of the presentation folder, creating a colorful tropical garden in vivid colors.

The menu design in Figure 6-18 provides individual folders for each menu section, each clearly identified by a color photograph of the appropriate plate presentations, as shown for the dinner selections. The inside panels of each section outline the menu offerings. The price list is printed separately. While this is an expensive presentation, it represents the perceived value that management wants to impart to the customer for the catering menu program. Prices can be easily changed by reprinting the separate pricing sheet, rather than the complete menu presentation.

The design in Figure 6-19 uses a horizontal layout with color food photography to illustrate menu offerings. This multipage book format, from the Radisson Airport Hotel and Conference Center in Columbus, Ohio, includes 24 design pages covering both social and business catering package information. This presentation clearly communicates quality and perceived value to the customer. Preprinted prices, however, create a challenge for management due to the high cost of reprinting for price changes. The menu page offers both à la carte and fixed price menus, providing guests with a choice between the flexibility of designing their own menus and with the convenience of selecting a preestablished menu.

A variety of design formats are outlined in Figure 6-20.

The Inn At Morrow Bay

BREAKFAST

Traditional Breakfast (plated or buffet)

SCRAMBLED EGGS WITH BACON AND SAUSAGE, O'BRIEN POTATOES, ASSORTED PASTRIES, STRAWBERRIES, BUTTER AND PRESERVES, ORANGE JUICE, COFFEE, DECAF, HOT TEA, AND WATER.

Fiesta Breakfast (plated or buffet)

SCRAMBLED EGGS WITH LINGUICA AND CHEESE, REFRIED BEANS, O'BRIEN POTATOES, TORTILLAS, SALSA, STRAWBERRIES, ORANGE JUICE, COFFEE, DECAF, HOT TEA, AND WATER.

Health Nut Breakfast (buffet only)

GRANOLA AND BRAN FLAKES, HOT OATMEAL WITH RAISINS AND BROWN SUGAR, YOGURT, STRAWBERRIES WITH CRÈME FRÀICHE, MUFFINS, BAGELS AND CREAM CHEESE, FRESH ORANGE JUICE, COFFEE, DECAF, HOT TEA, AND WATER.

Continental Breakfast (buffet only)

AN ASSORTMENT OF DANISH, MUFFINS, BAGELS AND CREAM CHEESE, BUTTER, PRESERVES, ORANGE JUICE, COFFEE, DECAF, HOT TEA, AND WATER.

The following items may be added to any buffet:

OMELETTE BAR (MINIMUM OF 25 PEOPLE)

CREPE BAR (MINIMUM OF 25 PEOPLE)

PASTA BAR (MINIMUM OF 25 PEOPLE)

EGGS BENEDICT (MINIMUM OF 25 PEOPLE)

BARON OF BEEF (MINIMUM OF 65 PEOPLE)

BRUNCH

Traditional Brunch Buffet

CREPE BAR WITH CHEF, EGGS BENEDICT, SAUSAGE AND BACON, O'BRIEN POTATOES, FRESH SEASONAL FRUIT, ASSORTED SALADS, ASSORTED PASTRIES, ORANGE JUICE, COFFEE, DECAF, HOT TEA, AND WATER.

Specialty Brunch Buffet

CHEF CARVED BARON OF BEEF, CHICKEN VOL AU VENT, SCRAMBLED EGGS, AU GRATIN POTATOES, FRESH SEASONAL FRUIT, ASSORTED SALADS, ASSORTED PASTRIES, ORANGE JUICE, COFFEE, DECAF, HOT TEA, AND WATER.

Dessert Buffet

CREPE BAR WITH CHEF, ASSORTED PASTRIES, ASSORTED CAKES, ASSORTED COOKIES, CHOCOLATE DIPPED STRAWBERRIES.

CHILDREN'S MENU

10 YEARS AND YOUNGER

Paradise Sand Dollars

SIX SAND DOLLAR SIZE BUTTERMILK PANCAKES SERVED WITH BUTTER AND SYRUP, MILK OR JUICE, AND WATER.

Junior Breakfast

ONE SCRAMBLED EGG, TWO PIECES SMOKED BACON, ONE SLICE OF TOAST, MILK OR JUICE AND WATER.

FIGURE 6-13 THE INN AT MORROW BAY SINGLE-PANEL MENU DESIGN FORMAT.
(Courtesy of The Inn at Morrow Bay, Morrow Bay, California.)

DINNER

ROSACE OF MAINE LOBSTER AND
SAFFRONED TURNIP
SEVRUGA CAVIAR IN A BLINIS CRÊPE

FOWL CONSOMMÉ WITH QUENELLES OF PHEASANT

BRAISED LOIN OF VEAL WITH OREGON MOREL CREAM
WILD RICE WITH PIGNOLI NUTS
YELLOW AND GREEN ZUCCHINI
SAUTÉED SPINACH

WINTER BABY LETTUCE WITH WHOLE GRAIN MUSTARD
WALNUT DRESSING
SELECTED FARMER CHEESES
STONE-BAKED SEMOLINA BREAD

PLAZA WEDDING CAKE

MACERATED GRAPEFRUIT AND ORANGE RINGS
AND MIGNIARDISES

COFFEE AND ASSORTED TEAS

FIGURE 6-14   PLAZA HOTEL, NEW YORK CITY, SINGLE-PANEL MENU.
("A Plaza Wedding" by Lawrence D. Harvey. Courtesy of the Plaza Hotel,
New York, New York.)

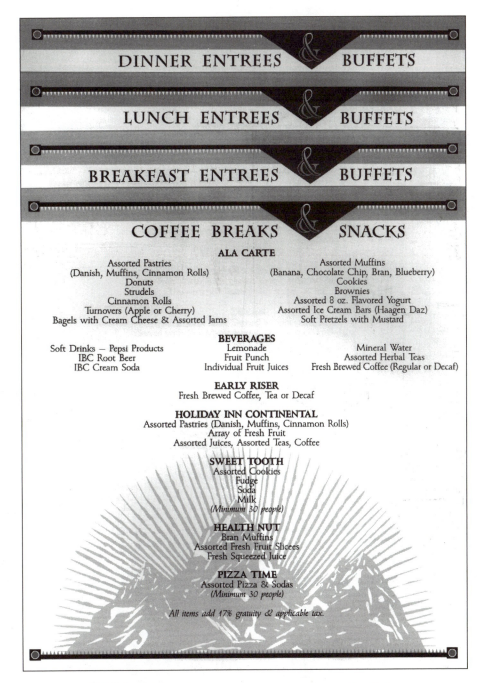

DINNER ENTREES & **BUFFETS**

LUNCH ENTREES & **BUFFETS**

BREAKFAST ENTREES & **BUFFETS**

COFFEE BREAKS & **SNACKS**

ALA CARTE

Assorted Pastries
(Danish, Muffins, Cinnamon Rolls)
Donuts
Strudels
Cinnamon Rolls
Turnovers (Apple or Cherry)
Bagels with Cream Cheese & Assorted Jams

Assorted Muffins
(Banana, Chocolate Chip, Bran, Blueberry)
Cookies
Brownies
Assorted 8 oz. Flavored Yogurt
Assorted Ice Cream Bars (Haagen Daz)
Soft Pretzels with Mustard

BEVERAGES

Soft Drinks – Pepsi Products
IBC Root Beer
IBC Cream Soda

Lemonade
Fruit Punch
Individual Fruit Juices

Mineral Water
Assorted Herbal Teas
Fresh Brewed Coffee (Regular or Decaf)

EARLY RISER
Fresh Brewed Coffee, Tea or Decaf

HOLIDAY INN CONTINENTAL
Assorted Pastries (Danish, Muffins, Cinnamon Rolls)
Array of Fresh Fruit
Assorted Juices, Assorted Teas, Coffee

SWEET TOOTH
Assorted Cookies
Fudge
Soda
Milk
(Minimum 30 people)

HEALTH NUT
Bran Muffins
Assorted Fresh Fruit Slicees
Fresh Squeezed Juice

PIZZA TIME
Assorted Pizza & Sodas
(Minimum 30 people)

All items add 17% gratuity & applicable tax.

FIGURE 6-15   INDEX FORMAT OF SINGLE-PANEL MENU.
(Courtesy of Holiday Inn Garden of the Gods,
Colorado Springs, Colorado.)

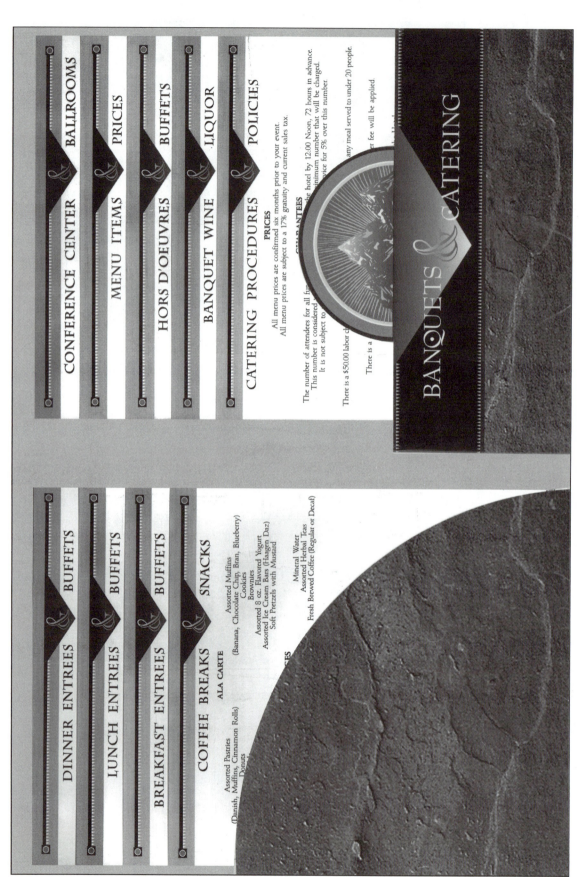

FIGURE 6-16 GARDEN OF THE GODS IN COLORADO SPRINGS, COLORADO MENU INDEX.
(Courtesy of Holiday Inn Garden of the Gods, Colorado Springs, Colorado.)

FIGURE 6-17   THE FLAMINGO HILTON MENU INDEX.
(Courtesy of The Flamingo Hilton, Las Vegas, Nevada.)

DINNER MENUS

FIGURE 6-18 THE HYATT REGENCY SCOTTSDALE'S MULTIPANEL MENU. (Courtesy of The Hyatt Regency, Scottsdale, Arizona.)

DINNER

All Dinners include Chef's accompaniment of Pasta, Rice or Potato, Fresh Seasonal Vegetables,
Specialty Rolls, Butter, Brewed French Roast Coffees, Specialty Teas and Milk

THREE-COURSE SELECTIONS

DINNER I

Chilled Sonoran Shrimp Cocktail
with Field Greens and Crisp Jalapeño Tortilla Chips

Tenderloin of Beef, Southwest Herb Butter
Roasted Garlic Marinated Chicken Breast
on Corn Stuffing with Cilantro Butter

Flourless Chocolate Cake
on Pecan Crust with Vanilla Ice Cream

DINNER II

Painted Southwest Shrimp Caesar Salad
with Roasted Corn, Tomatoes
and Horseradish Relish

Pistachio Roasted Lamb Chop
Steamed Halibut Roll
Cilantro Hollandaise

Tequila Lime Tart and Fresh Berry Tostada
Citrus Glace

DINNER III

Chilled Portabella Mushroom
and Barbecued Quail Napoleon
Baby Bok Choy
Three-Bean Relish

Grilled Swordfish with Crawfish Chili
Pancetta Roasted Porkloin
on Braised Fennel

Pecan and Cranberry Tart
in Graham Cracker Crust
with Vanilla Ice Cream

DINNER IV

Frisee, Radicchio, Bibb Lettuces
Ripe Red and Yellow Tomatoes
with Maytag Blue Cheese Fritter
Raspberry Walnut Dressing

Baked Sonoran Bass, Diced Onion,
Fresh Chili Peppers,
Calamata Olives and Capers
Soy-Ginger Sauce

Mascarpone Cheese Coffee Cake
Powdered Sugar Design
Chocolate Sauces

DINNER V

Grilled Lobster
on Saffron Risotto Cake
Buttermilk Mushroom Sauce

Mushroom Crusted Veal Loin
and Crisp Duck Leg Confit
on Cilantro Pasta
Lingonberry Demi

Toasted Hazelnut Parfait
and Flourless Chocolate Cake
Caramel Orange Sauces

DINNER VI

Smoked Shrimp on Pickled Napa Cabbage
and Daikon Slaw
with Fresh Watercress and Field Greens

Grilled Tenderloin of Beef, Southwest Herb Butter
Lobster Medallion on Creamed Orzo Cake

Warm Apple Cinnamon Strudel
and Caramel Ice Cream
Warm Raspberry Sauce

DINNER VII

Ranch Salad with Grilled Eggplant
and Saffron Linguine Salad

Rice Pepper Crusted Quail and Steamed Salmon Roll
Achiote Basil Lime Sauce

White and Dark Chocolate Chimney
with Raspberry Mousse
Painted Fruit Sauces

SORBETS

Served on a Powdered Sugar Design or Logo

Green Apple
Orange Campari

Pink Champagne
Lemon Lime

Raspberry Peppercorn
Orange Tarragon

Sorbets may be added to any Three-Course Menu for $5.50
or may be substituted for an Appetizer on any Four-Course Menu at no charge.

FOUR-COURSE SELECTIONS

DINNER VIII

Crabmeat and Piñon Nut Cakes
Roasted Red and Yellow Pepper Cream
Root Vegetable Slaw

Painted South Mountain Greens
Ripe Tomatoes, Calamata Olives
Cilantro Dressing

Baked Double Chicken Breast
Stuffed with Herb Boursin and Spinach
with Fried Tortilla
Ancho Chili Sauce

Fresh Berry and Chocolate Taco
with Vanilla Bean Mousse
Fruit Sauces

DINNER IX

Roasted Duck and Tomato Tortilla Wrap
on Spinach Salad
Peanut Dressing

Lobster Bisque
Crab Fritter

Smoked Bacon and Rosemary Roasted Pork
Tenderloin and Sautéed Veal Medallion
Porcini Mushroom Sauce

Warm Pear Tart in Hazelnut Crust
Caramel Ice Cream

DINNER X

Steamed Vegetables Pot Sticker
Consommé

Hearts of Romaine with Lobster,
Jicama and Sweet Potato Tower

Orange-Honey Barbecued
Chicken Breast
Fried Rosemary Crusted Veal Loin
Roasted Garlic Demi

Fresh Berry Crème Brûlée
in Cookie Cup on Chocolate Design

DINNER XI

Cream of Roasted Fennel and Garlic
in Ancho Puff Pastry

Blackened Lamb Loin Wrap
with South Mountain Greens

Roasted Garlic Marinated
Double Chicken Breast
on Wild Mushroom Risotto Cake
Morel Sauce

Fresh Berries on Navajo Fry Bread
with Fried Ice Cream

DINNER XII

Mixed Greens in Potato Basket
with Fresh Artichoke
and Heart of Palm Salad

Amber Beer and Cheese Soup
in Lime-Pepper Puff Pastry

Herb Rubbed Pork Steak
and Potato Crusted Mahi Mahi
Apple and Toasted Walnut Salsa

Checker Chocolate Mousse Terrine
Fresh Berries and Fruit Sauces

DINNER XIII

Wild Mushroom Ravioli with Shrimp and Scallops
on an Asparagus Skewer

Southwest Root Vegetable and Roasted Eggplant
in Cilantro Tortilla

Mesquite Honey Barbecued Capon Breast
Hoisin Marinated Double Lamb Chop
Minted Pear and Sweet Onion Relish

Tequila Lime Flan with Chocolate Piñon Nut Tart
Painted Chocolate Desert

DINNER XIV

Lobster and Corn Polenta Roll on Braised Fennel
Chive Butter

Red and White Endive on Bibb Lettuce
Ripe Tomatoes and Mushroom Salad
Raspberry-Walnut Dressing

Grilled Veal Chop
with Shrimp Tamale
Balsamic Demi Glace

Fresh Pear Tart with Vanilla Sauce
Pear Williams Ice Cream

DINNER

Appetizers

Fresh Seasonal Fruit Cup $2.25
Shrimp Cocktail $8.50
Shrimp & Scallops St. Jacques $6.25
Prosciutto/Melon $4.95

Soups

Soup du Jour $1.75
Chilled Fruit Soups $2.95
French Onion Soup $3.25

Salads

Caesar Salad $2.95
Spinach Salad $2.50
Bibb Lettuce with Raspberry Vinaigrette and Pine Nuts $3.25
Strawberry and Onion Salad $2.25

Entrees

All Entrees include our Garden Fresh Salad with Choice of
Dressing, Fresh Seasonal Vegetable, Choice of Potato,
Rolls and Butter and Selection of Coffee, Hot Tea,
Decaf or Iced Tea

Beef & Pork Entrees

Roast Prime Rib of Beef $19.95
Served in its Natural Juices with
Creamed Horseradish Sauce.

New York Strip $22.95
We cut our Strip Steaks from the Center of the
Loin for the most Tender Steaks and
crown them with Maitre d Butter.

Filet Mignon $24.95
Crowned with a Mushroom Cap and
accompanied with Bernaise Sauce.

Sliced Roast Top Sirloin of Beef $16.95
Served in its Natural Juices.

Stuffed Pork Chop $14.95
Center Cut Pork Chop, split and filled with Sage
Dressing and served with Cinnamon Apple Sauce.

Sliced Pork Loin $15.95
Roasted Boneless Pork Loin in a Dijon Au Julais
with Fresh Rosemary

Veal Entrees

Veal Marsala $19.50
Tender Veal Lightly Sauteed, served in
Marsala Wine Sauce.

Veal Piccata $18.95
Lightly Sauteed Veal Medallions served with Fresh
Lemon and Capers.

Seafood Entrees

Broiled Swordfish $19.95
A Center Cut Portion of Swordfish Broiled with
Lemon Butter accompanied with Dill Sauce.

Broiled Halibut $17.95
Broiled Halibut Steak topped with Herb Butter,
served with Fresh Lemon

Orange Roughy $16.95
A New Zealand Delicacy, broiled and served with
Lemon and Chive Butter.

Shrimp Scampi $18.95
Jumbo Shrimp sauteed in Garlic and Herb Butter,
served with Rice Pilaf.

Pasta
(Maximum 50 Persons)

Pasta Primavera $13.95
Tender Fettuccine Noodles sauteed with
Fresh Vegetables and served with a
Light Cream Sauce.
(Served with Salad, Rolls, Butter, Beverage)

Chicken and Pasta Primavera $15.95
Strips of Chicken Tenderloin sauteed with
Fresh Vegetables, tossed with Fettuccine
Noodles is a Light Cream Sauce.

Linguini Napoli $17.95
Succulent Gulf Shrimp flavored with Garlic and
served in a Basil Tomato Coulis with Pine Nuts.

Poultry Entrees

Chicken Lexington $19.95
Chicken Breast Stuffed with Fresh Zucchini, Squash,
Carrots, Celery. Rolled and Baked. Cut into
Medallions and served over an
Herbed White Wine Sauce.

Chicken Pizzolla $18.95
Baked Chicken Breast topped with Marinara Sauce,
Sliced Red Pepper, Green Pepper, Mushrooms,
Tomatoes and Purple Onion and topped with
Grated Provolone and Parmesan Cheese.

Chicken St. Clair $17.95
Chicken Breast topped with Broccoli Flourets,
Julienne Smoked Ham, Sliced Mushrooms.
Purple Onion and Mozzarella Cheese.
topped with a Light Supreme Sauce.

Chicken Amberly $19.95
Chicken Breast filled with Bacon, Artichokes,
Mushroom and Onion Mixture and Grated Monterey
Jack. Rolled in Cracker Crumbs and Fried.
Cut into Medallions and served with
a Marsala Mushroom Sauce.

Char-Broiled Free Range Chicken Breast $15.95
Topped with a Pomaroy Mustard Cream Sauce.

All Banquet Functions will be Charged a 17% Service Charge and Applicable Taxes.

11

FIGURE 6-19 RADISSON COLUMBUS, OHIO HORIZONTAL MENU LAYOUT WITH COLOR FOOD PHOTOGRAPHY.
(Courtesy of The Radisson Airport Hotel and Conference Center, Columbus, Ohio.)

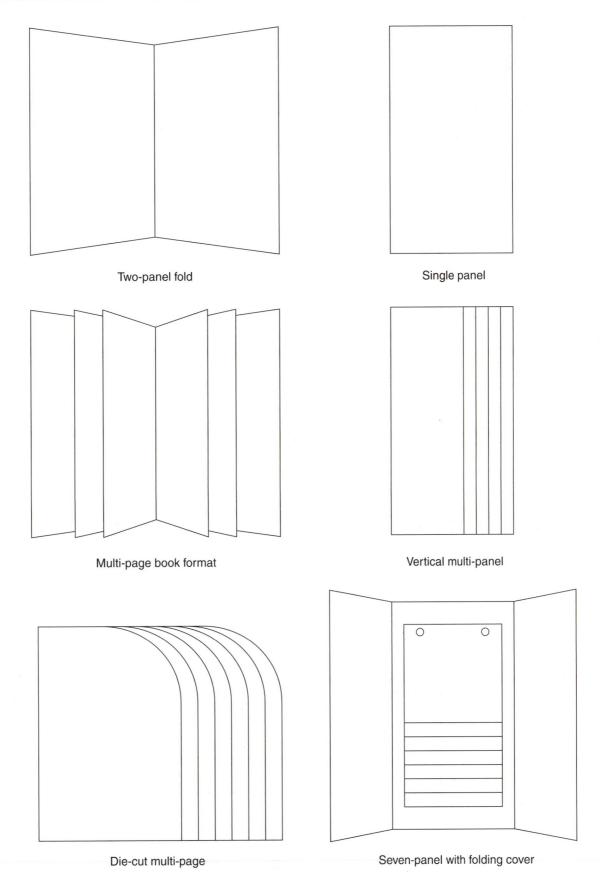

Two-panel fold

Single panel

Multi-page book format

Vertical multi-panel

Die-cut multi-page

Seven-panel with folding cover

FIGURE 6-20 VARIETY OF MENU DESIGN FORMATS.

Layout

Layout refers to the placement of typeface and illustrations on the design format. A catering menu, outlining the complete menu, lists items in the order in which they are served, as in Figure 6-21. Illustrations are often incorporated to add interest to the page presentation as seen on the Llangoed Hall menu in Figure 6-22.

Special design work can create dramatic and appealing layouts such as seen in Figure 6-23. A preprinted paper with bold vertical green stripes on a

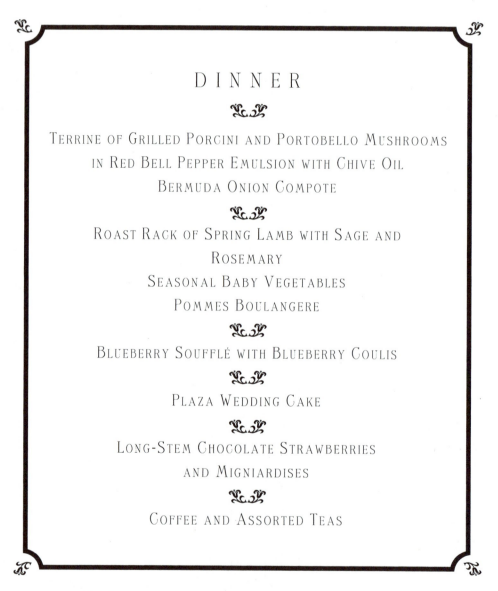

DINNER

TERRINE OF GRILLED PORCINI AND PORTOBELLO MUSHROOMS
IN RED BELL PEPPER EMULSION WITH CHIVE OIL
BERMUDA ONION COMPOTE

ROAST RACK OF SPRING LAMB WITH SAGE AND
ROSEMARY
SEASONAL BABY VEGETABLES
POMMES BOULANGERE

BLUEBERRY SOUFFLÉ WITH BLUEBERRY COULIS

PLAZA WEDDING CAKE

LONG-STEM CHOCOLATE STRAWBERRIES
AND MIGNIARDISES

COFFEE AND ASSORTED TEAS

FIGURE 6-21   PLAZA HOTEL CATERING MENU WITH ITEMS
LISTED IN THE ORDER IN WHICH THEY ARE SERVED.
("A Plaza Wedding" by Lawrence D. Harvey. Courtesy
of The Plaza Hotel, New York, New York.)

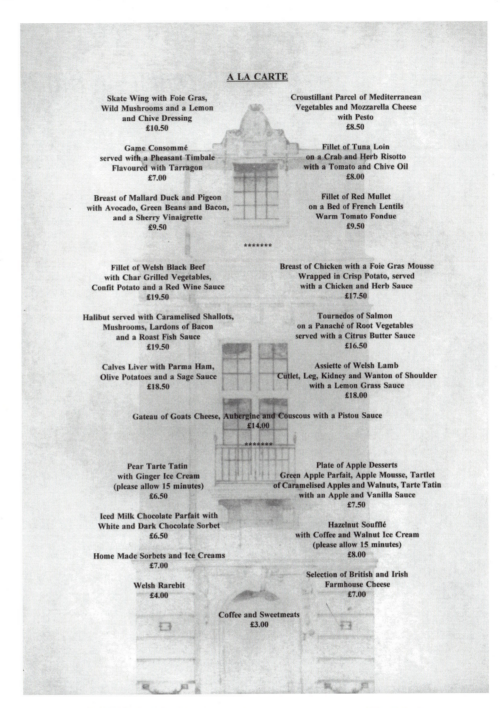

A LA CARTE

Skate Wing with Foie Gras,
Wild Mushrooms and a Lemon
and Chive Dressing
£10.50

Croustillant Parcel of Mediterranean
Vegetables and Mozzarella Cheese
with Pesto
£8.50

Game Consommé
served with a Pheasant Timbale
Flavoured with Tarragon
£7.00

Fillet of Tuna Loin
on a Crab and Herb Risotto
with a Tomato and Chive Oil
£8.00

Breast of Mallard Duck and Pigeon
with Avocado, Green Beans and Bacon,
and a Sherry Vinaigrette
£9.50

Fillet of Red Mullet
on a Bed of French Lentils
Warm Tomato Fondue
£9.50

****

Fillet of Welsh Black Beef
with Char Grilled Vegetables,
Confit Potato and a Red Wine Sauce
£19.50

Breast of Chicken with a Foie Gras Mousse
Wrapped in Crisp Potato, served
with a Chicken and Herb Sauce
£17.50

Halibut served with Caramelised Shallots,
Mushrooms, Lardons of Bacon
and a Roast Fish Sauce
£19.50

Tournedos of Salmon
on a Panaché of Root Vegetables
served with a Citrus Butter Sauce
£16.50

Calves Liver with Parma Ham,
Olive Potatoes and a Sage Sauce
£18.50

Assiette of Welsh Lamb
Cutlet, Leg, Kidney and Wanton of Shoulder
with a Lemon Grass Sauce
£18.00

Gateau of Goats Cheese, Aubergine and Couscous with a Pistou Sauce
£14.00

****

Pear Tarte Tatin
with Ginger Ice Cream
(please allow 15 minutes)
£6.50

Plate of Apple Desserts
Green Apple Parfait, Apple Mousse, Tartlet
of Caramelised Apples and Walnuts, Tarte Tatin
with an Apple and Vanilla Sauce
£7.50

Iced Milk Chocolate Parfait with
White and Dark Chocolate Sorbet
£6.50

Hazelnut Soufflé
with Coffee and Walnut Ice Cream
(please allow 15 minutes)
£8.00

Home Made Sorbets and Ice Creams
£7.00

Welsh Rarebit
£4.00

Selection of British and Irish
Farmhouse Cheese
£7.00

Coffee and Sweetmeats
£3.00

FIGURE 6-22 LLANGOED HALL MENU WITH ILLUSTRATIONS.
(Courtesy of Ashley Hotels.)

glossy cream colored paper uses a simple design to project an elegant yet casual image.

Many catering services use computer word processing programs to produce their own menus. The menus in Figure 6-24 are printed on paper that has been pre-printed with illustrations. This menu program incorporates

Breakfast Buffets

Breakfast Buffets include choice of two Juices (fresh-squeezed Orange or Grapefruit, Apple, Cranberry, Tomato),
Baker's Basket, whipped Butter, Preserves, fresh-brewed and Decaffeinated Coffee, Specialty Teas or Milk.
(For parties under 50, a set-up charge of $150.00 applies.)

The Coronet

Seasonal Fruit and Berries
Breakfast Cereal and Honey-toasted Granola
Fruit Yogurts
Scrambled Eggs
Double Thick Maple-smoked Bacon
Chicken Apple Sausage
Brioche
Cinnamon-Raisin French Toast,
Maple Syrup
Hash Browns
$20.00

The Windsor

Seasonal Fruit and Berries
Breakfast Cereal and Honey-toasted Granola
Fruit Yogurts
Scrambled Eggs, choice of Toppings: Sautéed
Mushrooms, Onions, Peppers, Cheese, Salsa
Sonoma Sausage Patties
Cheese Blintzes with Blueberry Coulis
Cottage Fries
$21.00

The Hanover

Seasonal Fruit and Berries
Breakfast Cereal and Honey-toasted Granola
Banana Pancakes, Macadamia Nut Syrup
Quiche Loraine
Housemade Corned Beef Hash
Lyonnaise Potatoes
$20.00

The Crown

Seasonal Fruit and Berries
Breakfast Cereal and Honey-toasted Granola
Atlantic Smoked Salmon, Cream Cheese
Omelettes cooked to order
Julian Apple Crêpes
Iowa Ham Steaks, Veal Sausage
Hash Browns
$22.00

Customized Buffet Brunch

We will be happy to create a memorable Brunch menu for your special event.

Prices are subject to Service Charges and applicable Tax.

Hotel del Coronado

1500 Orange Avenue, Coronado, California 92118 • (619) 435-0611

FIGURE 6-23   HOTEL DEL CORONADO MENU WITH SPECIAL DESIGN WORK.
(Courtesy of The Hotel Del Coronado, Coronado, California.)

three graphic designs to create an image that is a once distinctive and cost effective.

The layout in Figure 6-25 offers six complete luncheon menus, priced per person. The layout in Figure 6-26 is for a buffet clam bake menu. The menu in Figure 6-27 offers a selection of menu items for each course at one per person price.

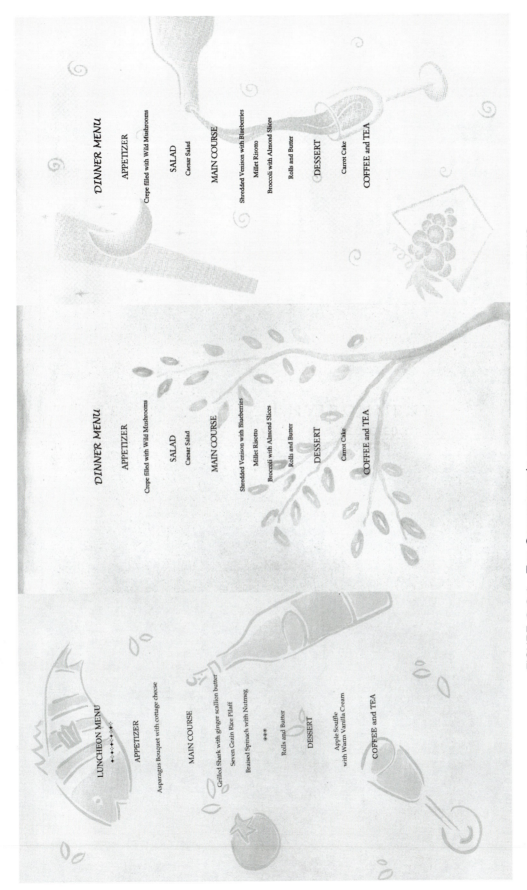

FIGURE 6-24 THE GREENBRIER'S MENU WITH PREPRINTED ILLUSTRATIONS.
(Courtesy of The Greenbrier, White Sulpher Spring, West Virginia.)

DINNER BUFFETS

New England Clam Bake

New England Style Clam Chowder
Oyster Crackers

Garden Greens with Cucumbers
Tomatoes, Radishes, Carrots and Grated Cheddar Cheese
Sprouts and Croutons Served with Creamy Peppercorn,
Herb Vinaigrette and 1000 Island Dressings

Smoked Fish with Spinach Salad
Warm Bacon Dressing

Jumbo Shrimp on Ice
Cocktail Sauce, Tabasco and Lemon
(based on 4 pieces per person)

Steamed Lobsters and Clams
with Drawn Butter, Tabasco and Lemon
Served by an Attendant at $25.00 per hour

Grilled New York Sirloin Steaks
Barbecued Chicken
*Chef Required at $75.00 per hour to Grill Outdoors
One Chef and Grill per 100 Guests*

Corn on the Cob
Salt Potatoes
Fresh Rolls and Butter

Assorted Cakes and Pies

Freshly Brewed Regular and Decaffeinated Coffee
Selection of Herbal Teas and Iced Tea

$60.00 per person

All prices are subject to 19% Hotel Service Charge and 5% Civic Assessment Tax,
both taxable to the state at a 4.5% rate
For a plated function of twenty (20) people or less a $50.00 labor charge will apply.
For a buffet function of fifty (50) people or less a $100.00 labor charge will apply.
All prices are valid through December 31, 1998

FIGURE 6-26 HYATT REGENCY, BEAVER CREEK
DINNER BUFFET MENU.
(Courtesy of The Hyatt Regency at Beaver Creek, Colorado.)

Luncheons

Luncheon. If you would prefer the intimacy of a sit-down service luncheon to break up your day of meetings and give your guests a chance to relax and enjoy a leisurely meal, you will want to review the following menu options.

L-1 Menu at $28.00 per person charge.

Melon with Prosciutto

Broiled Sirloin Strip Steak
with Buttermilk Fried Onion Rings
and Sauteed Wild Mushrooms

Chocolate Banana Pie

Coffee   Iced Tea

L-2 Menu at $30.25 per person charge.

Gazpacho

Grilled Yellowfin Tuna
Warm Nicoise Salad
Tomato Provencale

Greenbrier Cheesecake
with Fresh Berries

Coffee   Iced Tea

L-3 Menu at $29.00 per person charge.

Caesar Salad

Scallopini of Veal with Lemon Caper Butter
Wild Mushroom Risotto
Asparagus Spears

Dutch Apple Crumb Pie
Vanilla Ice Cream

Coffee   Iced Tea

L-4 Menu at $28.00 per person charge.

Mushroom Consomme

Grilled Atlantic Salmon
Saffron Cream
Pastina with Asparagus and Shiitake Mushrooms

White Chocolate Macadamia Nut Tart

Coffee   Iced Tea

L-5 Menu at $24.75 per person charge.

Fresh Melon in Season

Grilled Breast of Chicken, Raspberry Salsa
Red Pepper Orzo
Grilled Vegetables

Warm Espresso Brownie
with Vanilla Bean Ice Cream

Coffee   Iced Tea

L-6 Menu at $30.00 per person charge.

Soup du Jour

Chesapeake Bay Crab Cakes
Remoulade Sauce
Fresh Steamed Asparagus
Creamy Cole Slaw

Lemon Creme Brulee

Coffee   Iced Tea

1

FIGURE 6-25 THE INN AT PERRY CABIN'S SIX COMPLETE
LUNCHEON MENUS DONE ON ONE PAGE.
(Courtesy of Ashley Hotels.)

Lunch Menu

Butternut Squash Soup with Roasted Chestnuts and Cumin

Poached Oysters with Proscuitto Ham, Shredded Vegetables and Champagne

Marinated Wild Boar Terrine with Fresh Thyme, Quince Chutney, and Toasted Cinnamon Brioche

Gratin of Field Mushrooms with Fresh Leaf Spinach and Parmesan Cheese

Goats Cheese wrapped in Potato, with Apple and Beetroot Chutney and Arugula Oil

* * * * * *

Atlantic Salmon with a Scallion Crust, Fresh Kale and a Warm Potato Salad

Sautéed Rockfish on Parsley and Corn Crushed Potatoes with a Mussel, Cilantro and Tomato Broth

'Osso Bucco' of Monkfish on Vegetables and Barley with Shrimp wrapped in Bacon and Roasted Baby Onions

Lambs Loin with a Napoleon of Eggplant and Basil Oil

Cider and Honey Glazed Pheasant with Spiced Pickled Pears, Root Celery Pureé and Spaghetti Squash

Turkey Club with Proscuittio de Parma Ham and Crisp Potato Chips

Cold Roast Beef Salad with Horseradish Mayonnaise Pickled Cornichons and Caper Berries

* * * * * * *

Hot Fudge Sundae Cake with Vanilla Ice Cream

Granny Smith Apple Charlotte with a Dried Cherry Sauce

White Chocolate Bread Pudding with Pistachio Anglaise

Pecan Crusted Butterscotch Sweet Potato Pie

Autumn Sorbets and Ice Cream

Baked Brioche with Poached Fruits, Spiced Syrup and Chantilly Cream

Twenty-five dollars per person
(Excludes Beverage, Tax, and Gratuity)

FIGURE 6-27   SELECTION OF MENU ITEMS PRICED PER PERSON.

Typeface

The selection of a typeface for a menu layout is important to the overall success of the menu. Typeface style and size can influence the customer's menu selection. Menus that are difficult to read will be either passed over by customers or quickly skimmed and then discarded.

To create interest, establish a mood or character, and increase readability, a variety of the hundreds of different typeface styles and sizes should be incorporated into the overall design of the menu. Careful selection of UPPERCASE (capital) and lowercase letters is one method of providing useful contrasts. Another is varying the thickness, or typeweight, of the typeface. Depending on the message that is to be conveyed some bold typefaces are more efficient than thin ones. To analyze the uses of typefaces, the menu layout can be divided into four separate areas:

Area 1: Course headings separate the menu items into sections such as appetizer, entrée, or dessert. The primary use of typeface for this section is to create interest and unify the overall design. Readability is not a major concern.

Area 2: Menu item names must stand out on the menu page. The primary function of typeface in this section is to highlight menu items in a style that is easy to read and comfortable to the eye.

Area 3: Descriptive copy identifies menu item ingredients and provides other information of interest to customers. Typeface should be easy to read and be presented in a different style or weight than the menu item typeface.

Area 4: Merchandising copy provides catering service and special interest information. Merchandising copy is usually placed at the page bottom or on separate panels or pages. Type style can be decorative to highlight the overall menu design.

A variety of typeface styles that are commonly used in menu design are featured in Figure 6-28. Many of these typefaces are available in computer software programs for word processing and desktop publishing.

Typeface selection for each area of the menu should provide spacing, contrast, and design emphasis. A contrast in typeface size makes menu item selection easier for the customer. Descriptive copy should always be less emphasized than the menu item to create contrast (e.g., lowercase vs. uppercase, lightface vs. bold, and/or smaller type). Course headings should provide design emphasis and spacing between the menu sections. Figure 6-29 offers a menu from the Hotel Du Pont in Wilmington, Delaware, that takes advantage of four different typefaces to create the layout for a buffet menu. Using the hotel logo as the heading, the menu also includes a line, drawn ¾ of an inch in from the margin, which gives the layout the definition of a page. A distinctive upper case heading clearly identifies the menu. Typeface headings for the three courses create breaks in the page that are both decorative and draw the reader's eye to specific points on the page. The typeface for the menu items is very clear and easy to read. Prices and service information is in yet another typeface and sized smaller than any of the others on the page.

Sautéed Steaks Stuffed with Oysters

Beef with Almonds and Olives
Carne Machada à la Andaluza

Fried Meatballs
Keftedes Tiganites

Steak with Onions
Côte de Boeuf à la Marseillaise

Chicken Cacciatore

Poached Salmon with Hollandaise Sauce

Jambalaya

Chocolate Bavarian Cream

LENTIL SOUP
A wonderfully hearty, whole-meal soup

COLD CUCUMBER SOUP

CRAB AND TOMATO BISQUE
Serve this creamy pink treat in patty shells for a lovely luncheon.

LOBSTER AND AVOCADO SALAD

BAKED RED SNAPPER WITH SOUR-CREAM STUFFING

RED SNAPPER FLORIDIAN

SHERIFF HOUSE TROUT
(Sheriff House, Stockbridge, England)

TROUT GRENOBLOISE

RATATOUILLE

MAINE CHICKEN PIE

Schaschlik Spiess
(GERMAN STYLE KEBABS)

Bratwurst in Bier, Berliner Art
(PORK SAUSAGE LINKS IN BEER, BERLIN STYLE)

PETITS FOURS GLAZE

HOLLANDAISE SAUCE

Steak with Caper Sauce

Crab Meat Canapé
Fried Spring Turkey

Candied Sweet Potatoes   *Cauliflower, Tomato Meringue Pudding*
French Salad
Strawberry Baked Alaska

Pennsylvania Dutch Stuffed Shoulder of Pork

Gooseberry Tarts Crust

Crabmeat Cocktail

Broiled Lobster in Clam Shells

Shrimp Rounds

CRAB-MEAT CANAPÉ   **CANDIED SWEET POTATOES**

CAULIFLOWER, TOMATO MÉRINGUE PUDDING

FRIED SPRING TURKEY

Veal and Oyster Pie.   Quenelles of Veal.   Veal Kidney Pie.

Stewed Apples with Rice.   Gooseberry-and-Cream Tarts.

FIGURE 6-28 TYPEFACE STYLE SELECTIONS.

DELUXE BUFFET DINNER SUGGESTIONS

Designed for 30 guests or more

Appetizer Buffet

WILD MUSHROOM SOUP, HERB CROUTON GARNI
MIXED SEASONAL GREENS, BALSAMIC VINAIGRETTE
PASTA SALAD, SEAFOOD SALAD, VEGETABLE SALAD
PATE MAISON WITH SAUCE CUMBERLAND
FISH TERRINE WITH HERB SAUCE
BREAD BASKET & MELBA TOAST

Entree Buffet

ROASTED RACK OF BABY LAMB COATED WITH PECAN CRUST, DEMI GLACE
SALMON STRUDEL WITH CHAMPAGNE SAUCE—Carved at Buffet by Chef
BREAST OF CHICKEN PROVENCALE WITH MADEIRA SAUCE,
Stuffed with Wild Mushroom Mousse, Herb Crust
SHRIMP, CRABMEAT, SCALLOP RAGOUT NEWBURGH, PETITE PATTY SHELLS
BLENDED WILD RICE
FRESH SEASONAL VEGETABLE BOUQUET
SWISS STYLE ROSTI POTATOES

Dessert Buffet

ASSORTED PETITE FRENCH PASTRIES
CHOCOLATE MOUSSE, CREME CARAMEL
SEASONAL FRESH BERRIES CHANTILLY
HOMEMADE RASPBERRY SORBET AND RUM RAISIN ICE CREAM
MACAROONS, TRUFFLES

COFFEE, DECAFFEINATED COFFEE AND TEA

54.00 per person

Chef Attendant fee 30.00 per hour (two hour minimum).
Please add 5.00 per person for less than 30 guests.

Prices are subject to change and do not include service charges.

FIGURE 6-29   HOTEL DU PONT MENU FEATURING FOUR DIFFERENT TYPEFACES.
(Courtesy of The Hotel Du Pont, Wilmington, Delaware.)

Typeface Menu

Fresh Mesclun Greens with Mandarin Oranges & Toasted Almonds
tossed table side
Balsamic Vinaigrette dressing

Petit Filet Mignon, Sauce Chantrelles & Crepes
served with
Medallions of Grilled Swordfish,
Beurre Blanc Garni

Freshly Baked Dinner Rolls
and Butter

White Chocolate Mousse Cake
Strawberry Sauce

Freshly Brewed
Superior Colombian Blend Coffee
regular or decaffeinated
Assorted Bigelow Tea, Regular or Decaffeinated

FIGURE 6-30   MENU WITH STANDARD BUSINESS TYPEFACE, TIMES NEW ROMAN.

The menu in Figure 6-30 is an example of a menu that has been created on a personal computer with word processing using a standard business typeface, Times New Roman. By varying the typeface selections and the case size, this menu takes on a whole new look in Figure 6-31.

Paper and Color

While budget considerations are a factor in selecting package designs and paper stock, both play a major role in establishing the perceived value of a catering service to the customer. Management should define the image that the menu package will give to the customers before they select paper stock and colors. Inexpensive throwaway menus printed on light paper stock in black ink on white paper will convey a very different image than menus presented on a textured 24-weight bond paper in pastel colors with a contrasting print color.

Color is an important part of every menu design presentation. Color can be used in catering menus to elicit specific physical and emotional actions

Revised Typeface Menu

LUNCHEON

❧❧❧❧❧

Salad

Fresh Mesclun Greens with Mandarin Oranges & Toasted Almonds
tossed table side
Balsamic Vinaigrette dressing

❧❧❧❧❧

Entree

Petit Filet Mignon, Sauce Chantrelles & Crepes
served with
Medallions of Grilled Swordfish,
Beurre Blanc Garni

❧❧❧❧❧

Freshly Baked Dinner Rolls
and Butter

Dessert

White Chocolate Mousse Cake
Strawberry Sauce

❧❧❧❧❧

Freshly Brewed
Superior Colombian Blend Coffee
regular or decaffeinated
Assorted Bigelow Tea, Regular or Decaffeinated

FIGURE 6-31   SAME MENU WITH VARYING TYPEFACES.

from the reader. Bright reds and purples excite, soft pinks soothe, and light blues create a feeling of confidence. Shades of brown convey mediocrity, hues of green create unrest, and yellow tones indicate cheerfulness.

Regional and international cuisine themes can also be accented through the creative use of color. Bright reds, blues, and yellows reinforce the Mexican theme of a menu. Green, yellow, and orange symbolize freshness and natural flavors in healthy dining menus. Fine dining menus often use gold inks to contrast with a second print color on cream parchment stock, establishing a rich, formal tone.

An example of the skillful use of paper and color is provided in Figure 6-2. A dark rich green sets off the gold lion logo in the center of the presentation cover. The paper stock is exceptionally heavy, creating the perception of value and quality.

Illustration and Graphic Design

As is the case with catering menus in general, a number of the examples in this chapter incorporate graphic designs and illustrations into their overall format. Catering menus that use illustration are highly successful. Figure 6-18 focuses on illustration with color food photography. Figure 6-12 uses a garden theme and flamingos to reinforce the hotel theme while simultaneously creating a wedding sales presentation that sends a very definite message of sophisticated professionalism.

The marketing objectives of creating interest, reinforcing the theme, and directing customer attention can be achieved with illustration and graphic design. As mentioned earlier and seen in Figure 6-23, preprinted paper can supply an inexpensive source for illustration on menu pages.

Copy

Copy consists of the written words used to identify menu items and describe item contents for the customer. Menu copy is broken down into three categories:

> Accent copy
> Descriptive item copy
> Merchandising copy

Accent copy is used in course headings and menu item names to create customer interest. Figure 6-22 is a good example of the use of accent copy. In catering menus, accent copy, particularly foreign language terms, can help to establish themes and reinforce cuisine orientation. Historical reference and humor are other tools of accent copy.

Descriptive copy informs the customer about the contents of menu items. It is important, especially in catering menus, to keep this description as brief as possible. Ingredients that are highlighted by descriptive copy should encourage the selection of the menu item by creating interest or emphasizing the quality of preparation, such as in Figure 6-32. The descriptive copy in this dessert menu maximizes the use of ingredients to create customer interest with phrases such as "fire weed honey," "brown sugar glazed mango ginger," "caramelized Alsatian apple," and "sun-dried cherry cabernet."

Detailed sentences that overdescribe menu items are inappropriate for catering menus. Words such as crisp, fluffy, light, creamy, smooth, rich,

DINNER A LA CARTE SELECTIONS
Continued

DESSERTS

Brown Sugar Glazed Mango Ginger Crème Brûlée $9.00

Mascarpone Coffee Cream, Lady Fingers and Bitter Cocoa $8.00

Frozen Passion Fruit Chocolate Soufflé $8.00

White Chocolate Praline Mousse with a Sun-dried Cherry Cabernet Jelly $7.50

Marinated Plum Compote, Fire Weed Honey Ice Cream, Almond Tulip Crisp $8.00

Burgundy Poached Seckel Pear, Amaretto Pistachio Mousse, Cabernet Wine Jelly $10.50

Fruit Filled Almond Crepe, Hazelnut Meringue, Raspberry Kirsch Sauce $9.00

Caramelized Alsatian Apple Tart, Cinnamon Parfait, Haitian Vanilla Bean Sauce $11.50

Caravan of Chocolate to include:
Chocolate Crème Brûlée, Chocolate Termine,
Gjanduja Chocolate Marquise, Chocolate Orange Truffle $14.50

Trio of Sorbets:
Chocolate, Almond Tuile and Berry Compote $9.50

Our award winning pastry chef would be delighted to create a dessert to enhance your
special occasion. From your company logo incorporated in chocolate to pulled sugar
lovebirds to a dessert in the theme of your event, we want to make a lasting impression on
you and your guests.

Prices are subject to 7% tax and 18% gratuity

10/98

FIGURE 6-32   BELLAGIO HOTEL DESSERT MENU
FEATURING DESCRIPTIVE COPY OF ITEMS.
(Courtesy of Mirage Resorts, Incorporated.)

blended, and fresh can create a positive association with a customer's previous experience with food items. Superlatives such as "best ever" and "to perfection" should be avoided because they create customer expectations that may not be met by this menu item.

Merchandising copy provides information about catering services and/or the catering operation. Information about catering services should state policies and prices as clearly as possible to avoid misunderstandings that can result in customer relations problems during and after functions.

Well-written copy in all sections of the menu can have a positive impact on the total menu program. Customers who find information to be stated in a clear and interesting way will be more comfortable in their decisions and willing to consider additional services that can increase the caterer's overall revenues and profits.

Summary

The presentation of catering menus directly reflects the style of the catering operation. Package covers combine menus with other catering services and information to present customers with a complete overview of the business. Many catering services use the word processing capabilities of computer systems and a laser printer to create menus with a professional image. The design elements of layout, typeface, paper stock, color, and illustration can be utilized to create interest and develop sales. Menus that present items in entertaining and easy-to-read formats will be given more consideration by customers, ultimately increasing sales.

CHAPTER SEVEN

Catering Beverage Management

ESSENCE of QUAIL
Sesame Twists

SAUTEED SEA SCALLOPS
with SAUTEED POTATOES and BLACK TRUFFLE
Chive Butter Sauce
Chardonnay or Tuscan Varietal

PINOT NOIR and ROSEMARY SORBET

HONEY ROASTED LOIN of GREENBRIER VALLEY LAMB
Natural Jus
Baby Green Bean and Morel Mushroom Ragout
Creamy Chevre Polenta
Cabernet Sauvignon or Red Bordeaux

BIBB LETTUCE, TANGO and RADICCHIO LEAVES
BRIER RUN CHEVRE SOUFFLE
Aged Balsamic Vinaigrette

GREENBRIER CHOCOLATE DECADENCE
Buttermilk Vanilla Ice Cream
Port or Cream Sherry

DEMI TASSE
Cordials

PARADE of FANCY COOKIES and GREENBRIER CHOCOLATES

Beverage Management

Alcoholic beverages, when offered, constitute a major factor in catering operations. Beverages fall into two major categories, nonalcoholic and alcoholic.

Any beverage that does not include alcohol as an ingredient is classified as a nonalcoholic beverage. The service of nonalcoholic beverages at social and business functions is becoming increasingly popular. Foodservice operations that serve alcohol are promoting nonalcoholic versions of traditionally alcohol-based drinks with a high level of success.

Alcoholic beverages are categorized as wine, beer, and distilled spirits such as scotch, gin, bourbon, and rum. Alcohol in spirits results from the fermentation of ingredients such as fruit, grains, and sugar. Proof indicates the quantity of alcohol in a distilled spirit. In the United States proof is defined as twice the percent of alcohol by volume. For example, bourbon containing 45 percent alcohol by volume is 90 proof. Wine and beer have much lower proof designations than spirits.

Well-managed beverage sales can be a profitable extension of a catering operation. The relationship of food sales to beverage sales is called the food and beverage mix. Where a maximum of 60 percent of the revenue from menu item sales is retained as gross profit, as much as 80 percent of beverage sales may go to profit, depending on the maximum markup management chooses to take.

Catering beverage services and package pricing can be designed to incorporate the theme or concept of the function or convention according to customer needs. For all beverage programs the issues of server relations and liquor liability must be reviewed.

NONALCOHOLIC BEVERAGES

A heightened awareness of the negative effects of alcohol consumption, stronger drunk driving laws, and increased liability on the part of anyone dispensing alcohol have combined to decrease the overall consumption of alcohol in the United States.

Nonalcoholic versions of traditionally alcohol-based drinks mixed with creative substitutions of fruits and flavorings can be successfully promoted. *Mr. Boston Bartender's Guide,* a standard beverage recipe book for the foodservice industry since 1935, lists a number of nonalcoholic drinks. For example:

1. **Orange Smile:** Replaces grenadine syrup with raspberry syrup, mixed with orange juice and egg.
2. **Pineapple Cooler:** Adds powdered sugar and carbonated water to pineapple juice.
3. **Lady Love Fizz:** Combines egg whites, sweet cream, and lemon juice.

Drinks such as these, along with a variety of fruit-based daiquiris and margaritas, can prove to be profitable additions to catering beverage menus.

The catering department of the Chicago Hilton Hotel in Chicago, Illinois, offers a standard option for their beverage service with nonalcoholic bars serving fruit-based drinks, sodas, and bottled waters. Bottled waters, particularly sparkling varieties, have increased significantly in popularity as an alcohol alternative beverage. A comparison of beverage costs shows the potential for increased profit:

NONALCOHOLIC BEVERAGE COST COMPARISON

CATERING BEVERAGE	PRICE	BEVERAGE COST %	CGP*
VODKA MARTINI	$4.50	18%	$3.69
NONALCOHOLIC STRAWBERRY DAIQUIRI	4.50	10%	4.00

*CGP is contribution to gross profit.

In this example the cost of the nonalcoholic beverage is 8 percent lower than that of the alcoholic beverage, but the price is the same. For every dollar in sales, the strawberry daiquiri will contribute 90 cents to gross profit, whereas the vodka martini will contribute 89 cents. Although alcohol is often the highest cost factor in a beverage, customers perceive an equally high value for a nonalcoholic fruit-based beverage.

FOOD AND BEVERAGE MIX

The ratio of food and beverage sales to total sales is called the food and beverage mix. This measure of the result of sales is often referred to in terms of a ratio of 60/40—60 percent from food revenue and 40 percent from beverage revenue—or 70/30—70 percent from food revenue and 30 percent from beverage. Because beverage sales often generate higher profit margins than food sales, this relationship is important to overall profits.

Catering Beverage Pricing

Beverages for catering services are sold by the bottle, by the drink, or by the time period. Customers may choose to buy beverages for catering functions by the bottle to be served by bartenders from stationary bars. At the conclusion of the function customers are billed for every bottle opened and/or consumed. For functions where consumption will not justify setting up a full bar at bottle prices, customers are charged according to a record of each drink consumed. As shown in the beverage menu in Figure 7-1, hosted drinks range in price according to name brand content. Package beverage prices offer a flat fee over a given time period and are discussed later in this chapter.

Another option is a cash bar, where guests must pay for their own beverages. Pricing on cash bars reflects current individual drink prices for restaurants and lounges according to whether drinks are based on house or call brands. Wine can be purchased by the bottle to be served during the meal with one or more courses. The catering wine and beverage menu in Figure 7-2 lists a variety of beverage options.

Conditions for beverage services, such as those listed in Figure 7-2 and 7-3, are common to all catering operations. Bartender fees are subject to local

Hilton

in the WALT DISNEY WORLD® Resort

Banquet Beverages

Cash Bars (Per Drink/Inclusive of Gratuity & State Sales Tax)

House Brands 5.00

Hilton Scotch	Beef Barron Whiskey
Hilton Gin	Darnoc Vodka
Castillo Rum	

Name Brands 5.50

Dewar's Scotch	Old Grand-Dad Bourbon
Canadian Club	Beefeater Gin
J & B	Smirnoff Vodka
Bacardi	Cutty Sark
Seagrams Seven	Gordons Vodka

Premium Brands 6.00

Chivas Regal	Jack Daniel's
Crown Royal	Tanqueray
Finlandia	Bacardi
Wild Turkey	

Imported Beer 5.00

Heineken	Beck's Dark
Bass Ale	Amstel Lite
Sapporo	Fosters
Corona	

Domestic Beer 4.50

IceHouse	Michelob Dry
Coors Light	Miller Lite
Budweiser	

Frozen Tropical Drinks	6.00
House Wine	5.00
Wine Coolers	5.00
Non-alcoholic Beer - O'Douls, Sharps	5.00
Assorted Soft Drinks	2.50
Flavored Mineral Waters	3.25
After Dinner Cordials	7.00

All Beverage Prices Include Florida Alcoholic Beverage Surcharge

**An Additional $50.00 Supplemental Gratuity
Will Be Added to Cash Bars For Less Than 25 Guests**

*All Prices Subject To 19% Service Charge and 6% State Tax
Prices Effective As of June 1, 1997*

1751 Hotel Plaza Boulevard P.O. Box 22781 Lake Buena Vista, FL 32830-2781 407/827-3844 Fax 407/827-3805

FIGURE 7-1   HILTON BEVERAGE MENU FEATURING A RANGE OF HOSTED DRINKS ACCORDING TO PRICE.
(Courtesy of Hilton in the Walt Disney World Resort.)

Hilton
in the WALT DISNEY WORLD® Resort

Banquet Beverages

Specialty Station

Frozen Tropical Drinks: ....*87.00 Gallon*
  Margaritas, Piña Coladas, Rum Runners, Strawberry Daiquiris

Champagne Punch..*77.00 Gallon*
Mimosas..*77.00 Gallon*
Sherbet Fruit Punch ....*57.00 Gallon*
Sangria..*67.00 Gallon*

Non-alcoholic Bar

Perrier ....*3.25 Each*
San Pellegrino...*3.25 Each*
Evian..*3.25 Each*
Non-alcoholic Beer ....*4.25 Each*
Frozen Margaritas, Piña Coladas, Daiquiris..*4.00 Each*

Sponsored Hourly Bars

House Brands:
1st Hour...*9.00*
2nd Hour..*6.50*
3rd Hour...*4.50*

Name Brands:
1st Hour...*12.00*
2nd Hour..*9.00*
3rd Hour...*7.00*

Premium Brands:
1st Hour...*13.50*
2nd Hour..*10.50*
3rd Hour...*8.50*

Labor Charges

Bartenders {Per Bartender/4-Hours} *50.00*
Cashier {Per Cashier/4-Hours} *50.00*

All Beverage Prices Include Florida Alcoholic Beverage Surcharge

All Prices Subject To 19% Service Charge and 6% State Tax
Prices Effective As of June 1, 1997

1751 Hotel Plaza Boulevard P.O. Box 22781 Lake Buena Vista, FL 32830-2781 407/827-3844 Fax 407/827-3805

FIGURE 7-1   (CONTINUED.)

Banquet Bars
(Minimum of 15 People)

Cash Bar

Premium Well Brands	$5.00
Wine	$4.75
Imported Beer	$4.25
Domestic Beer	$3.50
Mineral Water	$3.00
Fruit Juices	$2.50
Soft Drinks	$2.00

Hosted Bar

Premium Well Brands	$4.75
Wine	$4.50
Imported Beer	$4.00
Domestic Beer	$3.25
Mineral Water	$3.00
Fruit Juices	$2.50
Soft Drinks	$2.00

Bartender Charges	$50 For the First Hour
	$10 Each Additional Hour.

Bartender Charges are Waived If Sales Exceed $300.

Self Service Beverage Stations are available.
Charged by the number of bottles opened.

Wine	$18 Bottle
Imported Beer	$4.25
Domestic Beer	$3.50
Mineral Water	$3.00
Fruit Juices	$2.50
Soft Drinks	$2.00

House Chardonnay	$18 Per Bottle
House Merlot	$18 Per Bottle
Italian House Champagne	$24 Per Bottle
Fruit Punch	$22 Per Gallon
	(Aprox. 18 Servings)
Champagne Punch	$75 Per Gallon
	(Aprox. 18 Servings)

Prices are Subject to Change.
*Tickets may be used in place of cash to limit drinks. Tickets are $4.50++/Per Ticket.
All Prices are Subject to 18% Gratuity and 7.3% Sales Tax

FIGURE 7-2   CATERING WINE AND BEVERAGE MENU.

union wage scale but are often reduced or eliminated as total beverage sales exceed established limits. In this example the $40.00 bartender charge for a cash bar is canceled if bar receipts reach $350.00 for a two-hour period.

BEVERAGE PRICING METHOD

The method used to price beverages for catering functions is similar to that used by restaurants. Prices for each type of grain alcohol or spirit range

Spirits

HOSTED BAR

Premium Brands $4.25
Deluxe Brands $4.75
Cordials and Brandy $5.50
Wine by the Glass $4.00
Champagne by the Glass $4.00
Beer - Domestic $3.25
Beer - Imported or Premium $4.00
Jack Daniel's Country Cocktail $4.25
Coolers and Breezers $4.25
Soft Drinks $2.50
Mineral Water $3.00
Draft Beer - Keg $300.00
Nonalcoholic Beer - Domestic $3.25

Please add 19% service charge and applicable sales tax to all above prices.

A minimum of $300.00 revenue per bar per 2-hour period is required or a $40.00 bar service charge will apply.

CASH BAR

Premium Brands $5.00
Deluxe Brands.. $5.25
Cordials and Brandy................................... $6.00
Wine by the Glass $5.00
Champagne by the Glass............................ $5.00
Beer - Domestic $4.25
Beer - Imported $5.25
Jack Daniel's Country Cocktail.................... $5.25
Coolers and Breezers $5.00
Soft Drinks... $3.00
Mineral Water $3.25
Nonalcoholic Beer - Domestic..................... $4.25

The above prices include 19% service charge and all liquor taxes. Please add on all applicable sales taxes.

A minimum of $350.00 revenue per bar per 2-hour period is required or a $60.00 bar service/cashier charge will apply.

The Hotel, as a licensee, is responsible for the administration of the sale and service of alcholoic beverages on its premises.

We will accomodate requests for special order liquor or wine when you assume full responsibility to pay for the entire amount ordered.

The Hotel reserves the right to refuse service to anyone who appears to be intoxicated.

10/98   All prices listed in our menus are subject to 19% service charge and applicable sales tax.

FIGURE 7-3   OPRYLAND HOTEL'S LIST OF CONDITIONS FOR BEVERAGE SERVICES.
(Courtesy of Opryland Hotel, Nashville, Tennessee.)

according to the type and quality of alcohol. Both bottle and drink prices are based on the established amount of profit management wants to realize from the sales on a bottle of alcohol. For example, assume that the purchase price for a fifth (1/8 gallon) of scotch is $15.00 and that the desired beverage cost percentage is 50 percent. Catering beverage sales must total $30.00 for the contents of the bottle, whether sold by the drink or by the bottle. If 2 ounces of scotch are poured for a single drink, this 25-ounce bottle will yield 12 drinks. If drinks are sold at $2.50 each, total revenue for the bottle will be $30.00.

$$\text{Beverage cost} \div \text{Beverage cost \%} = \text{Selling price per bottle}$$
$$\$15.00 \div .50 = \$30.00$$

$$\text{Bottle size} \div \text{Drink portion size} = \text{Yield}$$

$$\text{Selling price per bottle} \div \text{Yield} = \text{Selling price per drink}$$
$$\$30.00 \div 12 = \$2.50$$

This pricing formula assumes that each drink will be portioned correctly and that there will be no loss or waste from the bottle. Table 7-1 demonstrates how this pricing method is applied to achieve the objective of a beverage cost percentage of 27 percent.

The selling price of $4.15 per drink is raised to a menu marketing price of $4.25 per drink, which will actually yield a $170.00 beverage revenue and a 27 percent overall beverage cost. In order to make beverage pricing consistent it is advisable to standardize the per drink cost. To maintain an approximate 25 percent beverage cost management sets a standard drink price of $4.50 per drink. Table 7-2 calculates drink prices based on a range of beverage cost percentages.

Where the market will bear higher beverage prices, such as in large cities and metropolitan areas, beverage costs can be set as low as 18 percent. In Table 7-3 the same pricing methods as in Table 7-2 are applied to a situation in which the predetermined beverage cost percentage is 18 percent and the drink size for scotch and bourbon is 1 ounce. All beverage prices are calculated accordingly and adjusted for marketable menu price.

TABLE 7-1   BEVERAGE YIELD PRICING

TOTAL BEVERAGE COST	TOTAL BEVERAGE REVENUE	TOTAL PER DRINK YIELD
$15.00	$55.00	12
12.50	53.00	16
18.50	58.00	12
$46.00	$166.00	40

TOTAL SALES ÷ TOTAL DRINK YIELD = DRINK PRICE*
$166.00 ÷ 40 = $4.15

MENU PRICE × DRINK YIELD = TOTAL SALES
$4.25 × 40 = $170.00

BEVERAGE COST ÷ TOTAL SALES = BEVERAGE COST %
$46.00 ÷ $170.00 = 27%

*Drink price is rounded up to create a marketable price.

TABLE 7-2   CATERING BEVERAGE PRICING I

Beverage	Bottle Size	Drink Size	Bottle Cost	Beverage Cost	Drink Price	Bottle Price
Scotch	25 oz.	2 oz.	$15.00	25%	$3.75	$45.00
Gin	25 oz.	1.5 oz.	13.50	30%	4.00	40.00
Bourbon	25 oz.	2 oz.	18.50	26%	4.75	57.00

TABLE 7-3   CATERING MENU PRICING I

Beverage	Bottle Size	Drink Size	Bottle Cost	Beverage Cost	Drink Price	Menu Price	Bottle Price	CGP
Scotch	25 oz.	1 oz.	$15.00	18%	$3.36	$3.50	$84.00	$69.00
Gin	25 oz.	1.5 oz.	12.50	18%	4.25	4.25	68.00	55.50
Bourbon	25 oz.	1 oz.	18.50	18%	4.08	4.25	102.00	83.50

The calculations in this table have been carried out to include the contribution to gross profit (CGP) in order to show the profit potential in catering beverage pricing.

Spirit and wine sales by the bottle are commonly priced for a minimum of 100 percent markup or a 50 percent beverage cost. The wine selection in Figure 7-4 is priced by the bottle with an average markup of 150 percent per bottle.

PACKAGE PRICING

Catering beverage services are often combined with food and other services into pricing packages for a variety of business and social functions. In situations in which the customer would like a fixed price for beverages, prices are calculated based on the use of either house brands or name brands, on an hourly scale. The following guidelines are generally followed:
One-hour open bar at reception, per person:

    House brands: $5.00
    Premium brands: $6.00

Two-hour open bar after dinner, per person:

    House brands: $7.00
    Premium brands: $8.50

Hourly prices are based on an average of the probable consumption of alcoholic beverages in a one-hour time period. Women consume an average of 0.5 to 1 drink during the first hour and men 1.5 to 2. By basing the price per person for the first hour of a function on the current drink per price,

Banquet Beverages

Champagnes & Sparkling Wines

Cuvée "Dom Pérignon", Brut, V	210.00
White Star, Moët et Chandon	85.00
Blanc de Noirs, Chandon	42.00
Korbel, Brut California	40.00
Crystal Crest	28.00

White Wines

Chardonnay, Cuvaison	48.00
Chardonnay, Beringer Vineyards	44.00
Fumé Blanc, Robert Mondavi	41.00
Sauvignon Blanc, Sterling Vineyards	41.00
Fumé Blanc, Château St. Jean Vineyard	40.00
Chardonnay, Kendall-Jackson Vineyards	39.00
Chardonnay, Sonoma-Cutrer 'Russian River'	38.00
Sauvignon Blanc, Simi	37.00
Chardonnay, Meridian	36.00
Chardonnay, Robert Mondavi 'Coastal'	35.00
Chardonnay, Columbia Crest	34.00
Chardonnay, Geyser Peak	33.00
Chardonnay, "Woodbridge" Robert Mondavi Winery	30.00
Johannisberg Riesling, Chateau Ste. Michelle	26.00
Chardonnay, Stone Pine Vineyards	25.00

All Beverage Prices Include Florida Alcoholic Beverage Surcharge

All Prices Subject To 19% Service Charge and 6% State Tax
Prices Effective As of June 1, 1997

1751 Hotel Plaza Boulevard P.O. Box 22781 Lake Buena Vista, FL 32830-2781 407/827-3844 Fax 407/827-3805

FIGURE 7-4   HILTON BEVERAGE MENU FEATURING A WINE SELECTION PRICED BY THE BOTTLE.
(Courtesy of Hilton in the Walt Disney World Resort.)

Hilton
in the **WALT DISNEY WORLD®** Resort

Banquet Beverages

Blush Wines

White Zinfandel, Beringer	27.00
White Zinfandel, Sutter Home Winery	25.00
White Zinfandel, Stone Pine Vineyard	23.00

Red Wines

Cabernet Sauvignon, Kendall-Jackson Vineyards	46.00
Merlot, Rutherford Hill	44.00
Cabernet Sauvignon, Columbia Crest	43.00
Cabernet Sauvignon, Meridian	42.00
Merlot, Markham Vineyards	42.00
Merlot, Dunnewood	42.00
Pinot Noir, Robert Mondavi Winery	42.00
Pinot Noir, Estancia Estates	41.00
Cabernet Sauvignon, Vichon 'Mediterranean'	40.00
Merlot, Meridian	40.00
Merlot, Geyser Peak	40.00
Pinot Noir, Napa Ridge Winery	40.00
Merlot, Tessera	38.00
Merlot, Columbia Crest	38.00
Cabernet Sauvignon, Geyser Peak	35.00
Zinfandel, Montevina	34.00
Cabernet Sauvignon, "Woodbridge" Robert Mondavi Winery	30.00
Merlot, Georges Duboeuf	25.00
Cabernet Sauvignon, Stone Pine Vineyards	24.00

All Beverage Prices Include Florida Alcoholic Beverage Surcharge

All Prices Subject To 19% Service Charge and 6% State Tax
Prices Effective As of June 1, 1997

1751 Hotel Plaza Boulevard P.O. Box 22781 Lake Buena Vista, FL 32830-2781 407/827-3844 Fax 407/827-3805

FIGURE 7-4   (CONTINUED.)

management can be reasonably sure of accurately estimating consumption. In this example the following calculation was applied:

1 Drink (women) + 1.5 Drinks (men) = 2.5 Drinks ÷ 2
= 1.25 Drinks per person

House brands: $5.00 per person per hour
Premium brands: $6.00 per person per hour

It is important, however, to evaluate the type of function and the attendees before quoting a per person drink price. The consumption level of some groups can be considerably higher than others.

The pricing structure for additional periods of time is also based on the averaging of consumption levels and the format of the reception or meal. If guests are consuming a full meal, alcohol consumption after the meal will be less than if the party is a reception that continues for three to four hours. Most women will consume a small amount of alcohol after a meal. An average of 1.5 drinks over a 2.5-hour period is considered normal. Men will consume an average of approximately one drink per hour. For example, the beverage price for a two-hour period after the meal would be calculated as follows:

1.5 Drinks per woman + 2 Drinks per man = 3.5 Drinks ÷ 2
= 1.75 Drinks per person

House brands: $7.00 per person for two hours
Premium brands: $8.50 per person for two hours

Wine to be served with the meal is calculated by dividing the per bottle price by six (the average number of glasses yield from a bottle). In pre-priced packages, management can select a house wine on which to base the price. Wine prices can be set in terms of either one glass or two, with the latter based on a consumption level of 1.5 glasses per person:

WINE	BOTTLE PRICE	YIELD	PER PERSON
HOUSE	$18.00	6 GLASSES	$3.00
PREMIUM	24.00	6 GLASSES	4.00

A complete beverage package incorporating the examples in this section would be:

	HOUSE BRAND	PREMIUM
RECEPTION	$5.00	$6.00
WINE	3.00	4.00
TWO-HOUR BAR	7.00	8.50
TOTAL PER PERSON	$15.00	$18.50

These prices are then added to the total food package, gratuities, and taxes along with other catering services. Examples of beverage package price lists are seen in Figure 7-1.

Catering Beverage Menu Planning

Profitable catering services develop specialty menus to include appropriate wines and cordials. Depending on the formality of the meal, up to seven wines and cordials can be matched with menu items in each category of the menu format. Figure 7-5 offers a seven-course menu paired with a selection of four wines and a port. A sauvignon blanc is served with the appetizer course, a chardonnay with the fish course, a red merlot with the beef course, champagne with the dessert course, and port with the cheese plate.

WINE MARRIAGE DINNER
November 18, 1992

Appetizer

Shrimp Spaetzle w/Basil Crabmeat Sauce
Sterling Sauvignon Blanc

Salad

California Field Green Salad

Fish

Grilled Mahi Mahi w/Mango Chutney Rice
Lime Beurre Blanc
Sterling Winery Lake Chardonnay

Intermezzo

Tangerine Sorbet

Beef

Korean Grilled Beef Skewers served over
Braised Bean Sprouts
Sterling Three Palms

Fruit Dessert

Fresh Fruit Tostada served in Chocolate Shell
w/Sour Cream Sauce and Carmelized sugar
Mum Cruvee Napa Blanc De Noir

Cheese

Plate of Assorted Cheeses on Each Table
Port to be Served

FIGURE 7-5 SEVEN-COURSE MENU PAIRED WITH A SELECTION
OF FOUR WINES AND A PORT.

Each of the red or white wines paired with the menu items in Figure 7-5 will complement the food item with which it is being served. This blending of food with wine is often referred to as "marrying" foods and wines. When menus of this caliber are being planned, it is important that caterers work with beverage and wine experts to choose a variety of wines for the entire menu and achieve the marriage of food and wine. Distributors are the best resources for finding the best wines available within the desired price range. Figure 7-6 is the catering wine list from the Hyatt Regency, Beaver Creek,

---

CATERING WINE LIST
Effective May 15, 1999

SPARKLING WINES
*Domaine Chandon, Hyatt Cuvee, Napa Valley, NV	$28
*Moet Chandon, White Star, France, NV	$57
*Veuve Clicquot, Yellow Label, France,NV	$85

Due to the demand for champagne for the millennium celebration in 1999, the quantities for champagne may be limited

WHITE ZINFANDEL
Turning Leaf, CA, 1997	$26

JOHANNISBERG RIESLING
Chateau Ste. Michelle, Washington, 1997	$26

SAUVIGNON BLANC
Frogs Leap, Napa Valley, 1997	$35
Conumdrum, Caymus, 1997	$48

CHARDONNAY
Turning Leaf, CA, 1997	$26
Columbia Crest, Washington, 1997	$38
Kendall-Jackson, Vintner Reserve, Napa Valley, 1997	$36
Cakebread, Napa Valley, 1997	$60
Acacia, Carneros, CA, 1997	$48
Robert Mondavi, Napa Valley, 1997	$46
Stonestreet, Sonoma, 1995	$52

CLASSIC RED WINES
Beaujolais Villages, Louis Jadot, 1997	$34
Pinot Noir, Wild Horse, Carneros	$54
Fetzer Eagle Peak, Mendocino, 1997	$32
Shiraz, Rosemount Estate, Australia, 1998	$35
Zinfandel, Rodney Strong, Northern Sonoma, 1996	$45
Merlot, Canoe Ridge, Columbia Valley, 1996	$54

CABERNET SAUVIGNON
Turning Leaf, CA, 1996	$26
Columbia Crest, Washington, 1996	$38
Stonestreet, Sonoma, 1996	$65

Additional wines and vintage years available upon request. There may be a minimum case purchase if the wine is not a wine that the hotel carries on either Banquet or restaurant lists. Colorado Liquor Laws regulate that no alcoholic beverage be brought into the hotel from an outside source and that all alcoholic beverage must be delivered to the hotel guest room.

The above prices are subject to 19% Hotel Service Charge and 5% Civic Assessment Tax, both taxable to the state at a 4.5% rate.

FIGURE 7-6   HYATT REGENCY, BEAVER CREEK CATERING WINE LIST.
(Courtesy of The Hyatt Regency at Beaver Creek, Colorado.)

Colorado. Wine selections have been chosen to include sauvignon blanc, cabernet sauvignon, and sparkling wines, among others.

Figure 7-7 offers a five-course menu paired with three wines for a simpler version of a wine marriage menu from the Greenbrier's Gold Service dinner program.

ESSENCE of QUAIL
Sesame Twists

SAUTEED SEA SCALLOPS
with SAUTEED POTATOES and BLACK TRUFFLE
Chive Butter Sauce

Chardonnay or Tuscan Varietal

PINOT NOIR and ROSEMARY SORBET

HONEY ROASTED LOIN of GREENBRIER VALLEY LAMB
Natural Jus
Baby Green Bean and Morel Mushroom Ragout
Creamy Chevre Polenta

Cabernet Sauvignon or Red Bordeaux

BIBB LETTUCE, TANGO and RADICCHIO LEAVES
BRIER RUN CHEVRE SOUFFLE
Aged Balsamic Vinaigrette

GREENBRIER CHOCOLATE DECADENCE
Buttermilk Vanilla Ice Cream

Port or Cream Sherry

DEMI TASSE

Cordials

PARADE of FANCY COOKIES and GREENBRIER CHOCOLATES

FIGURE 7-7   THE GREENBRIER'S WINE MARRIAGE MENU FROM
THE GOLD SERVICE DINNER PROGRAM.
(Courtesy of The Greenbrier, White Sulphur Spring,
West Virginia.)

Poached Salmon and Gulf Shrimp
with Assorted Field Greens
Balsamic Vinaigrette
Chardonnay

Essence of Asparagus

Roast Tenderloin of Beef
Shiitake Mushroom Sauce
Vegetable du Jour
Wild Mushroom Bread Pudding
Cabernet Sauvignon or Red Bordeaux

Strawberry Ganache Tarte
Roasted Banana Cream
Demi-Sec or Sparkling Wine

Coffee   Tea

FIGURE 7-7   (CONTINUED.)

Alcohol Service and Liability

There is growing awareness, fostered by citizens groups, about the number of automobile accidents that are alcohol related, and that cause deaths and severe disabilities. This awareness has resulted in stricter drunk driving laws and increased liability for operators who serve alcoholic beverages. State liquor laws throughout the United States prohibit the sale of alcohol to a minor. Other laws regarding the sale of alcohol vary from state to state and are open to court interpretation.

According to John Sherry, in *Legal Aspects of Foodservice Management,* many states have statutes, called dramshop acts, that hold operators liable for deaths or for injuries to third parties resulting from the illegal sales of alcohol to customers. The susceptibility of foodservice operators to the legal ramifications of any alcohol-related accident that occurs after a patron has left their establishment is greatest in cases involving third party liability, primarily because these cases have few defenses. An injured third party who sues under the dramshop acts will try to prove that a licensed seller sold alcohol under conditions deemed illegal, thereby causing or contributing to the intoxication of the customer whose actions resulted in the victim's injury.

Third parties may also charge foodservice operations with common law negligence either for noncompliance with statutes prohibiting the sale of alcohol in certain situations or for failure to anticipate the effects of poor supervision on the premises. In some states, the common law rule is expanded to hold servers responsible for expecting that any sale to an obviously intoxicated person with a known intent to drive a motor vehicle poses a reasonably foreseeable threat to other drivers or pedestrians.[1]

Foodservice operators who offer catering beverage services face the same task of identifying minors and intoxicated patrons as do lounges and restaurants. The atmosphere of a private party does not absolve caterers from the legal responsibilities regarding the service of alcohol, even in situations in which the host purchases the alcohol from the operator, and then dispenses it to the guests. The liquor license of the business governs the service of all alcohol within the establishment and can carry over to off-premise functions. Off-premise operators should make themselves fully aware of the liquor laws governing their communities. Bartenders and servers are also responsible for identifying minors and exercising prudent judgment in the service of alcohol to individuals who exhibit any of the signs of intoxication. They will be held accountable for the knowledge that an intoxicated individual represents a danger on the roads because in a private party situation they can assume that all guests intend to drive a motor vehicle.

This pressure of liability increases the need for foodservice operators to initiate training programs and policies in their establishments that will help to protect them from lawsuits and liquor law violations. The use of training programs that are nationally recognized by insurance companies and the courts can act both to decrease premiums for liquor liability insurance and to provide evidence of intent and concern on the part of management for responsible alcohol service.

A number of alcohol service training programs have been developed by nationally known organizations. Of these, TIPS (Training for Intervention Procedures) and Bar Code—Responsible Beverage Alcohol Service are the most widely known.

The TIPS program concentrates on providing servers with keys to identify customers who are on the verge of becoming intoxicated. Some of these signs are:

1. Drinking too fast
2. Becoming loud, mean, argumentative, and obnoxious
3. Complaining about drink strength or preparation
4. Slurring words
5. Lighting more than one cigarette
6. Becoming clumsy and changing their walking pattern[2]

This program is made available through certified instructors who hold training programs locally.

The Bar Code—Responsible Beverage Alcohol Service Program is offered by the Educational Foundation of the National Restaurant Association. Its logo, which is often featured on table tents or beverage menus and manuals, is featured in Figure 7-8.

This program concentrates on training managers, either in formal training sessions or by distance learning. Written materials, videos, and CD-ROMs help managers to train servers in their own establishments, incorporating the individual needs of each business. Managers and servers must pass a written exam before receiving a certificate of completion. The Bar Code program covers many of the same issues as the TIPS program. In addition, the program helps managers to assess the level of liability risk for their individual businesses and provides servers with training to increase food and beverage profitability by promoting the sales of premium brands and food accompaniments to drinks.

FIGURE 7-8   THE BAR CODE—RESPONSIBLE BEVERAGE ALCOHOL SERVICE PROGRAM LOGO.
(Courtesy of the Educational Foundation of the National Restaurant Association.)

To effectively develop policies and training programs, management should research state and local liquor laws and discuss the level of risk that their operation carries in terms of third party liability. Insurance companies that specialize in alcohol liability insurance are an excellent resource.

Summary

Well-managed beverage sales can be a profitable extension of every catering operation. Both alcoholic and nonalcoholic beverages can contribute to the success of a beverage program.

Catering beverage sales contribute to overall profitability if properly evaluated and priced. Because catering beverages are sold by the bottle, drink, and time period, a variety of opportunities are available to create highly profitable beverage prices. Catering menus for special occasions can serve wine either by the bottle or glass to increase beverage sales. Catering foodservice operators must be aware of liquor liability laws and the need for server training programs. TIPS and Bar Code are two nationally recognized training programs for alcohol service.

Endnotes

1. Sherry, John. *Legal Aspects of Foodservice Management,* 1984, p. 53.
2. *Life Saving Training for Alcohol Serving Professionals.* New York: Insurance Information Institute, April 1988.

CHAPTER EIGHT

Food and Beverage Operational Controls

POACHED CHICKEN BREAST PRINCESSE

PORTIONS: 24	PORTION SIZE: ½ CHICKEN BREAST 2 OZ (60 ML) SAUCE, PLUS GARNISH		
U.S.	**METRIC**	**INGREDIENTS**	**PROCEDURE**
24	24	BONELESS, SKINLESS HALF CHICKEN BREASTS, FROM TWELVE 3-LB (1.2-KG) CHICKENS	1. SELECT A BAKING PAN JUST LARGE ENOUGH TO HOLD THE CHICKEN BREASTS IN A SINGLE LAYER. BUTTER THE INSIDE OF THE PAN.
AS NEEDED	AS NEEDED	BUTTER	2. SEASON THE CHICKEN BREASTS WITH SALT
AS NEEDED	AS NEEDED	SALT	AND PEPPER. PLACE THEM IN THE PAN,
AS NEEDED	AS NEEDED	WHITE PEPPER	PRESENTATION SIDE (THAT IS, THE SIDE THAT HAD THE SKIN ON) UP.
¼ CUP	60 ML	LEMON JUICE	3. SPRINKLE WITH THE LEMON JUICE AND ADD
1½ QT	1.5 L APPROXIMATELY	CHICKEN STOCK, COLD	ENOUGH CHICKEN STOCK TO BARELY COVER THE CHICKEN.
			4. COVER THE CHICKEN WITH A BUTTERED PIECE OF PARCHMENT OR WAXED PAPER.
			5. BRING TO A SIMMER ON TOP OF THE STOVE. FINISH POACHING IN A 325°F (165°C) OVEN OR OVER LOW HEAT ON THE STOVE. COOKING TIME WILL BE 5–10 MINUTES.
			6. REMOVE THE CHICKEN BREASTS FROM THE LIQUID. PLACE THEM IN A HOTEL PAN, COVER, AND KEEP THEM WARM.
		BEURRE MANIÉ:	7. REDUCE THE POACHING LIQUID OVER HIGH
3 OZ	90 G	BUTTER, SOFTENED	HEAT TO ABOUT 2½ PT (1.1 L).
3 OZ	90 G	FLOUR	8. KNEAD THE BUTTER AND FLOUR TOGETHER
2½ CUPS	600 ML	HEAVY CREAM, HOT	TO MAKE A BEURRE MANIÉ (P. 120).
TO TASTE	TO TASTE	SALT	9. WITH A WIRE WHIP, BEAT THE BEURRE MANIÉ INTO THE SIMMERING STOCK TO THICKEN IT. SIMMER A MINUTE TO COOK OUT ANY STARCHY TASTE.
			10. ADD THE HOT CREAM TO THE SAUCE. SEASON TO TASTE.
72	72	ASPARAGUS TIPS, COOKED, HOT	11. PLACE EACH CHICKEN BREAST, WELL DRAINED, ON A PLATE AND COAT WITH 2 OZ (60 ML) SAUCE. GARNISH WITH 3 ASPARAGUS TIPS. SERVE IMMEDIATELY.

Operational Controls

The success of an ongoing catering operation is dependent on the operational controls that management establishes in order to monitor the daily productivity and profitability of the business. Operational controls are functions carried out within a foodservice operation to ensure that food and beverage products meet established standards of quality as efficiently as possible. Operational controls cover the following areas:

- Costing
- Pricing
- Purchasing
- Production
- Presentation
- Service

Costing and pricing were discussed in Chapters Five and Six, and service is a major topic in Chapter Ten. The areas of purchasing, production, and presentation are the focus of this chapter. Quality control is the term used for the process employed to meet the standards set for purchasing, production, and presentation. The objective is to produce food and beverage products following standardized recipes using ingredients purchased at prices that meet established food cost guidelines.

Purchasing controls define the criteria for quality by which food items are selected. These criteria, combined with established food cost goals, determine which products are purchased. Professional purchasing requires a knowledge of a wide range of food products and their expected yields. An awareness of waste-reducing and labor-saving products and their applications can enhance the profitability of a catering service operation.

Production controls ensure consistency in the amount of each ingredient used, the set of directions followed, the number of portions yielded, and the taste and texture obtained each time a food product is prepared. To accomplish this goal a standard recipe for a predetermined portion size and yield must be developed for every item in the menu file.

Presentation controls establish guidelines for the size and type of dish or glass to be used, the portion size of the food or beverage product, and the sauce and/or garniture. Often called plate architecture, plate presentation is important for maintaining customer satisfaction as well as standardizing costs.

Purchasing Controls

Establishing and directing a purchasing program is an important part of effective foodservice management. The objectives of a purchasing program are to:

1. Purchase the quality of product available necessary to fulfill the production requirement at a price that will meet established food cost guidelines.

2. Minimize the cost of waste realized by loss of product in receiving, storage, or distribution by developing step by step procedures that maximize the shelf life of the product.
3. Follow purchasing procedures that help ensure that management purchases the desired quality of product at the best available price. These procedures are to include the following functions:
   - Establish written purchasing specifications for every product that is purchased.
   - Select purveyors who can best supply product, following the established guidelines for quality, pricing, delivery, and payment.

Purchasing controls, usually called purchasing specifications, outline the exact requirements for the quality and quantity of a food product as well as the purpose for which the food product is to be used. Specifications should include the following information:

- Product name, with preferred brand names if available.
- Quantity to be purchased, designated by purchasing unit, such as a case, pound, or bunch.
- Indication of federal grade, such as U.S. Grade A
- Unit by which prices are quoted, such as dozen, #16, or gallon.
- Identification of the intended use of the product and any factors that can further describe the item to be purchased.

The bid form in Table 8-1 lists the simplified purchasing specifications for four poultry items. The unit price and total amount are completed by the purchasing agent once the price has been received from the vendor bidding on this purchasing order.

The purchase of quantity food products that consistently yield a specified number of portions helps to control food costs not only for individual items, but also for the overall menu. In order for a menu price to generate a consistent food cost percentage, menu item costs must remain constant. Table 8-2 outlines purchase quantities for fish and shellfish.

In this example a 1-pound fillet of fish will yield two to three portions between 3.4 ounces and 5.1 ounces in size. A yield of one hundred portions requires between 19¾ pounds and 29½ pounds of fish fillets. The exact amount of fish fillets to be ordered depends on the actual production portion size, which is determined in the final production specifications.

Efficiency is an important consideration in purchasing. Advances in food technology have provided innovative food preparation methods for preprepared and/or preportioned food products. For catering menu management these methods can provide significant savings in both food product and labor costs. Food products from beef cuts to vegetable cuts are available in single or multiportion packs. A variety of sealing and packaging techniques, from the cryovac method to quick-chill, have made available food products whose quality and safety is assured over a long period of shelf life.

Quick-chill combines bulk food preparation methods with refrigeration and freezing to create specified portion packages of food products. This process is applied mainly to soups, sauces, vegetables, and bulk ingredients, and is used in large contract feeding situations, multichain restaurant food

TABLE 8-1 PURCHASING SPECIFICATIONS

ITEM	SUPPLIES	QUANTITY	UNIT	UNIT PRICE	AMOUNT
1.	CHICKEN, FRESH CHILLED FRYER, 2½–3 LB., READY-TO-COOK, U.S. GRADE A To be delivered	500	LB.		
2.	CHICKEN, FRESH CHILLED FOUL, 3½–4 LB., READY-TO-COOK, U.S. GRADE B To be delivered	100	LB.		
3.	TURKEY, FROZEN, YOUNG TOM 20–22 LB., READY-TO-COOK, U.S. GRADE A To be delivered	100	LB.		
4.	DUCKS, FROZEN ROASTER DUCKLING, 5–5½ LB., READY-TO-COOK, U.S. GRADE A To be delivered	50	LB.		
	VENDOR _____				

(*Source:* Kotschevar, *Quantity Food Processing,* 2nd ed., p. 34.)

distribution systems, and institutional foodservice operations. In the final cooking process water is drawn off from the product, reducing both weight and volume. The temperature is rapidly lowered as the product is quickly packaged and sealed. Refrigeration during processing under constant temperatures in an atmosphere relatively free of the bacteria that cause food spoilage reduces the risk of food-borne illness. Quick chilled food products can be easily shipped over long distances and stored with extended shelf lives.

Sous vide is a food processing method that is revolutionizing the foodservice industry, with dramatic implications for catering in particular. Raw food products are packaged in individual or multiportioned packs using the cryovac sealing method, in which air inside the package is drawn out and the package closure is heat-sealed. Packs are then marked for storage under refrigeration for specified periods of time. Sous vide food products are put into production by placing them in hot water for a designated cooking period.

Both the quick-chill and sous vide methods provide catering managers with cost-saving food products that meet quality and quantity purchasing standards.

TABLE 8-2 PURCHASE QUANTITIES

Item: Fish, Fresh or Frozen	Unit Weight of Purchase	% Yield as Cooked	Number of Cooked Portions per Unit	Size (oz.) of Portions per Purchase Unit	Number of Units per 100 Portions		
Fillets	1 LB.	64	2 TO 3	3.4 TO 5.1	19¾	TO	29½
Steaks	1 LB.	58	2 TO 3	3.1 TO 4.6	21¾	TO	32½
Dressed	1 LB.	45	2 TO 3	2.4 TO 3.6	28	TO	41¾
Drawn	1 LB.	32	2 TO 3	1.7 TO 2.6	39¼	TO	58½
Whole (round)	1 LB.	27	2 TO 3	1.4 TO 2.2	46½	TO	69½
Breaded, raw	1 LB.	85	3 TO 4	3.4 TO 4.5	22	TO	29¾
Breaded, fried	1 LB.	95	3 TO 4	3.8 TO 5.1	19¾	TO	26½
Lobster, in shell	1 LB.	25	16 TO 20	About one	100	TO	125
Lobster meat	1 LB.	91	2 TO 3	4.9 TO 7.3	13¾	TO	20¾
Oysters, shucked	1 LB.	40	2 TO 3	2.1 TO 3.2	31¼	TO	47
Scallops, shucked	1 LB.	63	2 TO 3	3.4 TO 5.0	20	TO	30
Shrimp, cooked	1 LB.	100	2 TO 3	5.3 TO 8.0	12½	TO	19
Shrimp, raw	1 LB.	50	2 TO 3	2.7 TO 4.6	25	TO	37½
Shrimp, raw	1 LB.	62	2 TO 3	3.3 TO 5.0	20¼	TO	30½

(*Source:* Kotschevar, *Quantity Food Processing,* 2nd ed., p. 447.)

Production Controls

A standard recipe consists of a written set of directions that act as a guideline for the combination of specified amounts of ingredients to produce a desired product. Recipes are standardized in order to control the consistency of taste, texture, and yield.

The ideal standardized recipe includes a list of ingredients, their appropriate weights and/or measures, and specific directions for incorporating them into the product. A card format works the best for most operations, although those using computer software programs can access a variety of recipe formats.

The recipe card divides the recipe into sections that are easy to identify, read, and follow while cooking. For example, the recipe card presented in Figure 8-1 is formatted into three sections, one for instructions on prepreparing the salad greens, a second for the salad ingredients, and a third for the beef preparation. In the middle section, directions are also given for the plate setup of individual salad plates. In the third section, directions are again given for a single portion of meat to be sliced and plated.

Figure 8-2 shows a recipe card for 24 servings of a full beef tenderloin. The first section identifies the ingredients, weights, measures, and directions for the sauce, while section two focuses on the preparation of the beef. Section three is concerned with the plating of the individual serving. Both cards offer photographs on the reverse side to help in standardizing plate presentation.

STEAK CAESAR SALAD

INGREDIENTS	WEIGHTS	MEASURES	DIRECTIONS
Torn Romaine lettuce leaves	5 pounds, 4 ounces		1. Combine ingredients. Chill.
Cherry tomatoes, halved	3 pounds, 6 ounces		
Red onions, thinly sliced	12 ounces		
Romaine lettuce leaves		As needed	2. For *each* serving: Line 1 dinner plate with whole lettuce leaves. In bowl combine 5 1/2 ounces lettuce mixture, 3/4 ounce croutons, 1/2 ounce cheese; toss with 2-ounce ladle salad dressing. Plate mixture on whole lettuce leaves.
Parmesan *and/or* Romano cheese, shredded	12 ounces		
Prepared seasoned croutons	1 pound, 2 ounces		
Prepared Caesar salad dressing		6 cups (48 fl. ozs.)	
Beef Loin, Top Sirloin Butt Steaks, Center-Cut, Boneless, (NAMP/IMPS 1184B)	6 pounds	24 (4-ounce steaks)	3. Lightly coat both sides of 1 steak with pepper. Grill steak to desired doneness, turning once. Thinly slice steak. Arrange steak slices on 1 plate salad mixture. Sprinkle with cheese, if desired. Accompany with lemon wedge; serve immediately.
Cracked black pepper		As needed	
Parmesan *and/or* Romano cheese, shredded		As needed	
Lemon wedges		24	

NOTE: Six pounds Beef Strip Steaks, Boneless, (NAMP/IMPS 1180A) *or* Beef Tenderloin Steaks, Skinned, (NAMP/IMPS 1190 or 1190A) may be substituted for Top Sirloin Butt Steaks.

Yield: 24 Servings

©1993 Beef Industry Council and Beef Board 69350 / 24033

FIGURE 8-1   RECIPE CARD FOR STEAK CAESAR SALAD.
(Courtesy of the National Cattlemen's Beef Association.)

Ingredients

Any food item that is included in the preparation of the recipe must be listed, regardless of the amount used. In order for a recipe to consistently produce taste, texture, and yield, the same ingredients and proportions must always be used. Each ingredient should be described accurately with limited preparation directions, such as *shredded* Romano cheese, *prepared* croutons, *cracked* black pepper, and red onions, *thinly sliced*.

Weight and Measure

Either the weight or the measure for each ingredient must be included in the recipe. Some cards list both in order to make production more accurate. For example, in Figure 8-1 Caesar dressing is listed in both liquid measure and standard measure. Weight for steaks is given as well as piece count.

Measure is listed by pieces, cans, slices, bunches, or by indication of standard measure. For example, in Figure 8-1, lettuce leaves are measured by the pound, dressing by the cup, and cheese by ounces.

THE CHURRASCO

INGREDIENTS	WEIGHTS	MEASURES	DIRECTIONS
Chimichurri Sauce:			
Fresh parsley, finely chopped	10 ounces		1. Combine ingredients; remove and reserve 2 cups sauce to serve with cooked beef.
Olive oil		2 cups (16 fl. ozs.)	
White wine vinegar		1 cup (8 fl. ozs.)	
Garlic, minced	3 ounces		
Black pepper		1 1/2 teaspoons	
Salt		1 1/2 teaspoons	
Beef Loin, Full Tenderloin, Side Muscle Off, Skinned (NAMP/IMPS 190A)	15 to 20 pounds	3 to 4 tenderloins, about 5 pounds *each*	2. Cut *each* tenderloin crosswise into 4-inch wide chunks. With sharp knife and starting lengthwise, cut *each* tenderloin chunk jelly-roll-fashion, "unrolling" tenderloin to lay flat.
			3. For *each* serving: Brush both sides of 1 piece tenderloin with 2 tablespoons Chimichurri Sauce. Grill over high heat to desired doneness, turning once. Plate steak; drizzle with generous 1 tablespoon reserved sauce.

*For smaller 5- to 6- ounce portions, prepare beef as above; cut *each* piece in half.

©1993 Beef Industry Council and Beef Board 69350/24034

Yield: 24 Servings*
(From Churrascos South American
Restaurant, Houston, Texas)

FIGURE 8-2   RECIPE CARD FOR THE CHURRASCO.
(Courtesy of the National Cattlemen's Beef Association.)

Directions

Directions should be stated as simply and as clearly as possible. As English is the second language in many kitchens, staff members may have difficulty in reading long preparation explanations. The directions in Figure 8-2, for example, are accurate and to the point.

Yield

The yield is the number of portions that a recipe will produce. A portion is the amount of food product that has been allotted for a single serving. Portions are given by weight or measure. For example, the recipes in Figure 8-1 and 8-2 yield 24 servings. In Figure 8-1 the determined portion of beef per serving is 4 ounces.

The recipe in Figure 8-3 yields 24 portions of Poached Chicken Breast Princesse. As an example of a professional cooking recipe, Figure 8-3 provides weight and measure for all ingredients as well as the conversion for U.S. metric measurement. It can be conveniently used by cooks and chefs from different backgrounds.

POACHED CHICKEN BREAST PRINCESSE

PORTIONS: 24	PORTION SIZE: ½ CHICKEN BREAST 2 OZ (60 ML) SAUCE, PLUS GARNISH		
U.S.	METRIC	INGREDIENTS	PROCEDURE
24	24	BONELESS, SKINLESS HALF CHICKEN BREASTS, FROM TWELVE 3-LB (1.2-KG) CHICKENS	1. SELECT A BAKING PAN JUST LARGE ENOUGH TO HOLD THE CHICKEN BREASTS IN A SINGLE LAYER. BUTTER THE INSIDE OF THE PAN.
AS NEEDED	AS NEEDED	BUTTER	2. SEASON THE CHICKEN BREASTS WITH SALT
AS NEEDED	AS NEEDED	SALT	AND PEPPER. PLACE THEM IN THE PAN,
AS NEEDED	AS NEEDED	WHITE PEPPER	PRESENTATION SIDE (THAT IS, THE SIDE THAT HAD THE SKIN ON) UP.
¼ CUP	60 ML	LEMON JUICE	3. SPRINKLE WITH THE LEMON JUICE AND ADD
1½ QT	1.5 L APPROXIMATELY	CHICKEN STOCK, COLD	ENOUGH CHICKEN STOCK TO BARELY COVER THE CHICKEN.
			4. COVER THE CHICKEN WITH A BUTTERED PIECE OF PARCHMENT OR WAXED PAPER.
			5. BRING TO A SIMMER ON TOP OF THE STOVE. FINISH POACHING IN A 325°F (165°C) OVEN OR OVER LOW HEAT ON THE STOVE. COOKING TIME WILL BE 5–10 MINUTES.
			6. REMOVE THE CHICKEN BREASTS FROM THE LIQUID. PLACE THEM IN A HOTEL PAN, COVER, AND KEEP THEM WARM.
		BEURRE MANIÉ:	7. REDUCE THE POACHING LIQUID OVER HIGH
3 OZ	90 G	BUTTER, SOFTENED	HEAT TO ABOUT 2½ PT (1.1 L).
3 OZ	90 G	FLOUR	8. KNEAD THE BUTTER AND FLOUR TOGETHER
2½ CUPS	600 ML	HEAVY CREAM, HOT	TO MAKE A BEURRE MANIÉ (P. 120).
TO TASTE	TO TASTE	SALT	9. WITH A WIRE WHIP, BEAT THE BEURRE MANIÉ INTO THE SIMMERING STOCK TO THICKEN IT. SIMMER A MINUTE TO COOK OUT ANY STARCHY TASTE.
			10. ADD THE HOT CREAM TO THE SAUCE. SEASON TO TASTE.
72	72	ASPARAGUS TIPS, COOKED, HOT	11. PLACE EACH CHICKEN BREAST, WELL DRAINED, ON A PLATE AND COAT WITH 2 OZ (60 ML) SAUCE. GARNISH WITH 3 ASPARAGUS TIPS. SERVE IMMEDIATELY.

FIGURE 8-3   EXAMPLE OF A PROFESSIONAL COOKING RECIPE.

Accurate and easy to read recipe cards are an important part of quality control. They help to assure a quality food product and are instrumental in maintaining food cost control.

PRODUCTION SHEET

The final step in reaching the goal of consistency in production is the production sheet. The information on a production sheet regarding the menu and the number of expected guests is taken from catering function sheets that present all of the details for each catering function (see Figure 8-4). For each menu item to be produced during a given meal service the production sheet (Figure 8-5) lists the number of portions to be prepared, the food cost, and the selling price. Following the function the actual number served is noted and the value of the waste from overproduction is calculated.

The production sheet also acts as a tool that allows management to organize the production of multiple parties, indicating where a duplication

Listing:				Person in Charge:		
Organization:				Bus. Phone		Res. Phone
Person Calling:				Bill To:		
Address:				Organization:		
City	State	Zip		Address:		
Bus. Phone		Res. Phone		City	State	Zip

DAY & DATE

Function	DINNER	RECEPTION		
Room	LAFAYETTE	LAFAYETTE FOYER		
Time	7:00 P.M.	6:00 P.M.		
Attend.	175	175		

Guar. 170 Set 180 | Guar.   Set | Guar.   Set | Guar.   Set

MENU:

Bibb & Frisee Salad

Filet of Sirloin
　　pecan-basil crust
　　Madagascar pepper sauce

Green Beans & pimento

Roasted Red Potatoes

Rolls & Butter

Grand Marnier Mousse

Coffee/Tea

NUMBER SERVED _____ CAPT. _____

SPECIAL INSTRUCTIONS:

- ☐ Auditorium _____
- ☐ Schoolroom _____
- ☐ Conference _____
- ☐ U Shape _____
- ☐ Rounds _____
- ☐ Hollow Sq. _____
- ☐ Lounge _____
- ☐ Head Table _____8_____
- ☐ Exh. Table _____
- ☐ Reg. Table _____
- ☐ Blackboard _____
- ☐ Easel _____
- ☐ Flip Chart _____
- ☐ Piano _____
- ☐ Platform _____
- ☐ Entert. _____
- ☐ Dance Floor _____
- ☐ Linen Color _____
- ☐ Flowers _____
- ☐ Incoming Mer. _____
- ☐ Candelabra _____
- ☐ Table Nos. _____
- ☐ Telephone _____
- ☐ Screen _____
- ☐ 16 MM _____
- ☐ 35 MM _____
- ☐ Overhead _____
- ☐ Other _____
- ☐ Projector Table _____
- ☐ Tape Recorder _____
- ☒ Standing Podium   ☒ Mike
- ☐ Table Podium   ☐ Mike
- ☐ Standing Mike _____
- ☐ Neck Mike _____
- ☐ Table Mike _____

- ☐ BAR _Cash Bar_
- ☐ HOUSE _____
- ☐ PREMIUM _Premium Brands_
- ☐ BEER _____
- ☐ BAR _____
- ☐ BARTENDER _____50.00_____
- ☐ CASHIER _____

- ☐ WINE (RECP.) _____
- ☐ WINE (MEAL) _____
- ☐ CHAMPAGNE _____
- ☐ MINERAL WATER _____
- ☐ SOFT DRINKS _____
- ☐ CORDIALS _____
- ☐ OTHER _____

FIGURE 8-4   CATERING FUNCTION SHEET I.
(Courtesy of Hotel Du Pont, Wilmington, Delaware.)

CATERING PRODUCTION SHEET								
TOTAL ESTIMATED CUSTOMER COUNT: 375						ACTUAL # SERVED:		
DATE: TIME:						CHEF:		
ITEM	# OF ITEMS TO BE SERVED	FOOD COST	TOTAL FOOD COST	ACTUAL # SERVED	ACTUAL # FOOD COST	SELLING PRICE	TOTAL REVENUE	F.C.%
Bibb Salad								
Sirloin/F								
Chicken/Br								
Salmon/F								
Green Beans								
Red Potatoes								
Rice Pilaf								
Cream Puff								
Mousse/GM								

FIGURE 8-5   PREFUNCTION PRODUCTION SHEET.

of menu items will make kitchen production more effective. Figure 8-6 shows a completed catering production sheet with items for three different menus posted. The total production count for this meal period is 375, and while three different entrées are being served, the salad and vegetables are duplicated on all three menus, and the rice pilaf and mousse on two each. Kitchen management for these three functions will be greatly simplified by the ability of the chef to review the combined menu requirements on the production sheet.

Both purchasing staff and the kitchen receive menu requirements well in advance of the functions. Two weeks of planning time is needed by most hotels and caterers. This allows last minute functions, changes, and emer-

TOTAL ESTIMATED CUSTOMER COUNT: 375						ACTUAL # SERVED:	
DATE: TIME:						CHEF:	
ITEM	# OF ITEMS TO BE SERVED	FOOD COST	TOTAL FOOD COST	ACTUAL # SERVED	ACTUAL # FOOD COST	SELLING PRICE	TOTAL REVENUE
Bibb Salad	375	$1.31	$491.25	380	$497.80	$3.75	$1,425.00
Sirloin/F	175	$4.59	$803.20	180	$826.20	$17.00	$3,060.00
Chicken/Br	145	$2.88	$417.60	148	$426.24	$11.50	$1,702.00
Salmon/F	55	$4.65	$255.75	53	$246.45	$17.25	$914.25
Green Beans	375						
Red Potatoes	175						
Rice Pilaf	200						
Cream Puff	145	$1.31	$189.95	147	$192.57	$3.75	$551.25
Mousse/GM	230	$0.88	$202.40	233	$205.04	$2.50	$582.50
	1875	$15.62	$2,360.15	1141	$2,394.30	$55.75	$8,235.00

FIGURE 8-6   COMPLETED CATERING PRODUCTION SHEET.

gencies to be handled as efficiently and cost effectively as possible by written catering function change memos. Figure 8-7 is an example of a function sheet format created by a computer software program.

Following production the actual number of items served and the actual food cost are entered in the appropriate columns. Total food cost and food cost percentage can now be calculated for each function as well as for the meal period by applying the food cost formulas presented in Chapter Five.

$$\text{Total food cost} \div \text{Total revenue} = \text{Food cost \%}$$

Event Order   **Whitehouse/Barnes Reception**

Customer:	**Jack Sullivan**	Contact:	Jack Sullivan
Date:	12/20/02	Phone:	313-884-2500
Time:	06:00 pm To 01:00 am	Company:	Grosse Pointe Yacht Club
# Guests:	125	Addr 1:	788 Lake Shore Drive
# Guarantee:	120	Addr 2:	Suite 2000
Setup Time:	04:00 pm	City, St:	Grosse Pointe Shores MI 48236
Event Type:	Reception Dinner		
Room:	Silver Ball Room		

Schedule

04:00 pm	Employees arrive at store
06:00 pm	Bar Opens
07:00 pm	Meal starts
08:45 pm	Meal ends
09:00 pm	Entertainment starts
01:00 am	Entertainment ends
12:00 am	Bar closes

Orders   **Staff**

Soup Du Jour	125	Russ Nelson - Setup Helper
Mixed Green Salad w/Crouton	125	Joseph Paulson - Setup Helper
Raspberry Vinaigrette	250 Ozs	Jessica Payton - Setup Helper
Snow Flake Rolls & Butter	16 Dozens	Jessica Payton - Bartender
Sliced Top Round of Beef Bordelaise	125 8 Ounces	Russ Neslon - Bartender
Franconia Roasted Potatoes	125 Ea	Joseph Paulson - Bartender
Whole Green Beans w/ Toasted Almonds	125 Portion	Erika Mann - Wait Staff
Cheesecake w/ Raspberry Sauce	125	Marie Denaston - Wait Staff
* Beer, Soda & Wine *	125 Package	James Seward - Wait Staff
Soda, Juice & Bottled Water	75	Vaclav Sonorak - Wait Staff
Draft Beer	22 Pitchers	Margaret Ann Pepperney - Wait staff
Bottles of White Wine	25 750ml Btl	Ellie Lourd - Wait Staff
Bottles of Red Wine	25 750ml Btl	Erika Mann - Manager
Coffee by the Gallon	4 Gallons	George Haverford - Chef
DeCaf by the Gallon	3 Gallons	Bob Carpenter - Cook
		Anna Kowalski - Cook Helper

Table Centerpieces	15	Starlight Productions

Set up head table with sound system and microphone.
Press tableskirts immediately before event.
Floral designer will set up 2 hours before event starts.

FIGURE 8-7 CATERING FUNCTION SHEET FORMAT II.
(Courtesy of Hotel Du Pont, Wilmington, Delaware.)

Fluctuations in individual item costs as well as food cost percentages can be identified for each function. Overage can also be analyzed and its source traced to either a reduction in the number of expected covers or overproduction in the kitchen. Most catering functions have a guarantee policy that requires payment for a predetermined guest count, helping the caterer to absorb food costs when actual guest counts fall short of the expected numbers.

The completed production sheet in Figure 8-8 details the actual food costs, revenues, and food cost percentages for the meal period. For the sirloin filet, 175 portions were prepared with an individual food cost of $4.59 for a total food cost of $803.20. The actual number served was 180, for an actual food cost of $826.20. The selling price was $17.00 with total revenue of $3060.00. Food cost percentage was calculated to be 27 percent. Production overage was five portions with a value of $85.00. The chef was required to locate five additional portions of sirloin filet to meet service needs. Total actual number served for the meal period was 381. Total actual food cost was $2394.30, and total revenue was $8235.00. Overall food cost percentage for all three functions was 30 percent.

SALES MIX EVALUATION

The sales mix is an evaluation of the sales pattern of major catering menu items. Item sales are recorded over an established period of time and evaluated on the basis of two major factors: popularity and contribution to sales. In Figure 8-9, the sales of appetizer, entrée, and dessert items for a hotel catering department are recorded. At the end of the period sales for each item are totaled and the percentage of sales that each item represents calculated. The item is then ranked according to total sales in order to rate its popularity. The final step in the sales mix process is to calculate the contribution to profit for each item. Decisions are then made as to which items will remain on the catering menu item list and which will be deleted.

CATERING PROUCTION SHEET											
TOTAL ESTIMATED CUSTOMER COUNT: 375					ACTUAL # SERVED: 381						
DATE: TIME:					CHEF:						
ITEM	# OF ITEMS TO BE SERVED	ITEM FOOD COST	TOTAL FOOD COST	ACTUAL SERVED	ACTUAL # FOOD COST	SELLING PRICE	TOTAL REVENUE	F.C.%	OVERAGE	OVERAGE VALUE	WASTE F.C. %
Bibb Salad	375	$1.31	$491.25	380	$497.80	$3.75	$1,425.00	35	5	$18.75	
Sirloin/F	175	$4.59	$803.20	180	$826.20	$17.00	$3,060.00	27	5	$85.00	
Chicken/Br	145	$2.88	$417.60	148	$426.24	$11.50	$1,702.00	25	3	$34.50	
Salmon/F	55	$4.65	$255.75	53	$246.45	$17.25	$914.25	27			
Green Beans	375										
Red Potatoes	175										
Rice Pilaf	200										
Cream Puff	145	$1.31	$189.95	147	$192.57	$3.75	$551.25	35	2	$7.50	
Mousse/GM	230	$0.88	$202.40	233	$205.04	$2.50	$582.50	35	3		
	1875	$15.62	$2,360.15	1141	$2,394.30	$55.75	$8,235.00	30	18		

FIGURE 8-8   COMPLETED PRODUCTION SHEET.

CATERING MENU SALES MIX					
Items	Week 1	Week 2	Week 3	Week 4	Week 5
shrimp cocktial					
crabmeat muhrooms					
vegatable crudite					
escargot					
soup: French					
soup:lobster bisque					
fruit w/yogurt					
Total Appetizer					
N.Y. sirloin					
chicken veronica					
veal oscar					
filet mignon					
prime rib					
sword fish					
stuffed flounder					
Total Entree:					
mousse					
chambard cake					
cheescake					
derby pie					
Total Dessert:					

FIGURE 8-9   CATERING MENU SALES MIX.

Presentation Controls

Presentation standards include three important elements that contribute to the maintenance of a consistent quality in the appearance of the finished product as it is presented to the guest:

- Size and type of dish
- Portion size
- Garnish

The visual appearance of the portion size of food items must fit the plate size so that kitchen staff do not add to the portion in order to fill up the plate. Consistent portion size is significant, having a profound effect on both guest satisfaction and profitability. The final garnish is often overlooked in the development and production of menu items.

Plate architecture is the design of the actual placement of food items on the plate. In addition to the elements listed above, these other concerns become important to the overall design of the plate presentation:

- Colors and textures are interesting and appetizing.
- Food is layered for height in the presentation.

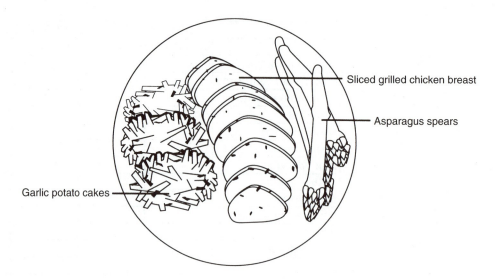

Sliced grilled chicken breast

Asparagus spears

Garlic potato cakes

FIGURE 8-10   EXAMPLE OF THE DESIGN SKETCH OF A PLATE DESIGN.
(Courtesy of the Idaho Potato Commission.)

- The plate is designed into the presentation.
- The overall presentation presents a balance of texture, height, and color.

Every plate design should be evaluated as to how well balanced the overall design is. The completed plate design is photographed as a standard presentation that accompanies the recipe card as a guide for the final step in the production process. Figure 8-10 is an example of the design sketch of a plate design and Figure 8-11 is a photograph of the final plate setup.

Many catered functions, particularly business occasions, are often attended by the same people on a routine basis. Whether as a guest or as a customer, people develop a level of expectation for the quality of food and service of catering operations. Maintaining a consistent presentation is an important part of meeting customer expectations.

Catering Menu Meeting

As an additional operational control, weekly catering menu meetings bring together key management personnel to review upcoming functions. Communication between production and service staff is necessary to successfully carry out a number of catering functions within the same time period.

Identifying possible logistical problems for multiple functions, such as shortages in service staff, timing schedules between functions, and availability of table service equipment, linens, tables, and chairs, is an important goal of menu meetings.

Purchasing is another area in which menu meetings are often highly effective. Function sheets are reviewed with the chef, purchasing agent, maître d'hôtel, and sales staff. Current fluctuations in the prices of main menu items

FIGURE 8-11   A PHOTOGRAPH OF THE FINAL PLATE SETUP.
(Courtesy of the Idaho Potato Commission.)

such as beef and fish can be recognized and steps taken to restructure menus to account for increased food costs.

Catering menu meetings should be held on a regularly scheduled basis as an ongoing method of operational controls. When key staff understands that they will have a formal means of discussing areas of interest and concern with other staff members, they will use this time effectively and reduce haphazard communications.

Beverage Controls

Profitable beverage management requires many of the same controls that are applied to food production including standard recipes, purchasing specifications, and presentation standards.

STANDARD RECIPE

A thorough knowledge of established beverage recipes is important if the desired taste, texture, and yield of beverages are to be consistently achieved. It is important for management to issue standard beverage recipe guidelines to enable the same beverage to be produced at the same time in a variety of different locations by different bartenders. The beverage recipes in Figure 8-12 are examples of one style of recipe format.

MARTINI		
MEASURE	INGREDIENT	DIRECTIONS
1 ¾ OZ.	GIN	1. CHILL STEMMED GLASS
¾ OZ.	VERMOUTH (DRY)	2. FILL MIXING GLASS HALF FULL ICE
	OLIVE OR	3. POUR GIN INTO MIXING GLASS
	LEMON ZEST	4. POUR VERMOUTH INTO MIXING GLASS
		5. USING STIRRER GENTLY MIX LIQUIDS
		6. USE SPRING STRAINER TO POUR MIX INTO CHILLED GLASS
		7. ADD OLIVE OR LEMON ZEST

WHISKEY SOUR		
MEASURE	INGREDIENT	DIRECTIONS
1 ½ OZ.	WHISKEY	1. FILL MIXING GLASS HALF FULL ICE
2 OZ.	LEMON MIX	2. POUR LEMON MIX INTO MIXING GLASS
	CHERRY	3. POUR WHISKEY INTO MIXING GLASS
		4. USE METAL CUP AS COVER, SHAKE IN QUICK EVEN MOVEMENTS
		5. USE SPRING STRAINER TO POUR MIX INTO SOUR GLASS
		6. ADD CHERRY

FIGURE 8-12   BEVERAGE RECIPE FORMAT.

Figure 8-13 offers an alternate format for beverage recipes. This format offers abbreviations to shorten the directions and provide workable bar recipe references. Beverages are broken down into categories.

PURCHASING

Purchasing for alcoholic beverages requires a knowledge of spirits and wines. A purchasing agent should be well informed about types of wines, vintages, and the appropriate marriage of wines and foods in order to construct a well developed wine list. Maintaining an adequate inventory is the most important factor of profitable beverage purchasing. Stock levels must be kept as low as possible while still providing sufficient beverages to service functions.

Alcoholic beverage purchasing specifications include the following information:

1. Product name with preferred brand names listed
2. Quantity to be purchased such as liter, fifth, gallon
3. Indication of proof, such as 80% proof, 100% proof, or 175% proof
4. Unit by which prices are quoted, such as case, keg, or barrel

The principle advantage to beverage purchasing for catering operations is that beverage requirements can be estimated well in advance of functions. Catering functions generally maintain standard bars, limiting the variety of drinks and liquors served. A standard catering bar will offer drinks made

2. Medium Cocktails

Name	Where	What/How	Glass
Daiquiri	SH / BL	1 / 4 MGL Lemon 3 / 4 MGl white Rum 1 - 2 BS Sugar Garnish: no	Cocktailglass
Side Car	SH / BL	1 / 3 MGL Lemon 1 / 3 MGL Cognac 1 / 3 MGL Cointreau	Cocktailglass
White Lady	SH / BL	1 / 3 MGL Lemon 1 / 3 MGL Gin 1 / 3 MGL Cointreau	Cocktailglass
Old Fashioned	DI	3 / 4 MGL Bourbon Whisky 3 D Angostura Bitter 1 D Lemon 1 Siger cube	Tumbler
Whisky Sour	SH / BL	3 / 4 Bourbon Whisky 2 BS Suger 1 / 4 Lemon / Soda Water Garnish: Orange/Lemon/Cherry on a Cocktailstick	Tumbler
Gin Fizze	SH / BL	3 /4 Gin 2 BS Suger 1 / 4 Lemon / Soda Water	Short Tumbler

3. After Dinner Cocktail

Alexander	SH / BL	1 / 3 MGL Cognac 1 / 3 MGL Creme de Cacao Liquor 1 / 3 MGL Cream Garnish: Muscat (Nutmeg)	Cocktailglass

4. Long Drink Cocktails

Champagne Cocktail	DI	1 Sugar cube 1 D Angostura Bitter 1 BS Grand Marnier Champagne Garnish: Cocktail-Cherry Lemonspiral	Champagne glass
Screw Driver	DI	3 / 4 Vodka 10 cl. Orangejuice	Long drink glass

FIGURE 8-13   ALTERNATE FORMAT FOR BEVERAGE RECIPES.
(Courtesy of the Swiss School of Hotel and Tourism Management.)

from scotch, gin, vodka, rye, bourbon, and wine. Additions are made at the discretion of the customer.

Theme bars are often popular for catering functions. Bars will feature either a regional theme, such as a Caribbean bar or a Southwest bar, or be focused on a particular type of spirit or drink such as a martini bar, a margarita bar, or a vodka bar. Figure 8-14 is the menu for a reception that features a variety of themed beverage bars to accompany food stations.

<u>Banquet Beverage Stations</u>

Vodka Station

A Selection of Premium Vodkas, chilled

Hors d'oeuvre Table

Imported Caviar Service

with Onions, Chopped Eggs and Crème Fraiche
Traditional Toast Points, Capers and Lemon Slices

Whole Smoked Salmon

English Cucumbers, Slivered Radishes and Fresh Dill
Served with a Cucumber and Dill Sauce

Scotch Bar

A Selection of Premium Single Malt Scotch

Hors d'oeuvre Table

Carving Station
to serve

Roast Sirloin of Beef with horseradish sauce
Roast Smoked Turkey with spiced cranberry relish
Honey Baked Ham with pineapple-mango chutney

Grilled Baby Lamp Chops and mint sauce

Sliced Beef Wellington En Croute

A selection of Fresh Breads and Condiments

FIGURE 8-14   MENU FOR A RECEPTION THAT FEATURES A VARIETY OF
BEVERAGE BARS TO ACCOMPANY FOOD STATIONS.

PRESENTATION

Beverage presentation is supported by an established selection of glassware that is associated with specific wines and drinks. Often the shape of the bowl of the glass has been developed to enhance the "bouquet" or supply adequate space for ice and liquid. Garniture can add to the customer's perceived value of the drink by creating a pleasing presentation. Theme drinks often include decorative stirrers or other items to create interest and highlight the beverage recipe or concept.

Summary

Three sets of controls important to establish in a foodservice operation cover the areas of purchasing, production, and presentation. The goal of these controls is to achieve a consistent quality of food and beverage production and service. Quality controls should be implemented to carry out the steps necessary to achieve and maintain the standards set by the operation.

Successful purchasing requires that specifications be developed for each food item identifying the desired quality and quantity of the food product. These specifications provide the basis for the bidding process, ensuring that the highest quality product is purchased for the lowest price.

Successful production requires that a standard recipe card be developed for every new item as a guideline to produce a food product with a consistent taste, texture, and yield. The production sheet outlines each menu item to be prepared prior to production and contains a record of the actual amounts produced and served as well as total costs and sales revenues. The catering sales mix uses the information from the production sheet to evaluate the sales and profitability of each menu item.

Successful presentation requires that the plate size, portion size, and garnish for each menu item be established in order to serve the same product on a consistent basis.

Profitable beverage management employs many of the same operational controls as food production, including beverage specifications, drink recipes, and established presentation styles.

CHAPTER NINE

Catering Computer Management

EVENT CALENDAR

Events: 9
Value: $8,013.60

SUN	MON	TUE	WED	THU	FRI	SAT
				1	2 *1*	3
4	5	6 *2*	7 *1*	8	9	10
11	12	13 *2*	14 *1*	15	16	17
18	19	20 *1*	21 *1*	22	23	24
25	26	27	29	30	31	

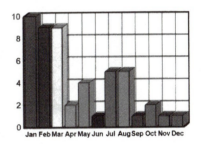

Events By Month

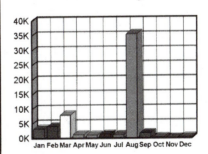

Event Sales By Month

In the business environment of the 2000s, the integration of computer systems into the management of any type of business is essential. The consistent application of management principles to restaurant and catering operations is necessary in order to generate the profits required to sustain a healthy business. Small catering businesses, in particular, often find the details of business the most difficult part of the operations to manage. Computer software systems offer a wide range of management options for accounting systems and contract and function booking management, along with sales and marketing activities.

Computer systems and software available to catering operations can range in both complexity and pricing, according to business needs and available finances. While restaurant operations require front of the house terminals, keyboards, and printers, independent catering operations can limit their investment to a microcomputer, software programs, a laser printer, and a modem. Desktop publishing software is available for any level of business volume.

Restaurants entering the catering business can integrate compatible software programs for catering management into their existing systems. Because many of these software programs are compatible with a variety of hardware systems, the catering department of a large hotel or restaurant can implement them just as effectively as an independent caterer or contract feeder. This chapter presents a sampling of the forms available through catering management software programs. The forms illustrated in the following figures have been provided by Horizon Business Services in Naples, Florida. The title of the software program from which they have been produced is Cater Ease.

Marketing

The application of computer foodservice management systems to the marketing process is invaluable in relation to time saving, customer follow-up, planning, and function follow-through. Software, such as Cater Ease, includes programs that track correspondence on individual client accounts, create future reminders, and compile account contact histories that can be accessed instantly. In addition, marketing efforts can be tracked and lost leads maintained in a file for future solicitation.

Generating letters using a merge-field function allows a standard letter format, such as shown in Figure 9-1, to become easily customized into a personal thank-you letter. Additional comments can be inserted into the body of the text to enhance the personal tone of the letter.

Sales contracts can be completed at the time of booking and delivered to the customers in a timely fashion by fax or in person. Figure 9-2 features a completed sales/catering contract. In this example, the menu has been identified along with the date, time, and location of the function. In addition, an estimated cost has been calculated for the customer. The sales contract information is calculated and posted as part of the software program, thereby eliminating errors in function cost calculations. By having the sales representative complete the contract at the time of booking, the necessity for secretarial assistance is minimized.

Holiday Inn
SELECT℠

October 23, 1998

{Booking Contact}
{Organization}
{Address}
{City, St, Zip}

Dear {Salutation},

We wish to thank you for the opportunity to host your {Event Theme} on {Event Date} in our {Function Room}. We hope that everything was satisfactory and that you and your guests thoroughly enjoyed your stay with us.

Please take the time to fill out the enclosed evaluation form and return it to us in the self addressed envelope provided. We value your input concerning our service. It will help us to better serve your needs in the future.

Thank you, once more, and we hope to see you again in the not too distant future.

Sincerely,

{Sales Rep}
{Title}

Holiday Inn Select · 2400 Mainsail · Clearview, FL 36609
Phone: (902) 783-0300   Fax: (902) 783-5525

FIGURE 9-1   STANDARD FORMAT FOR A THANK-YOU LETTER FOR THE HOLIDAY INN, CLEARVIEW, FLORIDA.
(Courtesy of Horizon Business Systems, Naples, Florida.)

Holiday Inn

SELECT™

SALES/CATERING CONTRACT

Order Number: <u>9698</u>

Day: Friday	Date: July 25, 2000
Starting Time: 07:00 PM	Ending Time: 12:00 AM
Company/Organization: Horizon Business Services, Inc.	Contact Person: George Kopriva
Street Address: P.O. Box 577	City, State Zip: Naples, FL 34102
Phone Number: (941) 261-5828	Fax Number: (941) 261-0067

ROOMS SELECTION

Room Name: San Diego	Est Count: 125	Gtd. Number:	125
Setup Style: Rounds			

FOOD & BEVERAGE REQUIREMENTS

Description	Cost	Qty	Total
Baked Sea Bass w/Julienne of Peppers & Prosecco Sauce	27.50	50	1,375.00
Cream of Carrot & Ginger Soup, Boston Salad w/Walnuts & Walnut Oil Vinaigrette, Saffron Rice, Seasonal Vegetables, Rolls & Butter, Chocolate Decadence w/Raspberry Sauce			
Breast of Chicken w/Champagne Vinegar Sauce	27.00	75	2,025.00
Lentil & Vegetable Soup, Mesclun Salad w/Hazelnut Oil Dressing, Wild Rice, Seasonal Vegetables, Rolls & Butter, Caramel Chocolate Torte			
Robert Mondavi Winery, Napa Valley (Chardonnay)	27.00	9	243.00
HOST BAR: Three Hours Call (/ppl)	17.50	125	2,187.50

AUDIO/VISUAL REQUIREMENTS

Description	Cost	Qty	Total
Overhead Projector	25.00	1	25.00
Screen	25.00	1	25.00
Lavalier Mic	35.00	1	35.00

SPECIAL REQUESTS/COMMENT SECTION

D.J. Elliot Cole to setup in corner of San Diego at 6:00 PM. D.J. to play soft rock and instrumentals from 7:00 PM - 9:00 PM, dance music from 9:00 PM to 11:00 PM.

Lobby Bar outside room entrance to serve drinks from 6:00 PM - 8:00 PM. Room bar to serve drinks from 7:00 PM until 11:00 PM.

ROOM RENTAL

Description	Cost	Qty	Total
Room Rental Charge (San Diego Room)	500.00	1	500.00

BILLING INSTRUCTIONS

SUBTOTAL:	6,415.50	DEPOSIT MADE:	1,000.00	BILLING TYPE: Credit Card	CARD NUM: 3811 4411 4876 6666
SERV CHG (18.00 %):	1,154.79	BALANCE DUE:	7.156.99	TYPE OF CARD: American Express	APPR: GFDI1105
TAX (7.75 %):	586.70	NEXT DEPOSIT:	2,500.00	CARDHOLDER: Chris Johns	EXP DATE: 10/10/1998
TOTAL:	8,156.99	DUE DATE:	7/20/97	CARD HOLDER SIGNATURE:	

CONTRACT TERMS

A $150.00 cancellation fee will be incurred for any cancellation within 7 days of event. A 100.00 fee will be incurred for any additional setup on the day of the event. All food and beverage is subject to a 15% service charge. I have read the above contract and the hotel's Catering Policies and Procedures printed on the reverse side of this contract (or attached) and agree to the terms and conditions as wells as any terms and conditions on any contract addendums which I may sign.

SALES MANAGER:_____   CLIENT:_____

DATE:_____   DATE:_____

Holiday Inn Select - 2400 Mainsail - Clearview, FL 36609
Phone: (902) 783-0300 Fax: (902) 783-5525

Page 1 Of 1

FIGURE 9-2   SALES/CATERING CONTRACT FOR THE HOLIDAY INN, CLEARVIEW, FLORIDA.

(Courtesy of Horizon Business Systems, Naples, Florida.)

Event Information and Reports

The event contract precedes the distribution of the event sheet, the principal form of event communication within a catering operation. By forwarding an event contract to the customer for approval and signature, the sales department is assured of the customer's agreement and compliance with the organizational features of the event as well as the menu, prices, and additional contract services. Figure 9-3 outlines the event order contract complete with menu, detailed costs, and charges. Figure 9-4 is an example of an additional event sheet that is distributed in-house. In this example, the timing of the event is detailed and staff members identified.

Figure 9-5 is a staffing requirement form for the function outlined on the event sheet in Figure 9-4. This form serves both as a staff work sheet and time form. Final hours worked by each staff member are posted to facilitate the calculation of labor costs for a particular function. If staff work on more than one function, labor costs can be divided and charged against each function to facilitate more accurate costing.

PURCHASING

On the format for the purchasing form in Figure 9-6, purchasing requirements for functions booked from November 14 to 16 have been detailed by item category. Quantities have been estimated based on the expected attendance for each function. Menu item details and guest counts have been taken from the individual function event orders. In this example, the software program has assimilated a summary of the food items required in report form from the data input on each event order.

To complete the purchasing process the software program will compare purchasing requirements against current inventories and issue a purchasing requisition from which orders will be placed. Figure 9-7 shows a purchasing specification form for each individual food item listed in the purchasing directory. This example, for the meat cut London broil, identifies the portion size, purchasing measure, and UOM (unit of measure) in pounds and established food cost ($2.29 per pound). Portion size is 8 ounces with the specification of two servings per UOM. The selling price per UOM is identified as $9.95. This is accompanied by a menu specification and cost outline. This is also known as a cost card and details the bulk food cost of each menu item and the quantity in which it is purchased. For example, the dessert item chocolate mousse cake is costed per person at $.35 with a selling price of $1.45 per portion. Yield from the purchased cake by unit is twenty portions. Cost for the total cake can be calculated as $7.00 with an estimated sales price of $29.00 if all twenty portions are sold. Oven-roasted potatoes are listed with a cost of $.65 for four portions. Cost per portion is $.16 and the unit of purchase is a 20 pound bag.

COST ANALYSIS

Following each function a cost analysis report such as shown in Figure 9-8 is issued. The total food cost for each item is listed and compared with the final selling price. The food cost percentage is determined for each menu

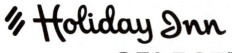

BANQUET EVENTS ORDER
Tentative

Booked: 05/15/97   Revised: 07/20/97

CLIENT/ORGANIZATION Sunset Technologies	EVENT DATE 8/09/1997 (Sat)	BOOKING CONTACT Douglas Weiner	SITE CONTACT Louis Trainor	ORDER 9701
ADDRESS 25 Davis Blvd, Concord, NH 03079 U.S.A.		PHONE (603) 271-5555	FAX (603) 271-5454	GUESTS 115 (Act)
PARTY NAME Office Party	THEME Dinner/Dance	CATEGORY Event Type 1	SALES REPRESENTATIVE Marv Truesdale	

ROOMS FOR THE FUNCTION

Room	Setup Style	Start	End	Serving	Guests	Room Date
San Diego	Rounds	07:00 PM	12:00 AM	07:30 PM	115 (Act)	07/25/1997

Setup Notes: *Room to be setup in rounds of 8. Wine glasses on each table. Room bar to be setup in S.E. corner of room.*

FOOD & SERVICE ITEMS

Description Of Item	Cost	Qty	Total
Food			
Succulent Prime Rib	21.95	50.00	1,097.50
Caesar Salad w/Vinegarette, 10 oz. Prime Rib w/Fresh Horseradish, Twice Baked Potato, Broccoli in Butter Sauce, Fresh Rolls, Chocolate Torte Cake.			
A Taste of the Sea	19.45	65.00	1,264.25
Spinach Salad w/Hot Bacon Dressing, Grilled Red Snapper, Rice Pilaf, Medley of Vegetables, Fresh Rolls, Key Lime, Pie			
Beverage			
Robert Mondavi Winery, Napa Valley (Chardonnay)	27.00	9.00	243.00
HOST BAR: 4 Call Hours	17.50	115.00	2,012.50

SPECIAL REQUESTS

D.J. Elliot Cole to setup in corner of San Diego at 6:00 PM. D.J. to play soft rock and instrumentals from 7:00 PM - 9:00 PM, dance music from 9:00 PM to 11:00 PM.

Lobby bar outside room entrance to serve drinks from 6:00 PM - 8:00 PM. Room bar to serve drinks from 7:00 PM until 11:00 PM.

COMMENTS

Wait Staff to arrive 1 hour prior to function to prep all tables. Wait Staff to stay after function to bus tables. Wait Staff shall wear formal attire.

Holiday Inn Select - 2400 Mainsail - Clearview. FL 36609
Phone: (902) 783-0300 Fax: (902) 783-5525

Page 1 Of 1

FIGURE 9-3   EVENT ORDER CONTRACT.
(Courtesy of Horizon Business Systems, Naples, Florida.)

Event Order

Whitehouse/Barnes Reception

Customer:	Jack Sullivan	Contact:	Jack Sullivan
Date:	12/20/02	Phone:	313-884-2500
Time:	06:00 pm To 01:00 am	Company:	Grosse Pointe Yacht Club
# Guests:	125	Addr 1:	788 Lake Shore Drive
# Guarantee:	120	Addr 2:	Suite 2000
Setup Time:	04:00 pm	City, St:	Grosse Pointe Shores MI 48236
Event Type:	Reception Dinner		
Room:	Silver Ball Room		

Schedule

04:00 pm	Employees arrive at store
06:00 pm	Bar Opens
07:00 pm	Meal starts
08:45 pm	Meal ends
09:00 pm	Entertainment starts
01:00 am	Entertainment ends
12:00 am	Bar closes

Orders

Soup Du Jour	125
Mixed Green Salad w/Crouton	125
Raspberry Vinaigrette	250 Ozs
Snow Flake Rolls & Butter	16 Dozens
Sliced Top Round of Beef Bordelaise	125 8 Ounces
Franconia Roasted Potatoes	125 Ea
Whole Green Beans w/ Toasted Almonds	125 Portion
Cheesecake w/ Raspberry Sauce	125
* Beer, Soda & Wine *	125 Package
Soda, Juice & Bottled Water	75
Draft Beer	22 Pitchers
Bottles of White Wine	25 750ml Btl
Bottles of Red Wine	25 750ml Btl
Coffee by the Gallon	4 Gallons
DeCaf by the Gallon	3 Gallons
Table Centerpieces	15	Starlight Productions

Set up head table with sound system and microphone.
Press tableskirts immediately before event.
Floral designer will set up 2 hours before event starts.

Staff

Russ Nelson - Setup Helper
Joseph Paulson - Setup Helper
Jessica Payton - Setup Helper
Russ Neslon - Bartender
Joseph Paulson - Bartender
Erika Mann - Wait Staff
Marie Denaston - Wait Staff
James Seward - Wait Staff
Vaclav Sonorak - Wait Staff
Margaret Ann Pepperney - Wait staff
Ellie Lourd - Wait Staff
Erika Mann - Manager
George Haverford - Chef
Bob Carpenter - Cook
Anna Kowalski - Cook Helper

FIGURE 9-4   ADDITIONAL EVENT SHEET FOR IN-HOUSE USE.
(Courtesy of Cater Mate, Indianapolis, IN.)

Staffing Requirements for Whitehouse/Barnes Reception on 12/20/2002

Customer:	GROSSE POINTE
Room:	SILVER
Contact:	Jack Sullivan
Guest Count:	125
Room Setup:	CT (Circle Tables)
Event Status:	B (Booked)

Name	Skill	Rpt Time	In	Out	Net Hour
Bob Carpenter	Cook	06:00 pm			
Marie Denaston	Wait Staff	06:00 pm			
George Haverford	Chef	06:00 pm			
Anna Kowalski	Cook Helper	06:00 pm			
Ellie Lourd	Wait Staff	06:00 pm			
Erika Mann	Manager	05:00 pm			
Erika Mann	Wait Staff	06:00 pm			
Russ Nelson	Setup Helper	04:00 pm			
Russ Nelson	Bartender	06:00 pm			
Joseph Paulson	Setup Helper	04:00 pm			
Joseph Paulson	Bartender	06:00 pm			
Margaret Ann Pepperney	Wait Staff	06:00 pm			
Jessica Payton	Setup Helper	04:00 pm			
Jessica Payton	Bartender	06:00pm			
James Seward	Wait Staff	06:00 pm			
Vaclav Sonorak	Wait Staff	06:00 pm			

FIGURE 9-5   STAFFING REQUIREMENT FORM.
(Courtesy of Cater Mate, Indianapolis, IN.)

Item Sheet

		Delivery Unit of Measure	
Description:	Assorted Dinner Rolls & Butter	Del UOM:	Dozens
Code:	BR001	Del UOM Cost:	$1.25
Category:	Breads	Serving UOM:	
Alternate Code:	0	Servings Del UOM:	8.0000
Prep Location:	Kitchen	Servings Person:	1.0000
Vendor:	ATLAS GROCERY	Price Del UOM:	$.00
Tax Table Field:	Food Items	Show When 'No-Charge':	No
Charge Method:	No Charge	Allow Item to Scale:	Yes
PLU Number:	0		
Quantity On Hand:	0		

Package Sheet

Code	Description	Item-Serves	Cost	Price	Qty	Del-UOM
AM01P	* Afternoon Break *					
DS009	Brownies	1.0000	$.28	$1.25	16	Each
DS010	Assorted Cookie	1.0000	$.17	$.75	12	Mixed
FR002	Whole Fruit	1.0000	$.35	$.95	18	Each
BV111	Assorted Regular & Diet Sodas	1.0000	$.27	$1.25	22	Mixed
BS006	Water, Avalon Each	1.0000	$.50	$.75	8	Each
PP008	Cup, Plastic Cold	1.0000	$.04		30	Each
PP011	Napkins, Dinner	1.0000	$.02		36	Each
PP009	Plate, 6"	1.0000	$.03		28	Each

FIGURE 9-7 PURCHASING SPECIFICATION FORM.
(Courtesy of Cater Mate, Indianapolis, IN.)

Items Required : Summary from Dec 15, 2002 To Dec 20, 2002 All Item Categories

Code	Category / Description	Quantity	Guests	Events
	Appetizer			
AP108	Soup Du Jour	125	125	1
	Breads			
BR001	Assorted Dinner Rolls & Butter	425 Dozens	425	2
BR006	Bakery Fresh Rolls & Butter	6 Dozens	35	1
BR005	Snow Flake Rolls & Butter	136 Dozens	245	2
	Buffet/Lunch/Dinner			
BU015	Carved Boneless Prime Rib	35 Portions	35	1
BU017	Carved Pork Tenderloin w/Mushroom Sauce	35 Portions	35	1
BU021	Fresh Salmon Filet	35 Portions	35	1
BU010	Ricotta Stuffed Pasta Shells/Marinara Sauce	35 Portions	35	1
	Beverages			
BV102	Coffee by the Gallon	4 Gallons	125	1
BV100	Coffee by the Pot	12 Pots	70	2
BV104	DeCaf by the Gallon	3 Gallons	125	1
BV103	DeCaf by the Pot	6 Pots	70	2
BV001	Hot & Cold Beverages	545	545	3
BV002	Hot Beverages	35	35	1
BV106	Hot Water by the Pot	6 Pots	70	2
BV003	Soda, Juice & Bottled Water	75	125	1
	Condiments			
CO003	Creamers	70 Each	70	2
CO001	Sugar Paks	42 Paks	70	2

FIGURE 9-6 PURCHASING REQUIREMENT FORM.
(Courtesy of Cater Mate, Indianapolis, IN.)

TOTAL COSTING ANALYSIS

Grosse Pointe Yacht Club
Jack Sullivan
Whitehouse/Barnes Reception
Dec/20/2002 At 06:00 pm   Contract #:   97000152
Guests: 125   Salesperson: AB

Tax Category	Cost	Price	Percent	Margin
Food Items	$0.00	$0.00	0.00%	$0.00
Items for All Lists	$0.00	$0.00	0.00%	$0.00
Bar/Liquor Items	$0.00	$0.00	0.00%	$0.00
Flowers/Decorations	$0.00	$0.00	0.00%	$0.00
Food Items	$2,609.65	$5,487.50	47.55%	$2,877.85
Equipment Items	$0.00	$0.00	0.00%	$0.00
Other Items	$0.00	$0.00	0.00%	$0.00
Audio/Visual Items	$0.00	$0.00	0.00%	$0.00
Beverage	$0.00	$0.00	0.00%	$0.00
Purchased Materials	$225.00	$675.00	33.33%	$450.00
Staffing	$611.50	$766.00	79.83%	$154.50
Outside Services	$400.00	$500.00	80.00%	$100.00
Room Charge	$350.00	$350.00	100.00%	$0.00
Additional Charges	$0.00	$0.00	0.00%	$0.00
Surcharge	$0.00	$0.00	0.00%	$0.00
Gratuity	$0.00	$0.00	0.00%	$0.00
	————	————	————	————
Subtotal Whole Proposal:	$4,196.15	$7,778.50	53.94%	$3,582.35
Subtotal Per Person:	$33.56	$62.22	53.94%	$28.65
Tax 1	$274.38	$274.38		
Tax 2	$329.25	$329.25		
Surcharge		$384.13		
Gratuity	$439.00	$439.00		
Discount		$493.88-		
	————	————		
Total Whole Proposal:	$5,238.78	$8,711.38	60.13%	$3,472.60
Total Per Person:	$41.91	$69.69	60.13%	$27.78

FIGURE 9-8   Cost analysis report.
(Courtesy of Cater Mate, Indianapolis, IN.)

item and a final contribution to profit margin calculated and posted. A similar calculation is made for the total function and for each guest. Both of these final calculations assist in analyzing the overall profitability of the function. This can help in developing pricing policies for future functions.

ACCOUNTS RECEIVABLE

An initial step in the accounts receivable process is to issue an invoice for payment. Figure 9-9 details each item, prices, quantities charged for, and totals. Credits to the account are itemized and reflected in the final amount due. Figure 9-10 is an alternative format for the invoice form. Figure 9-11 features an accounts receivable chart of the trial balance from 0 to over 120 days

---

Holiday Inn
SELECT ℠

10/27/98

Order Number: 9698

Horizon Business Services, Inc. - Office Party
P.O. Box 577
Naples, FL 34102 U.S.A.

INVOICE

Event Held On Friday, July 25, 1997

50	Baked Sea Bass w/Julienne of Peppers & Prosecco Sauce @ 27.50	1,375.00
75	Breast of Chicken w/Champagne Vinegar Sauce @ 27.00	2,025.00
9	Robert Mondavi Winery, Napa Valley (Chardonnay) @ 27.00	243.00
125	HOST BAR: Three Hours Call (/ppl) @ 17.50	2,187.50
1	Room Rental Charge (San Diego Room) @ 500.00	500.00
1	Overhead Projector @ 25.00	25.00
1	Screen @ 25.00	25.00
1	Lavalier Mic @ 35.00	35.00

	SUBTOTAL	6,415.50
18.00 %	Service Charge	1,154.79
7.75 %	Sales Tax	586.70
	TOTAL ORDER VALUE	8,156.99
	Paid	1,000.00
	BALANCE	7,156.99

Please remit the "Total Balance Due" within 30 days of the Event Date.
Address all corrrespondence to John Hurd, Catering Director.
Thank you for this opportunity to serve you.

Holiday Inn Select - 2400 Mainsail - Clearview, FL 36609
Phone: (902) 783-0300   Fax: (902) 783-5525

Page 1 Of 1

FIGURE 9-9   INVOICE FOR PAYMENT FROM THE HOLIDAY INN, CLEARVIEW, FLORIDA.
(Courtesy of Horizon Business Systems, Naples, Florida.)

outstanding. This allows management to identify the number of events for which invoices are still outstanding. In addition, it allows for a profile of payments showing that a total of $446,336.10 is outstanding, of which 11.9% is over 120 days in arrears. The sales department can be asked to assist accounting by calling these companies to try to expedite payments while still

10/28/98

Order Number: 9698

Horizon Business Services, Inc. - Office Party
P.O. Box 577
Naples, FL 34102 U.S.A.

INVOICE

Event Held On Friday, July 25, 1997

PARTY NAME Office Party	EVENT THEME Office Party		SALES REPRESENTATIVE Gail Snow	TELEPHONE (941) 261-5828
BOOKING CONTACT George Kopriva	SITE CONTACT Chris Johns		GUESTS 125 (Act)	FAX (941) 261-0067

	Food	Bev	Equip	Room	Other	Total
Subtotal	3,400.00	2,430.50	85.00	500.00	0.00	6,415.50
Service Charge:	612.00	437.49	15.30	90.00	0.00	1,154.79
Tax:	310.93	222.27	7.77	45.73	0.00	586.70
Total	4,322.93	3,090.26	108.07	635.73	0.00	8,156.99

Paid:	1,000.00
Balance:	7,156.99

PAYMENT METHOD Credit Card	APPROVAL GFDI1105	CARD NAME Chris Johns	EXP DATE 10/10/1998
CARD TYPE American Express	CARD NUMBER 3811 4411 4876 6666	CARD HOLDER SIGNATURE	

Please remit the "Total Balance Due" within 30 days of the Event Date.
Address all corrrespondence to John Hurd, Catering Director.
Thank you for this opportunity to serve you.

Holiday Inn Select - 2400 Mainsail - Clearview, FL 36609
Phone: (902) 783-0300   Fax: (902) 783-5525

Page 1 Of 1

FIGURE 9-10   ALTERNATIVE FORMAT FOR THE INVOICE FORM FROM THE HOLIDAY INN, CLEARVIEW, FLORIDA.
(Courtesy of Horizon Business Systems, Naples, Florida.)

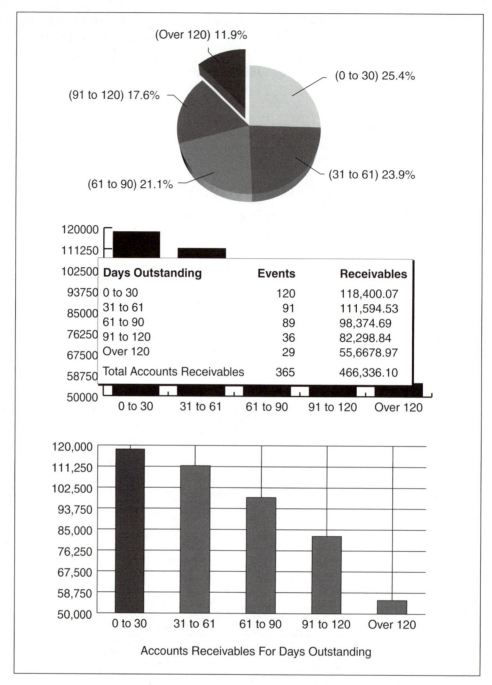

Days Outstanding	Events	Receivables
0 to 30	120	118,400.07
31 to 61	91	111,594.53
61 to 90	89	98,374.69
91 to 120	36	82,298.84
Over 120	29	55,6678.97
Total Accounts Receivables	365	466,336.10

FIGURE 9-11   ACCOUNTS RECEIVABLE CHART.
(Courtesy of Horizon Business Systems, Naples, Florida.)

maintaining a good client relationship. This analysis also flags accounts that should be evaluated before accepting for future bookings.

FORECASTING

An essential marketing tool for any organization is forecasting. For catering operations, forecasting is generally done on a quarterly basis for the upcom-

EVENT CALENDAR   **March, 2000**

Order #	Organization	Site Contact	Start	End	Theme	Pln/Act	Total
3-02-2000, Thursday							
T 9310	Florida Southern College	Brenda Lewis	08:00 AM	09:00 PM	Meeting	12/12	$186.14
							$186.14
3-06-2000, Monday							
9319	Alpha Delta Kappa	Sarah Johnson	09:00 AM	02:00 PM	Social	100/100	$1,384.36
9349	Erbes/Rogers Wed Recp	Edward Aaron	06:00 PM	12:00 AM	Reception	150/150	$556.50
							$1,940.86
3-07-2000, Tuesday							
9320	Royal Oak Reunion	Georgia Canover	10:00 AM	03:00 PM	Reunion	80/80	$170.66
							$170.66
3-13-2000, Monday							
9342	Allentown H.S. School	Charles Hills	01:00 PM	12:00 AM	Banquet	80/80	$356.58
9318	Guthrie/Davis Reception	Melissa Guthrie	03:30 PM	08:30 PM	Reception	150/150	$4,177.25
							$4,533.83
3-14-2000, Tuesday							
9343	Allentown H.S. School	Charles Hills	09:00 AM	11:00 AM	Banquet	30/30	$318.21
							$318.21
3-20-2000, Monday							
9317	DECHAMP/DONOHUE	Conrad Getts	05:00 PM	12:00 AM	Reception	150/150	$397.50
							$397.50
3-21-2000, Tuesday							
9346	Omega Psi Phi	Kent Swartz	03:00 PM	07:00 PM	Meeting	100/100	$466.40
							$466.40
							$8,013.60

Page 2 of 2

FIGURE 9-12   EVENT CALENDAR.
(Courtesy of Horizon Business Systems,
Naples, Florida.)

ing six-month period. In Figure 9-12 an event calendar for the period from March 2 to 21, 2000 forecasts expected revenue for a variety of functions. Each function is listed by account number and type of function. Figure 9-13 is the graphic representation of Figure 9-12. The number 2 or 1 in the lower right corner of various calendar boxes indicates the number of functions scheduled for that day. The two bar graphs compare the forecast of the number of events booked against estimated revenues for a twelve-month period.

Forecasting is a critical function for any business operation. Management needs to have an honest appraisal of future business both for volume and estimated value. This overview can produce marketing analysis and sales programs to increase business volume or analysis of costs and profitability margins to ensure that maximum profits are made from each function. Not having a valid understanding of future business can result in business failures.

EVENT CALENDAR
March, 2000

As of 10/26/1998

Events: **9**
Value: **$8,013.60**

SUN	MON	TUE	WED	THU	FRI	SAT
				1	2	3
					_1_	
4	5	6	7	8	9	10
		_2_	_1_			
11	12	13	14	15	16	17
		_2_	_1_			
18	19	20	21	22	23	24
		_1_	_1_			
25	26	27	29	30	31	

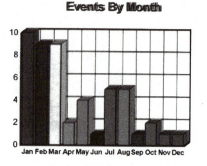

Events By Month

Event Sales By Month

FIGURE 9-13   GRAPHIC REPRESENTATION OF AN EVENT CALENDAR.
(Courtesy of Horizon Business Systems, Naples, Florida.)

Reporting Forms

A variety of additional reports and forms can be generated by catering software programs. Function room diagrams, booking allocation records, and calendar reports keep catering sales management and staff up-to-date on the current status of the sales of function rooms.

Off-premise catering functions can be assisted by packing sheets such as featured in Figure 9-14. In this form the function sheet in Figure 9-14 adds columns to indicate which items have been sent from the kitchen and subsequently received at the off-premise location. This system of checks and balances can help to quickly identify last minute missing items before the service time. In Figure 9-15, the software program has generated an overview of events scheduled for the period from December 17 to December 23, 1997. This form is issued to all departments on a weekly basis. Overviews help to

Packing Sheet   **Distinquished Service Awards**

Customer: **Dean White**
Date: Thursday May 30, 2002   Contact: Dean White   Cont #: 97000034
Time: 6:00 pm To   12:00 am   Phone: (317) 894-1564
Guests: 325   Cmpny: ABC Television
Event Type: Reception Dinner/Bar   Addr 1:   2709 Colonial Dr.
Svc Type: Sit Down   Addr 2:   Suite 2000
Setup: Circle Table & Chair   City, St: Indianapolis IN 46250
Room: Grand Ball Room

_____Times_____
4:00 pm   Setup Time on May 30, 2002
6:15 pm   Hors d'oeuvres served
6:00 pm   Bar Opens
7:30 pm   Meal starts
9:00 pm   Meal ends
7:30 pm   Bar Closes

_____Orders_____	Ordered	Sent	Returned
Jumbo Prawn on Ice	600	_____	_____
Crabmeat Stuffed Mushroom Caps	650	_____	_____
Crudite w/Mango Habanero Salsa	6	_____	_____
Turkey Cakes Presented With	325	_____	_____
Jumbo Prawn and Mustard			
Tarragon Sauce			
Spinach Salad with Sage Derby Cheese,	325	_____	_____
Pears and Toasted Pine Nuts			
Maple Cranberry Vinaigrette			
Brochette Of Tenderloin Dinner	325	_____	_____
with Maderia Wine Sauce			
Bed of Wild Rice		_____	_____
Grilled Baby Vegetables		_____	_____
Crusty French Bread	70	_____	_____
Sweet Cream Butter		_____	_____

Staff:
Joseph Paulson - Bartender
Margaret Ann Pepperney - Wait Staff
Jessica Peyton - Wait Staff
Russ Nelson - Wait Staff
Charlene Monihan - Chef
Mark Baker - Chef
Vaclav Sonorak - Wait Staff
Brian Anderson - Wait Staff
Marie Denaston - Wait Staff
Special Instructions:
Please remove all ash trays from tables per Mr. White's request.
Please press white skirts prior to event. Setup AV on north side with screen on north-east corner.
Mr. White will be sending place cards with floor plan.

FIGURE 9-14   OFF-PREMISE CATERING SHIPMENT FORM.
(Courtesy of Cater Mate, Indianapolis, IN.)

identify potential problems, conflicts, and overall business volume, in addition to assisting in future planning.

Catering and foodservice software programs can also provide recipe cards, sales mix analysis reports, inventory reports, and other information that provides vital information to management regarding the current status of business so important to successful management practices.

Holiday Inn Select

2400 Mainsail

Clearview, FL 36609

EVENT SHEET

Report Date: 12/17/1997

Organization	Order	Theme	Room		Start	End	Serving
			Wednesday - December 17,				
Riverside Rotary Club	4223	Lunch	Spanish Art Gall		11:30 am	02:00 pm	11:45 am
Inland Chapter of Accountants	8201	Cocktails/Dinner	S Juan Capistrano		05:30 pm	09:00 pm	06:30 pm
			S Juan Capistrano		06:00 pm	07:00 pm	06:00 pm
GTE	1425	Dinner/Dance	Glenwood Tavern		06:00 pm	11:59 pm	06:00 pm
			Music Room		06:00 pm	11:59 pm	07:00 pm
American Building Maintenanc	4290	Dinner	San Diego	50 (Act)	06:30 pm	11:59 pm	07:00 pm
			Thursday - December 18, 1997				
Airforce Audit Agency	C 1422	Lunch	Spanish Art Gall	80 (Act)	11:00 am	03:00 pm	12:00 pm
Life Care Center of Corona	1426	Dinner/Dance	Music Room	150 (Act)	06:00 pm	11:59 pm	07:00 pm
			Friday - December 19, 1997				
Republican Women	9613	Meeting	S Juan Capistrano	30 (Act)	11:00 am	01:30 pm	11:45 am
All American Asphalt	9673	Lunch	Santa Barbara	32 (Act)	11:00 am	03:00 pm	12:30 pm
Kaiser Mental Health	9616	Dinner	Glenwood Tavern	150 (Act)	06:00 pm	11:59 pm	06:00 pm
			Music Room	150 (Act)	06:00 pm	11:59 pm	07:00 pm
			Saturday - December 20, 1997				
Pamela Carrey/Robert Neice	1429	Wedding & Rece	St Francis	130 (Act)	10:00 am	12:00 pm	10:30 am
			Atrio	130 (Act)	11:00 am	04:00 pm	11:00 am
			Galleria	130 (Act)	11:00 am	04:00 pm	12:00 pm
B M W of Riverside	4553	Dinner	H O -O- Kan	50 (Act)	06:00 pm	11:59 pm	11:30 am
Southwest Controls	5217	Dinner/Dance	Santa Barbara	40 (Act)	06:00 pm	11:59 pm	
Luxfer, Inc	8202	Dinner/Dance	Galleria	150 (Act)	06:00 pm	11:59 pm	07:00 pm
			Sunday - December 21, 1997				
Cecil/Berninger	5222	Wedding Ceremo	St Francis	150 (Act)	03:00 pm	05:00 pm	
Madonna Knapik	1421	Wedding & Rece	St Francis	80 (Act)	06:00 pm	08:00 pm	06:30 pm
			Atrio	80 (Act)	07:00 pm	12:30 am	07:00 pm
			Galleria	80 (Act)	07:00 pm	12:30 am	08:00 pm
Nissan of Temecula	5218	Dinner/Dance	Music Room	150 (Act)	06:00 pm	11:59 pm	12:15 pm
			Tuesday - December 23, 1997				
K & N Engineering	5219	Dinner/Dance	Spanish Art Gall	80 (Act)	06:00 pm	11:59 pm	

FIGURE 9-15   AN OVERVIEW OF EVENTS SCHEDULED.

(Courtesy of Horizon Business Systems, Naples, Florida.)

Desktop Publishing

As discussed in the chapter on catering menu design, computer generated menus using design oriented software are especially effective in reducing the costs of catering menus. A number of examples have been reviewed and discussed in Chapter Six. Figure 9-16 is an example of a catering promotion for a wedding package that was prepared with a desktop publishing system. Photographs have been scanned and transferred to the page setup to act as a theme illustration. Printed in color, this concept creates an attractive page design that will stand out from other competitors' packages that are being considered.

FIGURE 9-16   CATERING PROMOTION FOR A WEDDING PACKAGE.
(Courtesy of the Hyatt Regency Albuquerque, New Mexico.)

Summary

Computer software programs provide catering management valuable tools with which to achieve profitable and efficient operations. A wide variety of software programs is available offering a range of reporting facilities and capabilities. Foodservice operators expanding into catering area will find that many of these programs are compatible with their existing computer systems.

The success of catering foodservice businesses is greatly enhanced by using software programs in the areas of marketing, purchasing inventory, production forecasting and analyses, sales mix, costing, and accounting. Word processing has numerous applications including sales files and contracts and correspondence. Desktop publishing software programs can assist marketing efforts with the production of newsletters, brochures, and menu package design. The ability to create menu design with typeface fonts and symbols offers every catering operation the ability to do its own in-house menu design.

Managing Catering Employees

CHAPTER TEN

Employee Organization

Managing any form of business organization requires an understanding of people in the workplace. The organization of management and line staff in catering operations is presented in the organizational chart in Figure 10-1. Whether catering services are incorporated into a restaurant or a hotel, or function as an independent operation, the organizational structure shown in Figure 10-1 is basic to them all.

A catering organization is made up of three primary areas: management, sales, and service. As seen in Figure 10-1, overall management is the responsibility of the director of catering or food and beverage director, catering sales and marketing by the catering sales manager, and catering service by the catering service manager. Responsibilities for the direction of the catering kitchen flow through the executive chef.

The catering organizational chart in a hotel flows from the food and beverage director's position and in a restaurant, the manager's position. A catering sales manager position is critical to a catering service organization whether those responsibilities are assumed by a restaurant manager or carried out by a designated catering sales director.

CATERING SALES

The director of catering or the catering sales manager is responsible for the overall sales and service of the catering department. Depending on the vol-

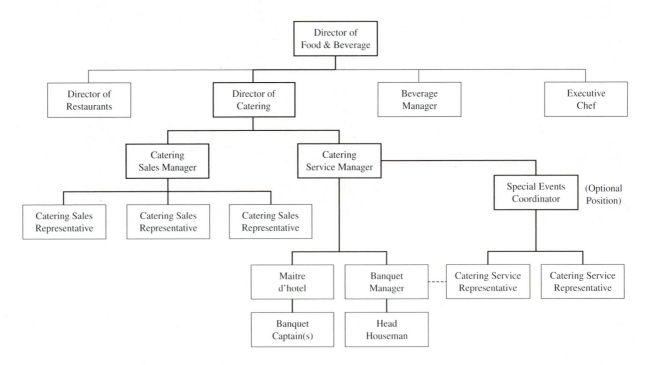

FIGURE 10-1   ORGANIZATIONAL CHART FOR A CATERING OPERATION, SHOWING MANAGEMENT, SALES, AND SERVICE.

ume of catering sales and service, this position may be supported by an assistant director and/or a number of catering sales representatives. Secretarial staff are present according to the needs of the business operation.

The director of catering is responsible for developing and implementing the marketing plan and creating sales programs. This position requires a wide range of product knowledge from food and wine to special events and current trends. In addition, the director must have a working knowledge of both business and social functions in the location of the business. If the catering operation is part of a convention property and/or hotel, the director will work closely with the director of sales and marketing to coordinate food and beverage functions for group meetings.

Catering sales representatives handle social and business accounts. Often, one or two sales associates will be assigned to the room sales division to assist with group meetings while another sales representative concentrates on local business and social functions. Again, the delegation of accounts and the number of staff available will depend on the overall volume of catering sales.

Catering Service

The catering service manager is responsible for scheduling all banquet service personnel. This includes banquet captains, servers, and room setup staff. The catering service manager is also responsible for banquet service training and the overall quality of service delivery. This includes both table service and function room setup. In large catering operations there may also be an assistant to the catering service manager.

In addition to scheduling service staff, the catering service manager will be responsible for planning linen and equipment requisitions and for maintaining a stock of table condiments and nonalcoholic beverages. Maintenance and storage of props, lighting, and special function equipment will also be included in overall responsibilities. In large convention halls and hotels this position works closely with engineering and audiovisual managers to ensure that guest requirements are met, that safety standards are maintained, and that special effects and audiovisual equipment are available.

Catering Food Production

In many hotel operations, the sous-chef is assigned responsibility for overseeing catering food production, often with the assistance of a chef familiar with volume production. In an independent catering operation, the executive chef must be experienced in volume food production, rather than à la carte restaurant food preparation. Catering function forms directed from the catering sales office form the basis for all food and beverage orders for catering functions.

As discussed in the section on catering menu development and menu planning, it is critical that menus be planned with an understanding of catering food production requirements. Whether a catering kitchen is producing for two or twenty functions, menus that are coordinated with one another to maximize food quality and costs are necessary for a successful operation.

CATERING BEVERAGE MANAGEMENT

In a hotel property the position of beverage manager is responsible for banquet beverages. This includes both wine and hard liquors. In addition, this position is responsible for the training of banquet bartenders as well as the equipment for banquet bar service. Purchasing of banquet beverages is based on the catering function forms issued by the catering sales office. In a restaurant or independent catering operation, beverage operations are managed by the restaurant manager or the catering service manager.

Employee Management

The labor market in the United States in the beginning of the twenty-first century poses many challenges for foodservice businesses. Unemployment rates are low and the economy is strong. These two factors combine to create an increased demand for both catering functions and the staff with which to service them.

In catering operations employees fall into one of two general categories: full- or part-time. Management personnel are generally full-time employees. Service and kitchen staff are often part-time employees.

Catering service offers part-time employment to a wide range of employee sources. Part-time catering employment, unlike many other part-time positions, offers the benefit scheduled in of highly flexible hours and advance scheduling. Banquet service managers maintain lists of part-time service employees who make themselves available according to their personal schedules. Homemakers, students, retirees, and those looking for second-job opportunities regard catering service as an ideal part-time employment. In today's marketplace, demand often exceeds availability and servers who associate themselves with more than one catering business can work as many hours a week as they can manage.

Catering service staff, in many cities, are organized through the office of the local union. As the labor unions have lost their power in the last decades of the twentieth century, catering service staff has become a mixture of union and nonunion members. The ability of banquet service managers to hire both union and nonunion staff members depends on the strength of a union contract with a hotel or convention facility. Figure 10-2 outlines the process of recruiting, hiring, training, and evaluating employees.

RECRUITING

In a nonunion market, banquet service managers begin to recruit their staff by advertising for service staff positions. As the service staff demand for a catering operation can fluctuate greatly from one day to the next, a large pool of part-time staff is needed to fill volume service requirements. In instances in which a minimum amount of catering service demand is always present, such as a hotel, a small core of catering service staff can be employed full-time. These individuals handle all types of catering service from meeting breaks and small functions to large parties. The catering service manager begins to determine his or her staffing needs based on the avail-

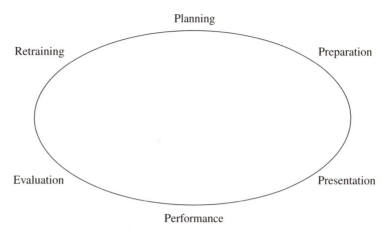

FIGURE 10-2   TRAINING CYCLE CHART.

ability of the full-time staff. From this core, the part-time staff are then scheduled according to availability.

An important responsibility in scheduling part-time help is not to exceed the maximum hours necessary to maintain part-time employment status. The cost of a part-time employee is significantly less that of a full-time employee. Part-time employees are not paid the benefits that full-time employees enjoy. Depending on the company, full-time employees can cost employers from 25 to 50 percent of their salaries in overall benefits ranging from health insurance to stock options.

Service standards are an important part of the overall success of any hospitality organization. Part-time status does not exclude employees from training. To ensure that general service standards are maintained, training is included in the overall staffing and evaluation process for part-time as well as full-time catering service personnel.

In a large business organization the human resources or personnel department will handle the operational processes of recruiting and selecting employees. The catering service manager advises the personnel director of the full- and part-time staffing needs. From this point on the recruiting and initial selection of acceptable candidates is handled by the personnel department. Immigration status, work permits, job history, criminal records, and other important selection criteria are covered in the initial review process.

Acceptable candidates are then referred to the catering service manager for interviews. During the interview process the applicant's ability to perform the level of service required is determined, along with other important qualifications such as attitude, appearance, and communication skills. The final list of acceptable candidates is then forwarded to the personnel office, who advises the prospective employees and completes the formal hiring process.

HIRING

In an operation that does not have a management position devoted to personnel issues, hiring is the responsibility of individual department managers or the general manager. Hiring employees is one of the most challenging management activities. Customer service employees play a key role in the operation and success of a hospitality business. Identifying candidates who are both qualified and capable of expressing a "hospitality attitude" is essential for customer service activities. In addition, the laws surrounding the hiring and firing of employees require that employers be well versed as to how they can be legally affected by the hiring and firing process.

The primary laws that can affect managers of catering operations are:

- The Americans with Disabilities Act (ADA)
- The Immigration Reform and Control Act of 1986
- Child labor laws (State and Federal)
- Fair Labor Standards Act of 1938

The Americans with Disabilities Act (ADA) protects the rights of individuals with disabilities to have equal opportunity to employment as people without disabilities. The Americans with Disabilities Act Questions and Answers (Washington, D.C.) p. 2, Office on the Americans with Disabilities Act, U.S. Department of Justice, states that an employer may not discriminate against a qualified person who can perform the necessary functions of a job position:

> *A qualified individual with a disability is a person who meets legitimate skill, experience, education, and or other requirements of an employee position that he or she holds or seeks, and who can perform the "essential functions" with or without reasonable accommodation. If the individual is qualified to perform essential job functions except for limitations caused by the disability, the employer must consider whether the individual could perform these functions with a reasonable accommodation. If a written job description is prepared in advance of advertising or interviewing applicants for a job, this will be considered as evidence, although not necessarily conclusive evidence, of the essential functions of the job.*

In the foodservice industry, in particular, employers should be well aware of the ramifications of not writing job descriptions that cover all eventualities of food service and production. Identifying future problems with prospective employees regarding their ability to perform tasks will require employers to recognize disabilities and understand how a disability may limit an individual's ability to perform specific tasks related to a job position. The ADA defines the term disability as follows:

- An impairment that substantially limits one or more major life activities, such as walking, hearing, speaking, seeing, learning, or working.
- A record of an impairment that substantially limits major activities from which the individual is recovering or has recovered.
- An assumption by others that an impairment exists which in actuality does not, such as the presence of hearing aids and severe scarring from accidents or burns.

Providing reasonable accommodation to employees requires that existing facilities be made accessible to disabled employees, by reorganizing job functions, modifying or adapting equipment, educational programs, and training materials.

While there are specific requirements that employers must meet in the practices of hiring, training, and firing under the Americans with Disabilities Act, employers are also given the right to reject applicants or fire employees who pose a significant risk to the health and safety of other individuals in the workplace. As this law is constantly being challenged, resulting court decisions change the context of the law. Therefore, employers are advised to make themselves aware of the current status of the law as it affects food and beverage businesses and catering operations in particular.

Immigration laws are another area in which employers who handle large volumes of part-time employees can put themselves at risk. To avoid heavy fines and criminal penalties for knowingly or unknowingly violating federal immigration laws, management should investigate current requirements thoroughly and:

- Require all employees to present valid documentation of their immigration and naturalization status, without exception
- Establish employment eligibility for all employees, without exception
- Maintain complete sets of required paperwork for each employee
- Maintain a copy of all documents in each employee file

Child labor laws can be especially challenging for food and beverage operators. In the United States, specific guidelines have been established by each state as to the minimum age and number of hours that a young person may work. As these guidelines differ from state to state, it is recommended that employers make themselves knowledgeable about guidelines and laws in their immediate area. Failure to comply with child labor laws can result in heavy fines. Part-time employment poses increased challenges; some jurisdictions hold an employer responsible for having knowledge of the total hours worked by a minor, even if the employee accumulates time with another part-time employer.

Interviewing a job candidate in the United States requires an understanding of the guidelines issued by the Equal Employment Opportunity Commission as to what a prospective employee can and cannot be asked. The interviewer may not ask questions that would require the applicant to supply information revealing the following:

Name: In so far as it might serve to indicate national origin, marital status, or original name.

Birthplace: Birthplace of applicant or applicant's parents.

Religion: Applicant's religious preference or affiliation as well as church or parish attended and religious holidays observed.

Age: Age or date of birth except where such information is necessary in order to satisfy state or local laws such as child labor laws and employee benefit programs.

Sex: Sex, marital status, or number of dependents.

Race: Applicant's race or skin color.

Marital status: Whether an applicant is single, divorced, married, or widowed or the number of children or intent to have children.

Citizenship: Applicant and applicant's family's citizenship or date of U.S. citizenship or status of naturalization.*

Military record: Eligibility for military service or date and conditions of discharge.

Arrest record: Arrest record unless directly related to the responsibilities of the job.

Handicaps: If a handicap exists and the extent of the handicap.

The increasing shortage of labor for foodservice operations discussed earlier in this chapter can cause managers to overlook federal and state laws in order to secure sufficient staff to operate their businesses. It is suggested, however, that by so doing they are putting both their employees and their interests in jeopardy.

Orientation and Evaluation

Orientation is the introduction of an employee to your business and its standards and operating procedures. Full-time and regular part-time employees should be required to attend an orientation program along with their initial training. It is during the orientation process that probationary or trial periods of employment are initiated. Guidelines for job orientation include:

- Employee policies and guidelines for each employee.
- A complete job description for each position.
- The formal training calendar.

The probationary employment period allow employers to set up a conditional employment time wherein new employees must perform to established standards as a condition of permanent employment. Failure to meet these standards is the basis for termination. Labor laws in the United States have been developed to protect the employee, rather than the employer. As a result, once an employee is considered a permanent member of a business staff it is difficult to fire that employee without having documented his or her failure to perform through a series of written reprimands along with coaching and counseling opportunities.

In addition, employees who feel that they have been terminated on insufficient grounds can, under the law, cause employers to keep them on the payroll during the time in which their case is reviewed by local and state employment agencies. With this in mind, it is important that provisional employment periods provide sufficient opportunities to evaluate and termi-

*A prospective employee's citizenship status may not be used as a criterion for offering a job position. However, the candidate must show valid evidence of his or her employment eligibility and be able to produce proof of citizenship or valid documentation of visas or naturalization status before the formal hiring process is completed.

TABLE 10-1 EMPLOYEE EVALUATION CALENDAR

	THIRTY-DAY PERIOD	NINETY-DAY PERIOD
WEEK 1	ORIENTATION/TRAINING	ORIENTATION
WEEK 2	TRAINING/EVALUATION	TRAINING
WEEK 3	JOB PERFORMANCE	JOB PERFORMANCE
WEEK 4	EVALUATION/PERFORMANCE JOB STATUS DETERMINED	EVALUATION/COACHING AND COUNSELING
WEEKS 5 AND 6		TRAINING AND JOB PERFORMANCE
WEEK 7		EVALUATION/COACHING AND COUNSELING
WEEKS 8 AND 9		JOB PERFORMANCE
WEEK 10		EVALUATION/RELEASE OR CONDITIONAL CONTINUED EMPLOYMENT
WEEKS 11 AND 12		JOB PERFORMANCE
WEEK 12		FINAL EVALUATION/JOB STATUS DETERMINED

nate employees who prove unsatisfactory before their positions become permanent.

Evaluations are scheduled during training and the initial service performance period. Table 10-1 outlines suggested thirty- and ninety-day probationary periods.

Training

Creating a consistent standard of service requires that a level of quality service be identified for the catering operation and a critical path of banquet service developed by which to deliver it, as discussed in Chapter Eleven under standards of operation.

The challenge for the catering service manager is to develop a team of full- and part-time employees who are trained to deliver a consistent standard of quality service. To accomplish this, all members of the catering service team must be scheduled to take part in a formal training program. It may be difficult to convince prospective part-time employees of the value of spending time in training programs for which they are paid a nontipped minimum wage. When the labor market is tight and demand is high, prospective employees feel that they can choose employers and may resist attending training programs. At this point it becomes the responsibility of a good catering facility to demand training as a condition of employment on the basis that consistent quality service generates business and results in greater financial rewards for all employees.

Employers must make the choice between sacrificing the immediate need for service staff for the long-term result of quality guest service. This may require that the current service staff stretch themselves to cover business service demands until the quality of additional staff can meet established standards. This is a problem common to all hospitality businesses, creating the challenge of providing consistent quality service to customers on a daily basis. Both individual companies and hospitality corporations that have chosen to create service standards that all employees are required to meet have benefited from the long-term financial results of customer satisfaction.

TRAINING PROGRAMS

Training programs are developed to meet the immediate and long-range goals and objectives of a catering business. A training program will need to respond to the complexities that a combined full- and part-time staff present.

The overall goal of a catering company may be:

To provide a consistent standard of quality banquet service

In order to accomplish this goal a training program will need to meet the following objectives of:

Objective One: Providing employees with basic banquet service skills for both American service and Russian service
Objective Two: Providing basic training for attitude, appearance, and communication for catering service
Objective Three: Providing employees with advanced catering service standard skills
Objective Four: Providing employees with catering product and sales knowledge for increased on-time sales*

Each of these objectives can be reached with the development of a training program that offers four individual training modules; these modules should be offered to current and new employees on a schedule that responds both to the employees' measured performance in meeting each module's objective and to management's ability to schedule training.

TRAINING METHODS

Training modules are designed to be presented in a variety of formats, depending on the objectives for the training. Basic training methods are classified as:

- Lecture format
- Individual and team activities

---

*On-time sales refers to sales made to the customer immediately prior to or during a function, such as additions to meeting breaks, alcoholic beverage services, and menu items.

Information can be offered in a variety of formats including written manuals, interactive computer software programs, CD-ROMs, video programs, and live presentations.

Training activities should be accompanied by a method of measuring the employees' understanding of the concepts presented. Measurement vehicles can include:

- Demonstration/performance
- Written and oral testing
- Interactive training materials
- Customer comment programs
- Tracking of sales records

The results of measurement activities provide employers with the documentation of employee performance and ability. Measurement provides employees with the evidence of their successes and can increase job satisfaction. Measurement also provides employers with the evidence of noncompliance or inability to perform job functions that is required to successfully terminate employees.

TRAINING BENEFITS

Employee participation and satisfactory performance of each training module can be recognized by a variety of methods ranging from incentive prizes to increases in hourly pay. All training activities should be accompanied by an identification of accompanying benefits. Benefits for the employee include financial return and job satisfaction in addition to planned incentives.

The "return on investment" for training activities to a catering business are significant. In addition to the obvious benefit of increased sales and profits, training also:

- Reduces turnover and increases job attendance
- Establishes a consistent standard of quality service product
- Develops employee loyalty and long-term employment
- Reduces customer complaints and accompanying losses

TRAINING CYCLE

Training programs are developed along a series of guidelines known as the training cycle, as seen in Figure 10-2.

The training cycle outline consists of:

- **Planning:** Establish the goals and objectives for every training activity.
- **Preparation:** Identify the amount of time required for each training activity. Design training to incorporate a variety of activities and teaching methods appropriate to the needs of those being trained.
- **Presentation:** Introduce training modules that present information in an interesting and effective manner and that have specific measurable objectives in employee performance.

- **Performance:** Create guidelines for trainees to effectively perform training activities during service.
- **Evaluation:** Design evaluation criteria that fairly measure the employees' understanding of the process for which they were trained.
- **Retraining:** Coach the employee in those areas in which performance did not meet the expected measurement of process understanding. Provide the opportunity for additional performance evaluations.

Summary

While catering operations provide the challenge of a mixed full- and part-time staff, management is required to effectively hire and train employees in a effort to contribute to the overall profitability of its operations. Employee recruitment, training, and maintenance is a major operating cost.

The staffing and evaluation process is critical to the effective management of the employment process. When hiring individuals it is important to be aware of the laws that govern employee rights. Failure to do so could result in a business suffering heavy fines for failure to comply with federal and state laws.

Training for all employees, regardless of full- or part-time status, is critical to achieving company goals and objectives. Maintaining a standard of quality service requires a well-developed training program and an ongoing training cycle that responds to the needs of both new and long-term employees.

uality
tandards

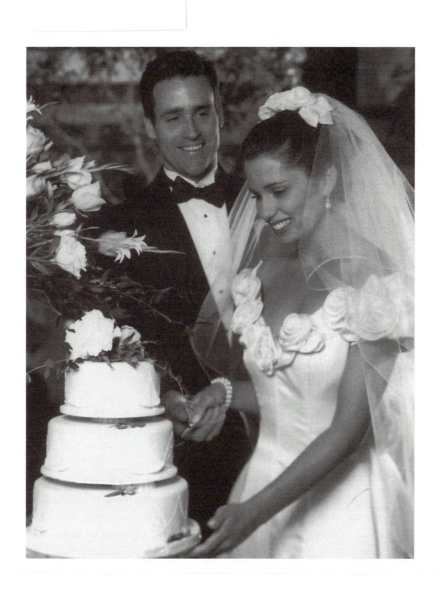

Quality

The term "Quality" is difficult to define in relation to hospitality operations but easy to recognize. Quality is a perception of how good or bad a product is based on an individual's points of reference. A "quality" experience for someone who has never stayed in a first class hotel may be completely different than for someone who regularly patronizes luxury level resorts and hotels. Customers whose foodservice experience has been limited to fast-food and casual restaurants will have a different perception of a "quality" experience than customers who regularly patronize full-service restaurants. Customers with a wide range of experience often have a higher standard of quality expectation and a much lower level of tolerance for erratic service and poor food. The more frequently customers patronize a business, the more critical they will be if the standard of quality that they have come to expect is not maintained.

The problem of meeting guests' expectations in regard to catering is especially problematic for large hotel companies. Business customers who book meetings and functions at a number of hotels in a particular chain expect to receive the same level of service at each hotel property. Unless service and food production standards are established company-wide, customers will be greeted with a wide range of levels of quality experiences.

Establishing Quality

The first step in establishing quality is to identify the level of "quality" to be produced. An overall level of quality for products and services should be determined for the particular target markets that a catering business services.

The initial way to identify a level of quality is financial value, both selling price and cost. The answers to the following questions can often establish the level of financial value of catering products:

1. Are selling prices in the low, medium, or high range of prices for similar services and items in the marketplace?
2. Is the cost of product low, medium, or high in respect to prices for similar items in the marketplace?

If selling prices are in the low end of the market, it can be assumed that the level of "quality" that customers expect and receive from your business is lower than that of other catering companies whose costs and prices are high. Catering businesses whose prices are mid-range can be assumed to provide a medium level of "quality" product and service.

Assumptions, however, are not always accurate. Some caterers offering prices in the low range sacrifice profit for volume business and produce high quality product and service. This type of operating standard can force other catering companies in the area to do the same, creating a price war that eventually results in profit being sacrificed by everyone until some operators either raise their prices or go out of business.

The location and type of facilities in which catering functions are held also helps to identify the quality level. Exclusive locations and expensively decorated interiors are a large part of the quality experience, raising both costs and prices. Expensive floral arrangements, entertainment, menu items, tableware, linens, and decorations all add to increased levels of quality and customer cost.

Not all customers want, or can afford, a high level of quality product and services. As discussed in the chapters on marketing and pricing, it is important for a business to determine at what level of the marketplace they are competing. The goal for a catering operation is to provide the best possible product and service at the level of quality that customers expect from the business.

The following keys to creating quality customer service successfully are common to all businesses and apply equally to catering service as well as to retail sales:

Keys to Creating Quality Customer Service

- Give the customers quality product and service.
- Match or exceed the customers' expectations of product and service.
- Provide the customers with what they want *and* what they need.
- Plan customer service recoveries.

Along with sound business practices, satisfying the customer is the key to overall success. Satisfied customers result in:

- Increased revenues and profits
- Increased function sales
- Long-term customer relationships
- Employee job satisfaction and retention

In addition to customer satisfaction, it is also important to set consistent standards for presentation and delivery of a number of elements in a catering operation:

- Quality of food
- Quality of overall service
- Pricing concepts
- Service styles
- Quality of function facilities
- Creative function planning

While food, pricing, facilities, and function planning are discussed in other sections of this book, service standards are covered in this chapter.

CATERING SERVICE

In a discussion of service for catering operations it is common to concentrate on food and beverage service delivery. Service, from the customer's point of view, however, begins at the first contact with a catering business. It is these initial experiences with a catering business that form a customer's first impressions of the overall level of "quality" that can be expected for meetings and functions.

In the training programs for Walt Disney Company theme parks, the opportunities that customers have to make a value judgment as to the quality of products and services are called "Magic Moments." These opportunities are perceived to be the critical customer contact points in which Walt Disney employees and facilities must meet or exceed customer expectations if the company is to maintain its competitive edge in the theme park industry. For the average theme park customers, the Walt Disney Company has identified the first two "Magic Moments" in their visit as the ability of guests to locate the park entrance from the highway and to park their cars. Park signage and the ease with which customers can both find parking spaces and transportation to the park ticket booths are critical to establishing quality expectations for the rest of their visit.

In a catering business the opportunities to meet customer expectations begin with the introduction to the business, either through personal reference or advertising. The second critical point is the quality of the initial phone contact or visit. Figure 11-1 outlines the critical path of customer service for the average catering business.

SERVICE GAPS

A service gap is the term used to identify those moments in which customer expectations are not met. These can be at any point in the service delivery when a customer does not receive the quality of service or product that he

1. POINT OF REFERENCE (PERSONAL REFERRAL OR ADVERTISEMENT)
2. INITIAL PHONE CALL AND/OR PROPERTY VISIT
3. TIMELINESS OF RESPONSE TO INQUIRY REQUESTS (BROCHURES, MENUS, APPOINTMENTS)
4. PROPERTY LOCATION SIGNAGE AND DIRECTIONS
5. PARKING
6. CURB APPEAL OF PROPERTY LANDSCAPING AND EXTERIOR
7. INITIAL WELCOME BY RECEPTION STAFF
8. SITE TOUR AND SALES MEETING
9. TIMELINESS AND COMPLETENESS OF FUNCTION PROPOSAL
10. PREFUNCTION ARRANGEMENTS
11. ACCURACY OF FUNCTION SETUP
12. QUALITY OF FOOD PRESENTATION AND PRODUCT
13. QUALITY OF FOOD AND BEVERAGE SERVICE
14. FOLLOW-THROUGH OF FUNCTION ARRANGEMENTS
15. INVOICING AND PAYMENT POLICIES
16. POSTFUNCTION FOLLOW-UP

FIGURE 11-1   CRITICAL PATH OF CUSTOMER SERVICE.

or she had been led to expect. To customers, "service gaps" can range from the way in which they are treated during a telephone call to the quality of a meal or the accuracy of the invoice for a catering function.

As service gaps are often perceived by the customer, rather than by management and service staff, they may go undetected, creating customer dissatisfaction and ultimately the loss of business. The first way to identify service gaps is to listen to customers and establish a policy that any customer complaint is documented and relayed to the responsible department and/or supervisor. The sooner that customer problems are identified, the faster they can be recovered from.

Often a service gap is not an actual complaint but a perception of a service not having been performed as the customer thought that it would be or of a product not being up to anticipated standards. It is these service gaps that are most difficult to recover from. In order to identify the "service gaps" in your operation ask the following questions:

- What products and services do customers complain about most frequently?
- What products and services do customers request most frequently?
- Can these services and products be provided more effectively?
- How are the needs and expectations of guests not being met?
- What steps need to be taken to reduce the "service gaps" in the operation?
- What are the "recovery plans" for service gaps? How is the customer reacted to and what steps are taken to "recover" customer disappointments or complaints?

SERVICE RECOVERY

A service recovery is a preplanned action in response to a customer complaint or comment. For example, if a customer complains that his or her eggs are cold, the planned recovery is to return the eggs to the kitchen and either reheat or replace the food item. If meat is undercooked, then it should be returned to the kitchen and brought up to the stage of doneness that the customer requests. If the guest continues to complain, the server is trained to turn the problem over to the banquet captain and to continue serving other guests. The banquet captain then has a variety of options to choose from in handling the problem, depending on a variety of circumstances that could be present.

Service recoveries can be easy or difficult to identify. In order to plan for effective service recoveries the steps management will take to satisfy a customer need to be determined. The most critical management policy to identify is the financial limit that management will put on satisfying a customer complaint.

The initial steps in the service recovery process are first to identify the primary areas of service breakdown and second, to empower servers with recovery tools up to a predetermined financial level. For example, in a restaurant situation a justified guest complaint about the length of time that it took for food to be delivered to the table can be recovered by offering a complimentary dessert. In catering service, it is difficult to apply these examples due to the simultaneous feeding of large groups of people. For this example, the customer who is responsible for booking and paying for the function might be recovered by a reduction of the bill for the meal or by a complimentary dinner in the hotel dining room. The individual circumstances surrounding each case will determine the recovery tactic. What needs to be predetermined is the financial amount that can be committed to this service recovery. Banquet servers may be allowed to offer a coupon for a reduced rate to the Saturday night buffet or Sunday brunch in the hotel or restaurant dining room if the service gap can affect the attitude of all of the guests attending the function. Couponing is a good way to create a perceived value for the guest from a service or production error. Coupons for future meal services bring the catering guest back as a customer, usually accompanied by from one to three other individuals, generating food and beverage revenues well beyond the cost of the coupon discount.

To plan for service recoveries begin by identifying four or five common customer complaints, that are service gaps in following the critical path of Figure 11-1. For each of these complaints determine two or three recovery situations that would be appropriate from both a service and financial perspective.

Establishing Standards

In order to meet customer needs and expectations in all of these areas, it is necessary to establish standard operating procedures for each function, from the process by which the telephone is answered to the language and attitude with which guests are greeted to the billing and payment process. The second step is to establish quality service and production standards.

International businesses in the twenty-first century are struggling to establish standards of operation by which to operate and manage their businesses. Often called standards of operating procedure, standards are guidelines to be followed for every activity in a business whether manufacturing or service related. An example of a standard of operation for an airline, for example, would be that a preflight check of all operating functions in an airplane be carried out before the takeoff of every flight.

The need for hospitality businesses to establish standards of operating procedures has grown with the need for multiunit franchise hotels and foodservice operations to be able to produce the same product for the traveling public in every location, regardless of ownership. Customers associate specific goods, services, and a level of quality with the name of the company. They are not concerned with the financial and legal arrangements that accompany franchise and management contracts.

On an individual level, established standards for service delivery are critical to providing the customers with the quality and style of service that they expect to receive, time after time. Customers become dissatisfied with inconsistent service that produces different levels of quality in each contact area. Regardless of the level of product quality, it is important to produce the same quality of delivery every time.

For banquet service, established policies and standards will maintain a consistent pattern of quality banquet service. Policies are general operating "rules" that are followed as a matter of procedure. Figure 11-2 identifies a list of "banquet policies" that help to ensure that overall quality standards are maintained.

CRITICAL PATH OF SERVICE

A critical path of service creates a standard level of quality table service consistently over an extended period of time. A critical path of service is a list of established service steps in the order in which they should be performed. The critical path of service also includes total quality service points (TQS). Total quality service points are those service activities that add to the overall perceived value of the function. Michael Hurst, former President of the National Restaurant Association and owner of the award winning restaurant 67th St. Fisheries in Fort Lauderdale, Florida, calls these "Wow Opportunities" to surprise guests with more than they expected in service quality. Total quality service points are inserted into the critical path of service at predetermined intervals to ensure that they, like the primary service steps, also happen on a consistent basis at a predetermined time in the service process.

The banquet breakfast meeting critical path of service in Figure 11-3 identifies each individual step in the banquet breakfast service process beginning with the initial greeting and finishing with the final offer of coffee. In this critical path it is assumed that the server will leave the room following the breakfast service while the meeting takes place.

An example of a critical path of service for full-service banquet dinner service is detailed in Figure 11-4.

- ALL SERVICE PERSONNEL ARE TO BE IN FULL UNIFORM WHENEVER THEY ARE IN THE SERVICE AREA.
- FRONT OF THE HOUSE FUNCTION ROOM DOORS ARE TO BE LOCKED UNTIL THE START OF A FUNCTION.
- NOISE BOTH DURING FUNCTION SETUP AND DELIVERY IS TO BE KEPT TO A MINIMUM.
- SERVERS ARE RESPONSIBLE FOR INSPECTING THEIR STATIONS. THIS INCLUDES THE QUALITY OF THE TABLE SETUP, GENERAL CLEANLINESS OF THE AREA, AND PLACEMENT OF TRAY STANDS.
- GLASSWARE IS TO BE HANDLED ONLY BY THE STEM, NEVER BY THE GLOBE.
- TRAY STANDS ARE TO BE DRAPED TO THE FLOOR WITH A LINEN CLOTH AND POSITIONED AROUND THE FLOOR ONLY DURING SERVICE.
- SERVICE FOR EACH COURSE WILL BE SIGNALED ONLY BY THE BANQUET CAPTAIN.
- FOOD WASTE AND SOILED DISHES ARE NEVER TO BE VISIBLE TO THE GUEST.
- FOOD SERVERS ARE RESPONSIBLE FOR RETURNING LEFTOVER FOOD TO THE KITCHEN AS QUICKLY AS POSSIBLE.
- THE BANQUET CAPTAIN IS RESPONSIBLE FOR THE OVERALL SANITATION OF ALL SERVICE AREAS AT THE CONCLUSION OF A FUNCTION.

FIGURE 11-2 BANQUET SERVICE POLICIES.

STEP 1:   SERVER INTRODUCES HIM OR HERSELF TO GUESTS.

STEP 2:   SERVER SERVES COFFEE AS GUESTS ARE SEATED.

STEP 3:   SERVER SERVES WARM BREAD BASKET.

STEP 4:   SERVER SERVES FRUIT COURSE, EITHER JUICE OR FRUIT PLATE.

STEP 5:   SERVER REPLENISHES WATER.

STEP 6:   SERVER CLEARS FRUIT COURSE.

STEP 7:   SERVER SERVES ENTRÉE.

STEP 8:   SERVER POURS COFFEE.

STEP 9:   TQS: ROVING SERVER REPLENISHES ROLLS AND BUTTER IF NEEDED.

STEP 10:   SERVER CLEARS ENTRÉE.

STEP 11:   SERVER REPLENISHES COFFEE AS NECESSARY.

STEP 12:   SERVER CLEARS BREAD AND BUTTER PLATES, BREAD, BUTTER, SALT AND PEPPER, AND OTHER FOOD ITEMS AND CONDIMENTS.

STEP 13:   SERVER OFFERS COFFEE BEFORE LEAVING THE MEETING ROOM.

FIGURE 11-3   BANQUET FULL-SERVICE BREAKFAST MEETING
CRITICAL PATH OF SERVICE.

STEP 1:   SERVER INTRODUCES HIM OR HERSELF TO GUESTS.

STEP 2:   SERVER SERVES WARM BREAD BASKET.

STEP 3:   SERVER SERVES SALAD AND DRESSING BOAT.

           TQS: TABLE SIDE SALAD PRESENTATION.

STEP 6:   SERVER POURS WINE OR BOTTLED WATER.

STEP 7:   SERVER CLEARS SALAD AND DRESSING.

STEP 8:   SERVER SERVES MAIN ENTRÉE.

           TQS: SERVE SAUCE TO EACH GUEST INDIVIDUALLY.

STEP 9:   SERVER POURS WINE OR BOTTLED WATER.

STEP 10:   SERVER REPLENISHES ROLLS AND BUTTER IF NEEDED.

STEP 11:   TQS: SERVER OFFERS COFFEE IF WINE IS NOT BEING SERVED.

STEP 12:   SERVER REPOURS WINE OR BOTTLED WATER AS NECESSARY.

STEP 13:   TQS: ROVING SERVERS OFFER SECOND PORTIONS OF ENTRÉE ITEMS WITH PLATTER SERVICE.

STEP 14:   SERVER CLEARS ENTRÉE, BREAD AND BUTTER PLATES, BREAD, BUTTER, SALT AND PEPPER, SAUCE BOATS, AND OTHER FOOD ITEMS, CONDIMENTS, AND WINE GLASSES.

STEP 15:   SERVER SERVES DESSERT.

STEP 16:   SERVER SERVES COFFEE SERVICE.

STEP 17:   SERVER OFFERS CORDIALS IF INCLUDED IN DINNER SERVICE.

STEP 18:   SERVER CLEARS TABLE LEAVING ONLY WATER GLASS, COFFEE CUP, SAUCER, TEASPOON, NAPKIN, AND CREAM AND SUGAR.

           *TQS IF THERE IS AN AFTER-DINNER SPEAKER WHO BEGINS BEFORE DESSERT IS CLEARED, COFFEE IS OFFERED BEFORE THE SERVER LEAVES THE ROOM.

STEP 19:   SERVER OFFERS COFFEE.

FIGURE 11-4   BANQUET FULL-SERVICE DINNER CRITICAL PATH OF SERVICE.

BANQUET BUFFET SERVICE

Buffet service can be presented in a variety of formats from casual picnic style to the traditional full-meal service and complete range of courses. Trends in buffet service design offer a variety of action stations located around the function space. These stations provide a way to break up the concentration of guests onto one buffet table and disperse them among a number of tables. Some of these tables can offer cooking stations such as pasta and shellfish or southwestern themes with fajitas or oriental menu items. Carving stations, salad buffets, and antipasto tables are among the wide variety of action station concepts that can be included. In addition to changing the flow of guests and creating a food entertainment venue, action stations can be highly decorative additions to a banquet function.

Buffet service in a banquet setting offers a variety of service challenges. While the concept of buffet service is that guests serve themselves food items for each course offered, the need for table service has not been eliminated. Servers are required to carry out the balance of the table service steps such as pouring beverages, clearing plates between each course, and other service acts as appropriate to the menu and formality of the function. Figure 11-5 outlines the critical path of service for a traditional sit-down buffet dinner where guests serve themselves food items from the buffet tables and servers provide the beverage and other associated table services. This is followed by a worksheet, in Figure 11-6, for catering operators to work with in establishing their personal critical paths for banquet service.

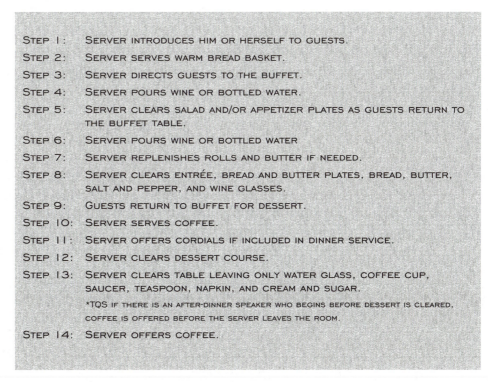

STEP 1:   SERVER INTRODUCES HIM OR HERSELF TO GUESTS.

STEP 2:   SERVER SERVES WARM BREAD BASKET.

STEP 3:   SERVER DIRECTS GUESTS TO THE BUFFET.

STEP 4:   SERVER POURS WINE OR BOTTLED WATER.

STEP 5:   SERVER CLEARS SALAD AND/OR APPETIZER PLATES AS GUESTS RETURN TO THE BUFFET TABLE.

STEP 6:   SERVER POURS WINE OR BOTTLED WATER

STEP 7:   SERVER REPLENISHES ROLLS AND BUTTER IF NEEDED.

STEP 8:   SERVER CLEARS ENTRÉE, BREAD AND BUTTER PLATES, BREAD, BUTTER, SALT AND PEPPER, AND WINE GLASSES.

STEP 9:   GUESTS RETURN TO BUFFET FOR DESSERT.

STEP 10:   SERVER SERVES COFFEE.

STEP 11:   SERVER OFFERS CORDIALS IF INCLUDED IN DINNER SERVICE.

STEP 12:   SERVER CLEARS DESSERT COURSE.

STEP 13:   SERVER CLEARS TABLE LEAVING ONLY WATER GLASS, COFFEE CUP, SAUCER, TEASPOON, NAPKIN, AND CREAM AND SUGAR.

*TQS IF THERE IS AN AFTER-DINNER SPEAKER WHO BEGINS BEFORE DESSERT IS CLEARED, COFFEE IS OFFERED BEFORE THE SERVER LEAVES THE ROOM.

STEP 14:   SERVER OFFERS COFFEE.

FIGURE 11-5   BANQUET BUFFET DINNER CRITICAL PATH OF SERVICE FOR A TRADITIONAL SIT-DOWN DINNER.

MEAL SERVICE: _____

STEP 1: _____

STEP 2: _____

STEP 3: _____

      TQS: _____

STEP 4: _____

STEP 5: _____

STEP 6: _____

STEP 7: _____

      TQS: _____

STEP 8: _____

STEP 9: _____

STEP 10: _____

STEP 11: _____

STEP 12: _____

STEP 13: _____

STEP 14: _____

STEP 15: _____

STEP 16: _____

STEP 17: _____

      TQS: _____

STEP 18: _____

FIGURE 11-6   CATERING OPERATOR'S WORKSHEET
FOR BANQUET CRITICAL PATH OF SERVICE.

Staffing Levels

The determining factor in whether "quality" service efforts are achieved is often the reality of there being enough service staff on hand to carry out the service steps. Staffing in the labor market of the early 2000s poses serious challenges to the management of all types of food and beverage operations. Catering staffing levels are often difficult to fulfill due to the use of part-time help to supplement full-time staff. Staffing levels for catering differ from restaurant staffing levels in that while restaurants may plan to serve an estimated number of guests over a four- or five-hour time period, catering functions require that all guests be served at the same time. Restaurant service timing can use fewer servers to serve the same number of guests in an evening than the larger number of servers it will take to serve a banquet function in a two-hour time period.

Staffing levels for catering are further complicated by the formality of the function, meal service, type of menu items being served, number of guests, seating arrangements, and size of tables, along with the required style of service. Plated American service to tables of ten or twelve guests takes fewer service staff than platter service to tables of eight. It is important to keep in mind that identifying staffing levels for catering functions is very different than for restaurants.

There are general estimates of staffing levels for a banquet dinner using American service to tables of ten for anywhere from fifteen to twenty guests per server, or 1½ to 2 tables per server. For tables of eight with platter service this can be reduced to one table per server with teams of two servers for every two tables. The overall service efficiency can also be influenced by the leadership skills of the banquet captain, the size of the function, and the facilities in which the function is being served.

Hotel companies and large independent caterers will often preestablish staffing guidelines for banquet captains to follow. Small independent caterers and restaurants will need to include the overall capabilities of their staff and facilities in the final staffing guidelines. Labor costs for both full- and part-time help can be a determining factor for staffing levels. Menu prices will need to reflect the labor costs for different staffing levels. Caterers also have the option of charging for labor as a separate item in proposals. From a competitive perspective it might be more successful to include the labor costs for a minimum staffing level in the menu price. Additional staff can be charged for on a per person/per hour basis as a way of upselling the quality of service to match a menu.

Staffing levels for buffet functions are dependent on the following factors:

- Number of guests
- Type of buffet table setups
- Menu

As discussed earlier, the fact that guests are serving themselves in a buffet line does not eliminate the need for table service. Service for traditional buffet service requires that plates be cleared between courses and beverages poured. For many functions, buffet tables will need to be staffed with service help. The concept of action stations for buffet presentation often requires service staff at each table and food preparation in the room by either service staff members or kitchen staff.

A general guideline for staffing standard buffet functions is one server for every two tables of ten to twelve guests. As with other styles of banquet service, the effectiveness of staffing levels is dependent on so many variable factors that every operation will need to finalize its own needs in relation to the level of "quality" service that is being offered.

Summary

Defining and creating quality standards for catering services and products is a key to long-term success for a catering business. Customer experience and expectations will help a catering operation to identify the level of "quality" product for which it can develop operating procedures along with standards of service and product. Making a decision to commit a business to "quality" standards requires the commitment to maintaining standards and to planning for service recoveries when service gaps happen in the process of delivering products and services to the customer.

Establishing banquet service policies and standards includes the development of critical paths of service for every type of banquet function from coffee breaks to formal dinners. Buffet standards also create challenges for service quality when customers expect table service activities while taking part in a self-service function.

The ultimate challenge for a catering operation is to create service steps that surprise the guest by providing an experience that is more than they expected to receive. Whether called "magic moments," "wow opportunities," or "total quality service points," preplanned service steps that consistently please and surprise customers will lead to increased revenues and profits in addition to employee satisfaction and retention.

Managing Catering Equipment

Catering equipment falls into two basic categories: front of the house service equipment and back of the house production equipment. Management of catering equipment is the responsibility of the catering manager for service needs and the executive chef for production and kitchen needs. While catering equipment for front of the house needs is by design highly portable for ease of transport and storage, some equipment can be designed for flexible use when outside catering is a service of the catering business.

Back of the house equipment, on the other hand, consists of a core of food production equipment that generally requires establishing a permanent food production area. Portable gas and electric stoves, refrigerator trucks, and other movable equipment permit off-site food production to fulfill outside catering needs.

Front of the House Equipment

Front of the house equipment is classified as service related. It creates the setting guests see, as shown in Figure 12-1. Equipment categories are:

TABLEWARE

This consists of china, glassware, stemware, and flatware.

SERVING PIECES

These will include silver, glass, and china.

BUFFET SERVICE

This will require chafing dishes and serving pieces.

FIGURE 12-1   SETTING FOR A CATERING FUNCTION.
(Courtesy of the New York Marriott Marquis,
New York, New York.)

TABLE LIGHTING

This might include candelabras, glass globes, candlesticks (both single and multiprong, short and tall), votive candle holders, candlestick shades, and oil lamps and shades.

TABLES AND MODULAR TABLE SECTIONS

Rectangular tables are available in a variety of lengths and widths ranging from 2½ by 4 feet to 2½ by 8 feet and can seat from four to eight people. The flexibility of modular tables allows catering functions table seating to be set up in a variety of table designs, as seen in Figure 12-1.

Round tables are generally available in diameters that range from 2 to 6 feet and seating from four to twelve persons. Modular units available in half moons and serpentine shapes allow a variety of table designs, some of which are seen in Figure 12-2.

CHAIRS

Chairs can range in design and function from collapsible painted wooden designs to metal frame upholstered chairs for formal banquets. The quality of the chair and overall design are selected based on usage and storage requirements. Outside catering needs require lightweight chairs that are easily stacked or collapsible designs.

LINENS

Linens include tablecloths, napkins, placemats, and lace overlays. Table linens can provide a wide variety of tabletop designs for private functions. Florists and special events companies often stock a wide variety of colored and patterned linens that can be rented. Rental charges include laundering and often delivery and pick-up service.

TABLE SKIRTING

Table skirting is used primarily for buffet tables and head tables for both formal and informal functions. In conference centers and hotels, foodservice break setups use skirting for buffet setups. Meal functions use skirting for a wide variety of buffet functions in addition to head tables. As with linens, a wide range of fabrics, colors, and patterns are available to accent special function themes and designs.

CHAIR COVERS

For special functions and themed events, chair covers have become a popular way to incorporate the chair into the overall design. Chair covers are available in a variety of fabrics and styles. Using the chair as a design component can also help set a theme for meetings and group gatherings. Chair covers can be sourced from local vendors or manufacturers and included in the function package prices in the same way as linens. Package pricing is discussed in detail in Chapter Thirteen. Skirting, chair covers, and modular table sizes are shown in Figure 12-3.

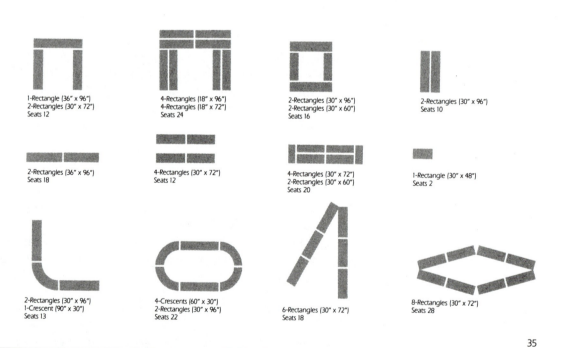

BUFFET/DISPLAY

4-Crescents (60" x 30")
Seats 16

2-Crescents (90" x 30")
Seats 10

4-Rectangles (30" x 96")
4-Crescents (60" x 30")
Seats 30

2-Crescents (90" x 30")
2-Rectangles (30" x 96")
Seats 17

2-Rectangles (36" x 96")
1-Quarter Round
"Buffet"

2-Rectangles (30" x 96")
1-Half Round
"Buffet"

6-Crescent (60" x 30")
"Buffet"

2-Rectangles (30" x 96")
4-Crescents (60" x 30")
Seats 20

4-Rectangles (30" x 72")
2-Crescents (90" x 30")
Seats 22

4-Rectangles (36" x 96")
Seats 30

2-Rectangles (30" x 96")
2-Half Rounds
"Buffet"

4-Half Rounds
"Buffet"

8-Rectangles (36" x 96")
Seats 60

CONFERENCE/MEETING

1-Rectangle (36" x 96")
2-Rectangles (30" x 72")
Seats 12

4-Rectangles (18" x 96")
4-Rectangles (18" x 72")
Seats 24

2-Rectangles (30" x 96")
2-Rectangles (30" x 60")
Seats 16

2-Rectangles (30" x 96")
Seats 10

2-Rectangles (36" x 96")
Seats 18

4-Rectangles (30" x 72")
Seats 12

4-Rectangles (30" x 72")
2-Rectangles (30" x 60")
Seats 20

1-Rectangle (30" x 48")
Seats 2

2-Rectangles (30" x 96")
1-Crescent (90" x 30")
Seats 13

4-Crescents (60" x 30")
2-Rectangles (30" x 96")
Seats 22

6-Rectangles (30" x 72")
Seats 18

8-Rectangles (30" x 72")
Seats 28

35

FIGURE 12-2   TABLE DESIGN.
(Courtesy of King Arthur®, a division
of Shelby Williams Inc.)

FIGURE 12-3   SKIRTING, CHAIR COVERS, AND MODULAR TABLE SIZES.
(Courtesy of the Peabody Hotel, Orlando, Florida.)

DANCE FLOOR

Portable dance floors help to expand the possibilities for function space use. Outdoor spaces, rooms that are completely covered in carpeting, tent floors, and pool decks are examples of where portable dance floors are often used. The fee for dance floors can be incorporated into the overall function price. If a customer has made a specific request for equipment that the catering business does not have on property, then the rental and service charges are normally added to the bill.

PORTABLE BARS

For receptions and parties it is often necessary to have portable bars available. Portable bars are available in a variety of designs and can include sinks, pour wells, storage areas, and other features. For outside catering it is helpful to work with units that are as lightweight as possible.

SPECIALTY ITEMS

To complement a catering business a wide range of service and special event items can be used. From coat racks to ice buckets, catering companies either own or rent appropriate service equipment to meet their specific needs. The following list of specialty items might be used for both in-house and outside catering functions:

> Fountain, electric
> BBQ grill, gas or charcoal
> Coffee maker
> Baskets, large and small
> Table stands
> Banquet trays
> Carving boards
> Ice carving pans with lighting
> Table spot lights
> Coat rack/hangers and coat checks
> Ice buckets, standing and table
> Ashtrays

PROPS

As discussed throughout this book, theme party plans can be critical to the success and profitability of a catering operation. Theme parties require a wide variety of props and often large stage set pieces for decoration. The number of props as well as set and lighting requirements required for a function will depend upon the customer's budget. A simple party theme may be satisfactorily carried out using colored and patterned linens, a table centerpiece, a few props on the buffet table and/or around the function area, and appropriate music.

Large budget parties, however, often require a complicated setup of props and sets along with linens, chair covers, table centerpieces, and entertainment. The inventory of props and other theme party equipment that a catering business owns is often dependent on both budget and storage space. Most catering companies maintain a small inventory of basic theme props and supplement for special functions by renting from larger catering or prop rental companies.

In U.S. cities such as New Orleans, for example, theme parties are in constant demand at the large convention hotels. Companies such as Fancy Faces supply centerpieces and specialty props to area hotels and caterers; a selection of their wares is shown in Figure 12-4a. Working directly with either the hotel or the client, Fancy Faces will use in-stock items or create custom special event centerpieces and props. For example, popular theme props are the jazz musicians in Figure 12-4b, available as table centerpieces or as full, life-size figures boarded with tubular lighting. Combined with signature china setplates, menus, and additional musical props, these figures

JZ10: Jazz Man Centerpiece (38" High)

Jazz Tiles
Top to Bottom: (6" x 6")
5803: Drum/Clarinet
5802: Drum/Tuba
5801: Sax/Trumpet
5800: Second Line/Trombone

Jazzmatazz

JZ20: Marching Band Silhouettes, 18" - 22" High

Napkin Rings:
5030: Mini Mask
5810: Flat Tile Jazz Silhouettes/Pin

JZ30: Life-Size Jazz Silhouettes, 5' - 6' High

(A)

(B)

FIGURE 12-4   (A) CENTERPIECE AND PROP COMPANY, FANCY FACES. (B) JAZZ MUSICIANS AS A MENU COVER.
(Courtesy of Fancy Faces, New Orleans, Louisiana.)

create an entertaining and high energy decorative theme to accommodate a wide range of customer interest and budgets. Another New Orleans company, Pete Fountain Productions, specializes in theatrical set designs and lighting for elaborate theme functions. Companies such these two work together to supplement a hotel's prop inventory and create themed events for hundreds of conventions and private parties annually.

THE PROP INVENTORY

An effective prop inventory requires that the catering operation identify a core of themes for which they can provide decorations in-house. As discussed in Chapter Thirteen, themed events can be included in package plans for special events and convention/meeting functions. In addition, meetings and individual reception and meal functions may also be "themed." Figure 12-5 is themed meeting break menu featured by Loews Georgio Hotel in Denver, Colorado. The following is a list of specialty theme functions offered by the Marriott at Sawgrass near Jacksonville, Florida. These functions require from minimal to very elaborate setup and props.

Breaks
A Break with A Flair
(10 Person Minimum)

"Pit Stop"	"Hole in One"	"Take Me Out to the Ball game"
Assorted Candy Bars	Bite Size Club Sandwiches	Peanuts in The Shell
Corn Chips and	Licorice	Popcorn
Chili Con Queso	Pistachios	Large Hot Pretzels
Assorted Cookies	Iced Tea	Sodas
Sodas	Sodas and Mineral Waters	$5.50 + +
$6.50+ +	$6.50+ +	

"The Chocaholic"	"The Health Food Break"	"The Soda Fountain Break"
Chocolate Chip Cookies	Fruit Kabobs	Chocolate and Vanilla
M&M's	Granola Bars	Haagen Dazs Ice Cream
Chocolate Dipped	Powerades	with 6 Different Toppings
Strawberries	Mineral Waters	Assorted Sodas
Milk and Chocolate Milk	$6.50 + +	$6.50 + +
$6.00+ +		

"Movie Time"	"A Day in the Park"	"A Day at the Beach"
Dots and Milkduds	Fruit Salad	Cheese and Crackers
Popcorn	Potato Chips and Dip	Fruit Tray
Assorted Sodas	Oatmeal Cookies	Assorted Sodas
$5.50+ +	Assorted Sodas	$5.50+ +
	$6.50+ +	

FIGURE 12-5 LOEWS GEORGIO HOTEL MEETING BREAK MENU.
(Courtesy of Loews Giorgio Hotel, Denver, Colorado.)

Specialty Function Themes

Western Cookout	That's Italian
Night in the Islands	Evening at Tara
Seatown	Around the World Cruise
Golf Tee-Off	Garden Party
Oldies But Goodies	Tacky Tourist Clam Bake
Florida Fantasy Feast	Hollywood Extravaganza
Alligator Alley	The Diner
Trailblazer's Fiesta	Bahama Baby

The hotel maintains a basic prop inventory to support these themes. When customers request similar themes for large functions, the hotel relies on outside vendors for additional equipment and materials.

Back of the House Equipment

The equipment for the central kitchen for any food service operation is dependent largely on the basic food production needs for menu items. The number of food production methods required to prepare foods will determine the overall equipment needs.

The requirements of food service operations are based on how and where food products are:

- Received
- Stored
  - Refrigeration
  - Dry
- Preprepared
- Prepared
- Served
- Cleaned up
- Disposed of

Added to these major considerations are the requirements for food sanitation and safety.

THE BASIC KITCHEN

The most basic kitchen setup for food production will require:

- Separate work surfaces for both food contact and nonfood contact areas
- Work sinks for both preparation and cleanup
- Sufficient cutting surfaces to prevent cross-contamination of food products during preparation
- Storage for utensils
- Storage for cooking equipment

- Storage for dry food product
- Adequate refrigeration and freezer space
- Food disposal equipment and area

For prepreparation of a standard full-service menu, the average production kitchen will generally require the following equipment:

- Mixer
- Steam kettle
- Chopper
- Food cutter
- Food slicer
- Tilting fry pan
- Ovens:
  - Convection
  - Microwave
  - Conventional
  - Deck
- Fryer
- Steamer
- Range
- Broiler

This equipment is supplemented by hand cooking utensils and small appliances. In addition, rolling racks, utility carts, storage containers, and cooking pans will be needed, along with a variety of other cooking equipment depending on the individual needs of the operation.

For off-premise catering functions, large open grills provide food production capability for a wide variety of vegetable, fish, poultry, and beef items. Many regional and international cuisine items are appropriate for open grill cooking, and can be accompanied by side dishes that have been preprepared at a central commissary kitchen and stored in portable banquet boxes. These dishes, accompanied by cold items and desserts, can make up a range of menus that can be successfully prepared in portable kitchen units.

REFRIGERATION

Adequate refrigeration for both raw food product and prepared foods is essential for all foodservice operations. Catering operations serve such a range of functions and customers on any given day that it is often difficult to maintain enough refrigeration for occasional large parties. Hotel and restaurant kitchens maintain adequate refrigeration to handle their requirements.

Permanent refrigeration units are available in a variety of sizes and designs. A commercial kitchen generally includes a combination of reach-in and walk-in refrigeration and freezer units. Walk-in units are used for storage of bulk items and are available in both closed box and pass through designs. These units are often located away from the central preparation area. Reach-in refrigerator units, both stand up and under the counter, are located adjacent to the preparation and production areas. Bulk food items that have been portioned out to preparation requirements are stored on trays in the reach-in refrigerators, along with other perishable food items, until they are needed for production.

Small catering companies and independent catering halls may find refrigeration capacity a recurring problem. For these situations refrigerator trucks or portable refrigeration units can be rented. This solution also applies for outside catering functions, both for transportation and for service of food items.

DISHWASHING

Dishwashing is a critical element of all foodservice operations. Hotels and restaurants have dishwashing equipment in place to handle loads appropriate to the size and needs of their facilities. Independent catering halls will also have dishwashing machines in place. Local food safety regulations may require that machines be inspected periodically and hot water temperature levels checked.

Small catering companies and caterers who handle outside catering functions face an additional challenge. Dishwashing is a critical area for food sanitation and safety. Washing dishes by hand is neither efficient nor acceptable as a way of handling this area of foodservice. All dishes must be scraped, sorted, and stacked to minimize breakage on the return trip to a foodservice facility. Dishwashing should be handled as soon as possible after trucks return from outside catering functions; this will reduce problems such as food smell, dishes that are hard to clean due to dried and caked on foods, or infestation by insects and rodents. Occasionally locations for outside catering functions will be provided with dishwashing facilities. For smaller functions, portable dishwashers can be rented.

WASTE REMOVAL

Waste removal is another critical area for food sanitation. Hotels, restaurants, and catering halls are equipped with combinations of compactors, garbage disposals, and/or pulpers. Off-site catering will require that all waste, both organic and nonorganic, be handled efficiently. Waste that will be returning to central production facilities will require covered containers and equipment in which to transport it. Arrangements for waste removal for off-premise catering should be planned for and determined prior to the function.

ICE MACHINES

Ice is a requirement for both beverage and food service. Ice machines are sized according to the need of a foodservice operation for ice on demand during a 24-hour period. Ice machines include three major components; production, storage, and dispensing. Ice is generally available in either cubes or flakes.

Ice requirements include beverages as well as cooling and/or holding foods for buffets and salad bars. For outside catering purposes, ice may also be needed for food storage and chilling beverages. Storage bins for ice machines should hold at least 50 percent more than the ice machine can produce. As ice machines will not produce ice when the bins are full, the amount of ice needed on hand for a function may not be available until the bins have been emptied enough to allow for the machine to produce more ice. Small catering companies may well find it more efficient to make arrangements with local ice companies to provide ice in large quantities for functions instead of investing in ice-making equipment.

Summary

Managing catering equipment requires a range of knowledge of both service and production techniques and procedures. The initial inventory of service-related equipment for a catering operation will need to be both maintained and brought up to par on scheduled intervals. Inventories should also be scheduled on a quarterly basis to identify both equipment losses and maintenance needs. At this time staff training can be implemented, if it is appropriate, to reduce losses and equipment breakage.

Back of the house equipment requires constant maintenance and inspection for both operating needs and employee safety. Kitchen equipment that is not inspected and maintained on a regularly scheduled basis can break down at critical times, affecting both production and the quality of product and service delivery to the guest.

Both front of the house and back of the house equipment represent a sizeable portion of the overall investment in any foodservice business. Managing supply and maintenance can be a time consuming operational detail, but is one that should not be overlooked in a busy catering operation. Assigning responsibility for equipment to one or two individuals can help to maintain the inventory and maintenance schedules and reduce replacement costs and expensive emergency mechanical repairs.

Catering
Marketing

CHAPTER THIRTEEN

WEDDINGS BY
BELLAGIO

IMAGINE THE PERFECT WEDDING.

It would, of course, have an utterly romantic ambience,

enchanting music, intimate service from beginning to end,

artful photography and lush, fragrant flowers.

When you exchange vows at Bellagio,

every one of these will be yours.

Choose between two classically styled chapels,

one holding over 100 guests and the other 35.

Both are beautifully appointed in palettes of cream,

rose, green, peach and bride's blue.

When your ceremony is concluded,

Bellagio is ready to host your reception and

honeymoon as well. You'll have at your disposal

rooms and suites for wedding guests, a world-class spa and salon,

a new Cirque du Soleil production, exclusive shops and exquisite dining.

Why just imagine the perfect wedding

when it can be a reality—at Bellagio.

Marketing is the key to the successful growth and development of catering businesses of all sizes, both in the United States and internationally. Marketing is the overall process of developing sales plans, recognizing industry trends, identifying customer needs, and developing products, prices, advertising and promotion, and sales, both direct and indirect; marketing also includes the measurement of your success in all of these combined efforts.

Marketing is the activity that, for small businesses, is most often sacrificed to daily operations. It is also a process for which most small business operators are undertrained or inexperienced. Unfortunately, since marketing is a major key to the ongoing success of any business, weaknesses in the development and follow-through of marketing plans can bring about business failure.

The principal goals of the marketing process are to recognize trends in cuisine, entertainment, customer lifestyle, and other concepts that shape customer needs and to develop products and services in response to those needs. Accompanied by appropriate pricing strategies and measurement vehicles, this process is called the marketing cycle. The ability to be flexible and to respond to customer needs in a timely manner is one of the primary reasons for the overall growth of the catering segment of the foodservice industry.

The success of a catering business is also dependent on management's ability to measure profitability and customer satisfaction. While profitability is a measure of the success of business practices, customer response is an accurate gauge of quality performance.

The Marketing Cycle

The American Marketing Association defines marketing as:

The process of planning and executing the conception, pricing, promotion, and distribution of ideas, goods, and services to create exchanges that satisfy individual and organizational objectives.[1]

The process of achieving these objectives is called the marketing cycle, shown in Figure 13-1. In the marketing cycle process, customer needs are identified, products and/or services are developed to satisfy those needs, customer interest in the product or service is created, and the success of these efforts is measured against both financial goals and customer satisfaction. The information identified and developed in this process is the basis of a marketing plan, the detailed outline of how and when a business will reach its target market with products and services that respond to specific needs. Also included are prices that have been determined to be both acceptable to customer value perceptions and simultaneously profitable to the business. The ability of catering services to adapt to customer demands with an extensive product line and broad service appeal produces dynamic and profitable results.

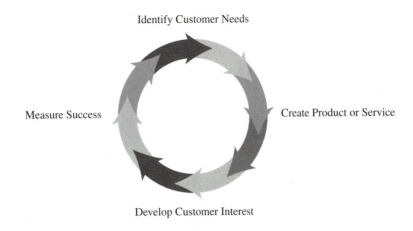

FIGURE 13-1   MARKETING CYCLE.

IDENTIFY CUSTOMER NEEDS

Customer needs are shaped by demographic and social trends. The ability to perceive these trends and apply them to a catering service expands marketing opportunities. Trends contributing to the current growth in catering opportunities are the demographic increases in two-income families, working mothers, and the age of the overall population. These three factors, combined with increased retail food costs, have created a trend toward a demand for preprepared food items.

Customers will often choose to purchase preprepared food items when they perceive that the cost of retail food, including the indirect costs of preparation time, becomes close to or equals the price of preprepared products. These satisfy the two major customer priorities for foodservice in the beginning of the twenty-first century: convenience and time management.

CREATE A PRODUCT OR SERVICE

The identification of customer needs provides an opportunity to create new catering products and/or services. Customer surveys, focus groups, and function comment forms, combined with national and local trends, will present a range of idea options from which to choose new products and services. Before responding to perceived customer needs ask the following question: Will there be enough sales volume to justify both the purchase of support materials and advertising materials, and the time and labor costs dedicated to research and development of new product design and the initial trial of product/services? It is tempting to respond to an interesting product idea with a frenzy of activity before measuring the return on an investment of time and resources. For small catering companies in which time and finances are limited, this can be especially costly.

DEVELOP CUSTOMER INTEREST

Customer interest for catering functions is developed through a combination of advertising and in-house promotions. The broad range of clients served by catering operations necessitates the use of a variety of promotional vehicles. Hotel and conference facilities have the ability to post display boards advertising new catering services. A direct mail campaign of brochures or newsletters to a customer list is an effective way of advertising specials and promotions. Internet technology applications such as interactive websites and E-mail can also be excellent methods of reaching both new and old customers. Figure 13-2 features two samples of custom promotional postcards, both of which are directed at prospective brides. One is for wedding cakes made by Mim's Bakery. The other advertises wedding packages at the Holiday Inn in Palo Alto, California. This type of advertising material is particularly effective when sent to newly engaged couples, sent in response to general inquiries, or included in billing statements and with other promotional literature.

MEASURE SUCCESS

The success of catering functions is measured by customer response. Interest from guests who have attended a function is one indication of success. Another is requests for additional functions from clients who plan business functions on an ongoing basis. Financial success can be directly measured by sales volume in the periods during and following promotions. Additional measurement formats are discussed under Measuring Customer Satisfaction, below.

The Marketing Mix

The marketing mix includes the marketing strategy elements and may be conducted either as an alternative to the marketing cycle or as a continuing activity in the marketing process. As illustrated in Figure 13-3, the marketing mix incorporates product, place, promotion, and price into the overall strategy of marketing a product/service.

PRODUCT

While this element has been discussed on a general level in the marketing cycle section, product, in the marketing mix, can refer to separate details of a larger product concept. For example, entertainment can be a highly profitable service product created through a series of strategic alliances with external resources. A wide variety of customer needs for entertainment can be met with quality musicians, entertainers, and DJs that a catering company is comfortable in arranging for as part of their overall product/services.

PLACE

In this process, place refers to how and where the product will be made available to the customer. This includes not only the physical environment in which the product/service is presented, but the reservation process. By including the reservation process as part of place, it becomes a functional component of the process, planned into the overall design of the product.

MIM'S BAKERY
CHICO, CALIFORNIA

For Wedding Cakes of every kind
Mim's Bakery can create a cake to
remember. We can tailor a cake to
your wishes, and your budget

Please Call for an Appointment
530.345.3331

(A)

We'll Capture
the Joy While You
Cherish the Moments

Two indoor/outdoor ceremony &
reception facilities for 75 - 350 guests

Flowing waters, fountains,
colorful gardens and gazebo

Award winning Chef

Special overnight rates
for out-of-town guests

Complimentary room for bride
& groom with chilled champagne

Complimentary
anniversary package

Professional bridal coordinator
combined with superb service

625 EL CAMINO REAL
PALO ALTO, CA 94301
(415) 328-2800

(B)

FIGURE 13-2   CUSTOM PROMOTIONAL POSTCARDS.
(*a*) Courtesy of Mim's Bakery. (*b*) Design: Michael Maystead/Cowper Graphics.
Photo: Genesis Photography. (Both © 1993 Modern Postcard.
All rights reserved. Website: www.modernpostcard.com)

Product   Place   Promotion   Price

FIGURE 13-3   MARKETING MIX: THE "FOUR PS" OF MARKETING.

PROMOTION

Promotion refers to the advertising and public relations activities surrounding a product/service. For example, the wedding segment of a catering business is often treated as an individual product, accompanied by separate promotional material, displays, advertising, and promotional calendar within the marketing plan. Figure 13-4 shows the wedding package brochure for the Colorado Springs Garden of the Gods, Holiday Inn. This mailing piece is sized to fit into a standard business envelope with a personalized letter in response to an inquiry for information. New Year's Eve and holiday functions are further examples of individual catering products that are treated in a similar manner. The regional location of a catering business will provide a product promotion calendar reflecting local holidays and events in addition to traditional catering function demands.

PRICE

As the financial measurement of successful product planning and promotional effort, the development of pricing strategies is a critical business activity. Price in the marketing mix is concerned primarily with identifying a price that both reflects the profit and cost needs of the business and responds to the needs of the consumer as acceptable on a perceived-value basis.

Cuisine, Entertainment, and Concept Trends

Trends, as they relate to catering menu management, reflect changes in the patterns of customer requests for catering services. Current trends in catering functions incorporate media technology, computerized laser light shows, and indoor fireworks displays, often simultaneously, in the production of entertainment performances and corporate presentations. Social functions such as bar mitzvahs and weddings include video presentations of the participants. Reception themes use interactive guest activity to create an entertainment atmosphere in a traditional food and beverage function format. Function locations have expanded far beyond the catering facility to create unique venues and events. Manufacturer's designs have responded to the need for portable and flexible service and production equipment. Simple meal functions have become theme parties complete with stage sets, lighting, costumed service personnel, music, and entertainment. The biggest trend in

Wedding Hors d'oeuvres Buffet

❖ Fresh Vegetables & Herb Dip
❖ Assorted Cheese & Cracker Display
❖ Mixed Variety of Deli Meats & Cheeses served with Assorted Breads & Condiments
❖ Seasonal Fresh Fruit Platter

Choice of Three Hot & Two Cold Hors d'oeuvres:

❖ Stuffed Mushrooms
❖ Breaded Hot Buffalo Wings
❖ Chicken Finger Filets served with a Honey Mustard Dipping Sauce
❖ Miniature Quiche
❖ Honey-Mustard Shaved Ham served with Cocktail Rolls
❖ Beef & Shrimp Kabobs
❖ Swedish Meatballs

❖ Marinated Artichoke Hearts
❖ Flaked Cucumber with Cream Cheese
❖ Assorted Cold Canapes
❖ Chile Con Queso served with Corn Tortilla Chips, Salsa & Guacamole
❖ Salami Coronettes

$13.95 Per Person
Plus 17% gratuity & applicable tax

Also Available:

❖ Carved Steamship Round of Beef served with Horseradish Cream, Imported Mustard & Cocktail Rolls

$14.95 Per Person
Plus 17% gratuity & applicable tax

Wedding Dinner Buffet

❖ Tossed Green Salad
❖ Crudite of Vegetables & Dip
❖ Chilled Pasta Salad
❖ Imported Cheese Display
❖ Seasonal Fresh Fruit Display
❖ Choice of Potato or Rice Pilaf

Choice of Two Entrees:

❖ Carved Roast Baron of Beef
❖ Chicken Marsala
❖ Sliced London Broil served with a Sherry Mushroom Sauce
❖ Chicken Dijon

Served With:

❖ Steamed Fresh Vegetables
❖ Assorted Fresh Baked Rolls
❖ Coffee or Tea

$16.95 Per Person
Plus 17% gratuity & applicable tax

The Holiday Inn, Garden of the Gods, specializes in wedding receptions. Our team of experienced professionals are here to assist you in planning this important occasion.

Whether you want a small intimate gathering of just 25 close friends, or a gala affair for up to 400, rest assured that we can provide the quality service that you need to make it the most special day of your life. We offer a complete range of plated and buffet meals as well as a selection of hot or cold hors d'oeuvres to meet your needs and your budget.

You will be able to take advantage of the following special wedding reception services:

Your private banquet room will be set with table linens in colors closely matching your wedding colors.

We will provide floral arrangements and candles for all tables at no charge.

Complimentary use of our parquet dance floor.

Champagne fountain (based on availability, minimum of 150 people).

Your wedding cake displayed on our special cake table - decorated with lace skirting, complimented with lights.

Full private bar set-ups available for hosted or cash cocktails.

Complimentary honeymoon suite and bottle of champagne waiting for you on your wedding night (based on availability with minimum of 150 people attending reception).

Free use of our private banquet room for your rehearsal dinner with a minimum of 25 persons attending reception.

All receptions are serviced with full chinaware, glass and linen.

Ice Carvings - 1 Block (heart, swan or dove) with a minimum of 150 attending reception.

FIGURE 13-4 GARDEN OF THE GODS, HOLIDAY INN'S WEDDING PACKAGE BROCHURE.
(Courtesy of The Holiday Inn, Garden of the Gods, Colorado Springs, Colorado.)

We're here to
make sure your
Wedding Day
goes just the way
you planned it!

❧

If there is any way that we
may be of assistance to you
please contact our
Sales Department at:

719-598-7656 Ext: 744
1-800-962-5470 Ext: 744

Or write to us at:
Holiday Inn
Garden of the Gods
Attn: Sales Department
505 Popes Bluff Trail
Colorado Springs, Co
80907

Banquet
Punch & Beer

Punch
❖ Non-alcoholic Fruit Punch $15.00 gallon
❖ Champagne Punch $28.75 gallon

Beer
❖ Domestic $2.75   ❖ Imported $3.25

Bar Services

Cash Bar
❖ $150 minimum in bar sales at the bar
❖ $50 in sales each hour after minimum
sales is attained or a $30 bartender fee
will be applied

Host Bar
❖ $150 minimum in bar sales at the bar
❖ $50 in sales each hour after minimum
sales is attained or a $30 bartender fee
will be applied
❖ All host bar sales are subject to a 17%
gratuity charge at the end of the evening

Banquet
Liquor & Wine

Call Liquor & Schnapps $3.25
❖ Amaretto   ❖ Smirnoff
❖ Bacardi   ❖ Canadian Club
❖ Tanqueray   ❖ Dewars
❖ Jack Daniels   ❖ Seagrams V.O.
❖ Kahlua   ❖ Jim Beam
❖ Peach Schnapps   ❖ Peppermint

Well Liquor $3.00
❖ Bourbon   ❖ Gin
❖ Rum   ❖ Scotch
❖ Tequila   ❖ Brandy

Liqueurs & Drinks
❖ White Russian or Black Russian $3.75
❖ Creme De Menthe $3.75
❖ Long Island Iced Tea $5.50
❖ Margarita $3.50
❖ Mixed Drinks $3.25
❖ Juices $1.25
❖ Sodas $1.25

Wine
❖ House Wine/ Glass $2.75
❖ House Wine/ Carafe $9.00
❖ Wine Coolers $3.00
❖ Premium Wine/ Glass $3.50
❖ Champagne/ Bottle $9.25

FIGURE 13-4 (CONTINUED.)

the catering industry of the early part of century 2000 is special events and "The Show."

The menu in Figure 13-5, featuring a Caribbean cuisine buffet, provides the central focus for an island party whose theme is further enhanced by decorations, music, entertainment, and costumes. Guests are advised of the theme in advance and tropical shirts are made available for those who came without costumes. The opening reception features specialty beverage bars and island drinks, while action stations serve the hors d'oeuvre menu in Figure 13-6. Guests are offered the opportunity to take part in beach volleyball,

---

DINNER BUFFETS

CARIBBEAN BUFFET
Tropical Fruit Salad with Papaya Seed Dressing

Mixed Salad Greens with Heart of Palm

Pickled Seafood Salad with Avocado

• • • • •

Grilled Mahi Mahi
Served with Mango and Scotch Bonnet
Pepper Beurre Blanc

*Roast Loin of Pork with
Jerk Spices and Island Rum

Tamarind Glazed Chicken, Fruit Chutney

Candied Yams, Seasonal Vegetables,
and Fried Plantains

Authentic Paella to Include
Shrimp, Chicken, Mussels and Spicy Sausage

• • • •

Key Lime Pie, Coconut Cream Pie and Banana Mousse

• • •

Freshly Baked Peabody Rolls and Butter

Freshly Brewed Coffee, Decaffeinated Coffee and Tea

*Carver Required
$85.00

$53.25 Per Person
Minimum 50 People

Please add 19% service charge and 6% tax to all prices.
All prices are subject to increase until signed Banquet Event Orders
are received by the Catering Office.

FIGURE 13-5   THE PEABODY HOTEL'S CARIBBEAN CRUISE BUFFET MENU.
(Courtesy of The Peabody Hotel, Orlando, Florida.)

CARIBBEAN RECEPTION ACTIVITY STATIONS

HOT BEACH STATION

Coconut Shrimp
Oysters Rockafeller
Clams Casino
Lobster Turnovers
Crabmeat Rangoon
Petite Crabcake, Roasted Red Pepper Remoulade

ICED ISLAND STATION

Jumbo Shrimp on Ice
Iced Crab Claws
Oysters on the Half Shell
Little Neck Clams
Smoked Mussels
Marinated Scallop Brochettes

ISLAND VEGETABLE MEDLEY

Roasted Red and Yellow Peppers
Carrot, Asparagus and Green Squash Baskets
Island Flavor Dressings
Jamaican Tomato Relish on Sweet Bread Rounds

WILD MUSHROOM STATION

*Assorted Wild Mushrooms Sautéed with Lemon
and Garlic, served with Mango Chutney*
Red Pepper Corn Cakes

FIGURE 13-6   ACTION STATIONS SERVING THE HORS D'OEUVRE MENU.
(Courtesy of The Peabody Hotel, Orlando, Florida.

create personalized "island" favors, and take a try at playing the steel drums with the band. A beach scene is established with a stage set featuring full size tropical trees, plants, and flowers, and including sand and a shallow wading pool. The dinner buffet allows guests to circulate throughout the room while the band provides Caribbean background music. After-dinner entertainment includes a Calypso floor show in which guests are invited to participate. Dancing to island themes follows with a more traditional dance band.

Concepts and themes can also be worked into small off-premise and on-premise catering functions. For example, the meeting breaks and lunches "to go" shown in Figure 13-7 can be packaged in baskets, boxes, bags, and other colorful containers for delivery to offices and conference centers, or sent

CONTINENTAL BREAKFASTS AND MID-MORNING REFRESHERS

FEELING DUCKY HEALTH BREAK
Assorted Fruit and Vegetable Juices

Multi-grain Muffins and Assorted Low Fat Fruit Muffins

Whole and Sliced Fruit

Breakfast Bars

Jellies, Jams, Cream Cheese and Honey

Assorted Yogurt

Assorted Dried Fruit and Nuts

Mineral Water

Freshly Brewed Decaffeinated Coffee Herbal Teas Skim Milk
$16.50 Per Person

PEABODY DRAKE BREAK
Orange and Grapefruit Juice

Cranberry Pecan Bread

Southern Style Biscuits with Shaved Ham and Cheddar Cheese

Assorted Muffins with Honey

Buttered Croissants

Jams, Jellies and Duck Butter

Sliced Fresh Seasonal Fruits

Whole Fresh Strawberries

Nut and Fruit Bars

Freshly Brewed Coffee, Decaffeinated Coffee and Tea
$16.50 Per Person

CITRUS BREAK
Orange Juice, Grapefruit Juice, and Lemonade

Fresh Fruit Cubes and Citrus Segments

Orange Muffins
Lemon and Poppy Seed Bread

Freshly Brewed Coffee, Decaffeinated Coffee and Tea
$13.00 Per Person

Please add 19% service charge and 6% tax to all prices.
All prices are subject to increase until signed Banquet Event Orders are received by the Catering Office.

3/99

LUNCHES TO GO

STANDARD BOX LUNCH
Choice of Roast Beef, Smoked Turkey or Ham and Cheese Sandwich
Potato Chips
Fresh Fruit
Oatmeal Cookie
$16.75 Per Person

EXECUTIVE BOX LUNCH
Rolled Lavosh with Turkey, Ham or Roast Beef and your Choice of Cheese
and
Chicken on a Whole Grain Roll with Sprouts, Avocado and Tomato

Jumbo Amaretto Cookies
$25.00 Per Person

DELUXE BOX LUNCH
Fresh Flaked Yellowfin Tuna Salad on a Kaiser Roll
and
Chicken or Beef Fajita Sandwich
with Cheddar Cheese, Guacamole and Roasted Peppers rolled in a Flour Tortilla

Fresh Vegetable Slaw or Pasta Salad

Fresh Fruit
Amaretto Cookies & Chocolate Pirouettes
$21.25 Per person

FITNESS BOX LUNCH
Sliced Fresh Fruit, Low Fat Cheddar or Cottage Cheese and Low Fat Fruit Muffins
or
Low Fat Cheese and Veggie Sandwich on Whole Grain Bread with Fruit Salad and Chips
$16.50 Per Person

All box lunches include appropriate condiments, napkins and cutlery.

Please add 19% service charge and 6% tax to all prices.
All prices are subject to increase until signed Banquet Event Orders are received by the Catering Office.

3/99

FIGURE 13-7   THE PEABODY HOTEL'S MENU OF LUNCHES "TO GO."
(Courtesy of The Peabody Hotel, Orlando, Florida.)

International Gala Dinner

Lobster Salad with Green Asparagus
Hazelnut Vinaigrette

◆▨◆▨◆▨◆▨◆▨

Warm Tomato Essence with Curried Indian Quark Dumplings

⋇◆⋇◆⋇◆⋇

Greek Cheese Baked in Phyllo with Calamata Olives

Chinese Peking Duck with Spring Onion Pancakes and Plum Sauce

⋇◆⋇◆⋇◆⋇

Crispy Cookie Shell filled with Three Flavors of Sorbet
and Fresh Berries

▨◆▨◆▨

FIGURE 13-8   MENU FOR THE BLACK-TIE GALA DINNER IN SWITZERLAND.
(Courtesy of the Swiss School of Hotel and Tourism Management.)

along with off-property meetings. Figure 13-8 details the menu for a black-tie gala dinner set in the dining room of a mountain retreat in Switzerland.

Menus for off-premise events are developed around food items that can be prepared in a central commissary or fully prepared on site. Consideration is given to items that can withstand adverse weather conditions and lengthy holding times. The menus should be coordinated to reduce the overall number of food items to be prepared while still providing corporate sponsors with customized cuisine themes.

Package Pricing

The function package most common to catering services is the wedding reception. The wedding reception plan in Figure 13-9 offers a one-hour bar, a selection of hot and cold hors d'oeuvres to be passed during the cocktail reception, a sit-down dinner entrée selection, wine to be served with dinner,

ROMANTIC RECEPTIONS
MENU PACKAGES

The Hotel del Coronado offers a variety of spectacular menus for your special occasion. Our menu packages include cocktails, hors d'oeuvres, a three-course meal with wine, and a champagne toast. Or, if you prefer, the Wedding Department can help you customize one of our menus or even create an entirely new menu according to your preferences.

BEVERAGE RECEPTION
Up To One Hour Hosted Bar Serving:
Standard Brands
Domestic Beer
Hotel del Coronado Chardonnay, Cabernet and White Zinfandel Wines
Soft Drinks
Mineral Waters
(Bartenders are based on one per 100 people.)

HORS D'OEUVRES
(Tray Passed)
Four Pieces Per Person for Lunch
Six Pieces Per Person for Dinner
Select Three From the Following:

COLD HORS D'OEUVRES
Dilled Cucumber with Shrimp
Duck Liver Mousse
Beef Carpaccio with Fresh Parmesan
Crab Bouchées
Smoked Salmon Canapés

HOT HORS D'OEUVRES
Spinach and Feta Cheese in Phyllo
Spring Rolls with Soy and Hot Mustard Dip
Sesame Shrimp Toast
Crab Stuffed Mushrooms
Mini Gourmet Pizzas

LUNCH OR DINNER
Choose a lunch or dinner selection
from the menus that follow on pages 13 through 17.
All Plated Selections Include:
Chef's Selection of Rice or Potatoes and Fresh Market Vegetables
Homemade Rolls, Butter
Hotel del Coronado Chardonnay
(Two Bottles Per Table)
Hotel del Coronado Sparkling Wine Toast
Freshly Brewed Coffee, Decaffeinated Coffee, Specialty Teas

FIGURE 13-9 THE HOTEL DEL CORONADO'S WEDDING RECEPTION MENU PACKAGES.
(Courtesy of The Hotel Del Coronado, Coronado, California.)

and a champagne toast. Wedding cake is offered as a separate item, as seen in Figure 13-10, and priced according to style and size.

The Hotel DuPont offers a variety of wedding packages based on the day of the week and/or time period. The wedding reception plan shown in Figure 13-11 includes a five-hour open bar, the champagne toast, a selection of hors d'oeuvres, a four-course sit down dinner, wine with dinner, wedding

WEDDING CAKES

Below is a sampling of our more popular wedding cakes. Our standard wedding cakes are covered with white shaved chocolate and decorated with fresh flowers or frosted with whipped cream icing and traditionally decorated in your choice of color accents. Our professional pastry chef can do a variety of other designs and decorations; please check with your Wedding Coordinator for additional information.

Michael Cornish Photography

FRENCH BAVARIAN
Layers of white or chocolate cake filled with a French Bavarian custard and raspberry filling.

SWISS BLACK FOREST
Made with layers of rich chocolate cake filled with a rich chocolate mousse and whipped cream.

CHOCOLATE MOUSSE
Four layers of white or chocolate cake filled with a rich chocolate mousse flavored with Grand Marnier syrup.

WHITE CHOCOLATE MOUSSE
Four layers of white or chocolate cake moistened with Creme de Cacaoand filled with a mousse of white chocolate and macadamia nuts.

MOCHA HAZELNUT MOUSSE
Four layers of white or chocolate cake moistened with Kahlua and filled with a rich coffee flavored mousse mixed with hazelnuts.

FIGURE 13-10   WEDDING CAKE SELECTION.
(Courtesy of The Hotel Del Coronado,
Coronado, California.)

1999 Wedding Reception Plan III
Exclusively designed for Saturday Evening

Bar Service
Five hour open Bar offering Deluxe Selections of Beverages and Imported House Wines

Toast
MUMM, CUVEE NAPA, BRUT PRESTIGE, NAPA VALLEY, N.V.

Hors d'Oeuvres—Buffet Style and Butlered

Appetizers • Salads • Desserts
Large variety available for your consideration; inclusive

Entree Selections—Featured on following pages

Imported House Wines—Served with Entree

Wedding Cakes
MARBLE, CHOCOLATE CHIP, GRAND MARNIER, LEMON
TRADITIONAL POUND CAKE, SWISS CHOCOLATE CAKE, HAZELNUT OR ALMOND NUT CAKE
Wedding Cake Knife and Individual Cake Boxes

Gourmet Coffee Table
FRESHLY BREWED COFFEE, AMARETTO COFFEE, IRISH CREME COFFEE
Cinnamon Sticks, Chocolate Shavings, Chantilly, Orange and Lemon Peels, Sugars
SWEET DELIGHTS FROM OUR PASTRY SHOP
FANCY FRIANDISES, PETIT FOURS, CHOCOLATE DIPPED STRAWBERRIES

Miscellaneous Services
Professional planning and guidance throughout Reception
Complimentary Self Parking at Hotel CarPark
Special Valet Parking for Bridal Party and Parents
Cloakroom Attendant
Choice of Color–Floor Length Linens
Complimentary Accommodations for Bride and Groom

Room Rental—May apply, please inquire with your Wedding Consultant

From 110.00 per person
(Including Gratuity)
Prices are subject to change.

10/98

1999 Wedding Reception Plan III
Exclusively designed for Saturday Evening

Hors d'Oeuvres Selection
BUTLERED
PHYLLO FLORENTINE
YAKITORI CHICKEN SKEWERS, with Dipping Sauce
SMOKED DUCK WITH SHIITAKE MUSHROOM in Wonton Cups

BUFFET
DOMESTIC AND IMPORTED CHEESE DISPLAY
Garnished with Fresh Fruits, Assorted Crackers and Home Baked French Bread
SEASONAL CRUDITEE SELECTIONS
Herb Garlic, Dill, Roquefort Dips in Pepper Shell Presentation
DELUXE CANAPE SELECTIONS—Chef's Selection
PETITE BOUCHEES FILLED WITH SHRIMP SALAD
PLUM TOMATO AND MOZZARELLA WITH PESTO ON CROUTON
BELGIUM ENDIVE HEART WITH BOURSIN AND OLIVES

Appetizers
SEASONAL FRESH FRUIT AND BERRIES
Melon Balls and Mint Leaf Garni
CHILLED FRUIT SOUP, Cinnamon Croutons
CHILLED VICHYSSOISE, Fresh Chives Garni
IMPORTED SMOKED WESTPHALIAN HAM
Medley of Seasonal Melon Garni
IN-HOUSE SMOKED SALMON with
Asparagus Cream Garni, (served hot)

WILD MUSHROOM SOUP
Herb Crouton Garni
CREAM OF ASPARAGUS SOUP
Asparagus and Chantilly on Lemon Garni
BRANDIED SEAFOOD BISQUE
Steamed Shrimp and Fresh Chives Garni
HOTEL DU PONT WEDDING SOUP, Asiago Cheese
Spinach and Miniature Meatballs Garni
CHICKEN CONSOMME CELESTINE
Parslied Julienne of Crepe Garni

Salads
MESCLUN SALAD, Raspberry Vinaigrette, Aluette and Chive Rosette
CAESAR SALAD, prepared tableside
SPINACH SALAD, Warm Balsamic Vinaigrette Dressing, Mushroom, Red Onion, Croutons,
Feta Cheese and Plum Tomatoes Garni

Desserts
"TIMBALE LES PARISIENNES"—Griottins in Chocolate Bavarian, topped with Hazelnut Creme, Chocolate Butterfly Garni
LEMON CREAM CHARLOTTE—Seasonal Berries and Raspberry Sauce
BITTERSWEET CHOCOLATE TART—Orange Sauce
CHOCOLATE ORANGE BOMBE—Chocolate Mousse enrobed in Dark Chocolate Glace, Orange Center
BAKED ALASKA FLAMBEE • CHERRIES JUBILEE FLAMBEE, Vanilla Timbale
CZARINA PARFAIT WITH STRAWBERRIES GRAND MARNIER FLAMBEE—Vanilla Parfait with Marinated Strawberries
"PAINTERS PALLET WITH TRIO OF SORBET"—Raspberry, Lemon, Apricot

Prices are subject to change.

10/98

FIGURE 13-11 THE HOTEL DU PONT'S
EVENING WEDDING RECEPTION PLAN III.
(Courtesy of The Hotel Du Pont, Wilmington,
Delaware.)

1999 Wedding Reception Plan III
Exclusively designed for Saturday Evening

Entree Selections

BAKED BREAST OF CHICKEN "MAITRE D'HOTEL", WILD MUSHROOM CREME SAUCE	110.00
Stuffed with Herb Mousse–Parmesan Crust	
BAKED SALMON FILET FLORENTINE, TARRAGON SAUCE	112.00
Stuffed with Spinach, Garnished with Fleuron	
PAN SEARED SEA BASS, BASIL SAUCE	112.00
Oven Roasted Tomatoes Garni	
BAKED SUPREME OF CHICKEN AUERSPERG AND SAUTÉED SHRIMP SCAMPI, MADEIRA SAUCE	117.00
Chicken with Duxelles of Mushrooms, Glaced–Scampi Provencale	
BROILED FILET MIGNON WITH A MUSHROOM CRUST, CABERNET SAUCE	119.00
Assorted Mushroom Garnish	
SAUTÉED VEAL MEDALLION CHAMPIGNONES, CREME SAUCE	120.00
Garnished with a Wild Mushroom Ragout	
ROASTED SLICED TENDERLOIN OF BEEF, SHIITAKE AND SHALLOT SAUCE	122.00
Carved at Tableside	
ROASTED BABY RACK OF LAMB PROVENCALE, LAMB DEMI GLACE	122.00
Carved at Tableside	
BROILED FILET MIGNON AND BAKED SALMON FILET WITH TWO SAUCES	122.00
Filet with Mushrooms—Salmon with Spinach and Fleuron, Madeira and Chervil Sauces	
BROILED FILET MIGNON AND SHRIMP SCAMPI PROVENCALE, MADEIRA SAUCE	123.00
Filet with Mushroom—Sautéed Shrimp Scampi	
GRILLED VEAL CHOP WITH TOMATO COULIS	123.00
Whipped Potato Garni	
MEDALLION OF VEAL LOIN AND SALMON FILET, EN CROUTE, TWO SAUCES	126.00
With Layers of Spinach, Wrapped in Pastry, Veal Creme and Nantua Sauces	
Carved at Tableside	
SAUTÉED VEAL MEDALLION WITH CRAB AND SHRIMP MOUSSE CAKE, TWO SAUCES	128.00
Veal with Asparagus Glaced–Crab Cake with Tomato Coulis,	
Marsala and Sweet Champagne Mustard Sauces	
SAUTÉED TOURNEDO OF BEEF WITH LOBSTER AND SCALLOP TIMBALE, TWO SAUCES	140.00
Tournedo with Herb Crust–Lobster and Scallop Timbale, Madeira and Nantua Sauces	

For a choice of (2) Pre-Selected Entrees, Please Add 5.00 per person

Prices are subject to change.

10/98

cake, and a gourmet coffee and dessert table. In contrast, Figure 13-12 is the mid-afternoon reception plan offering a four-hour open bar, a champagne toast, hors d'oeuvre stations, wedding cake, and a gourmet coffee and dessert station. The per person price for these receptions is based on the packaging of all of the selling prices and gratuities as follows:

Wedding Package Pricing

Five-hour open bar, premium brands	$ 20.00
Hors d'oeuvres	$ 15.00
Four-course dinner	$ 40.00
Wedding cake	$ 3.00
Wine with dinner	$ 6.00
Gourmet coffee table	$ 8.00
Complimentary parking	$ 3.00
Subtotal	$ 95.00
Gratuity	$ 15.00
Total per person	$110.00

In some situations, one item, such as the wedding toast or wedding cake, will be sold at cost in order to offer a more competitive package price.

1999 WEDDING RECEPTION PLAN V
Recommended for Mid-Afternoon

Bar Service
Four hour open Bar offering Deluxe Brands, including Imported House Wines

Toast
FRENCH GRATIEN & MEYER BRUT CHAMPAGNE, SAUMUR

Hors d'Oeuvres—Featured on following pages

Pasta Station—Featured on following pages

Tenderloin Station—Featured on following pages

Wedding Cakes
MARBLE, CHOCOLATE CHIP, GRAND MARNIER, LEMON
TRADITIONAL POUND CAKE, SWISS CHOCOLATE CAKE, HAZELNUT OR ALMOND NUT CAKE
Wedding Cake Knife and Individual Cake Boxes

Gourmet Coffee Table
BREWED REGULAR DEMI-TASSE, AMARETTO COFFEE, IRISH CREME COFFEE
SWEET DELIGHTS FROM OUR PASTRY SHOP
FANCY FRIANDISES, PETIT FOURS, CHOCOLATE DIPPED STRAWBERRIES

Miscellaneous Services
Professional planning and guidance throughout Reception
Complimentary Self Parking at Hotel CarPark
Special Valet Parking for Bridal Party and Parents
Cloakroom Attendant
Choice of Color Linens: White or Ivory
Complimentary Accommodations for Bride and Groom

Room Rental—May apply, please inquire with your Wedding Consultant

From 84.00 per person
(Including Gratuity)

Prices are subject to change.

10/98

1999 WEDDING RECEPTION PLAN V
Recommended for Mid-Afternoon

Hors d'Oeuvres Selections

BUTLERED
FOUR CHEESE AND ROASTED GARLIC PUFF
MINIATURE GOURMET PIZZA, Assorted Selection

BUFFET
DEEP FRIED SHRIMP, Cocktail Sauce
YAKITORI CHICKEN AND PINEAPPLE SKEWER, Dipping Sauce
KENNETT SQUARE MUSHROOM CAP, STUFFED WITH SAGE SAUSAGE
CLAMS CASINO
PLUM TOMATO AND MOZZARELLA WITH PESTO ON CROUTON
BELGIUM ENDIVE HEART WITH BOURSIN AND OLIVES
PETITE BOUCHEES FILLED WITH CRAB SALAD
DELUXE CANAPE SELECTION
Chef's Selection
DOMESTIC AND IMPORTED CHEESE DISPLAY, Fruit Garnish
BAKED BRIE WHEEL EN CROUTE, Raspberry Sauce
SAGA BLUE WHEEL, Grape Garnish
MINIATURE FRENCH BREAD, ASSORTED CRACKERS
SEASONAL CRUDITEE SELECTIONS
Herb Garlic, Dill, Roquefort Dips in Pepper Shell Presentation

Pasta Station
With Chef to Assist

SPINACH AND VEAL TORTELINI, Saffron and Pine Nuts
ZITI WITH BLACK OLIVES AND SUNDRIED TOMATOES, Lobster Sauce

Tenderloin of Beef Station
With Chef to Assist

Silver Dollar Rolls
Mustard, Horseradish Sauce, Chipolte Mayonnaise

Prices are subject to change.

10/98

FIGURE 13-12   MID-AFTERNOON WEDDING RECEPTION PLAN V.
(Courtesy of The Hotel Du Pont, Wilmington, Delaware.)

PACKAGING CATERING SERVICES

Packaging catering services into one price for customers can provide additional sources of revenues and profit by capturing a percentage of the income that would otherwise go to outside contractors such as florists, photographers, entertainment, prop and staging companies, and printers. The wedding reception plan in Figure 13-13, from the Hotel del Coronado in Coronado, California, offers a wide variety of service by its staff ranging from theme receptions to limousine service.

THE Wedding Department
AT THE HOTEL DEL CORONADO

At the Hotel del Coronado, our wedding services are as romance-enhancing as our setting. After all, we know that today's wedding couple is busy; we know you don't have time to devote to the millions of details that wedding preparations demand. We also know that today's wedding couple is exacting; we know you want your celebration to be perfect in every way.

The Wedding Department at the Hotel Del Coronado will help you plan your celebration from start to finish—and take care of every detail in between. Our professional Wedding Coordinators will help you create the wedding of your dreams. Whatever you need, we can do, so that your picture-perfect day unfolds perfectly, the way you always dreamed it would.

WE WILL CUSTOM DESIGN A WEDDING CELEBRATION JUST FOR YOU...

• Special requests are our specialty. You can decide the "look" you want; we'll make it happen. From "small and elegant" to "daring and dramatic" to "timeless and traditional," we can help you put all the pieces together so that the result is all you—and all you want your wedding to be.

• We can also create special wedding theme celebrations. Perhaps you'd like an authentic Victorian wedding, or an "island paradise" wedding (with a beachside tropical luau), or even a sophisticated "black and white" wedding. Whatever you can imagine, we can create.

WE WILL HELP YOU PLAN AND ORCHESTRATE EVERY ASPECT OF YOUR WEDDING CELEBRATION...

• We will take care of all your wedding arrangements for menus, music, flowers, photography, decorations, and everything else—every detail every step of the way!

• On your wedding day, we will oversee your entire wedding ceremony and reception activities according to your requirements and schedule.

• We will also coordinate additional wedding festivities such as bridal luncheons, bachelor/bachelorette parties, or even anniversary parties in the years to come.

• And, for a romantic Hotel del Coronado honeymoon, we will help you plan everything from breakfast in bed to champagne at sunset. Or, if you prefer, we will work with the Hotel's Del Coronado Travel to help with your out-of-town honeymoon arrangements, as well as travel arrangements or general tourist information for your out-of-town guests.

WE WILL TAKE CARE OF ALL YOUR FOOD AND BEVERAGE ARRANGEMENTS...

• From hors d'oeuvres to the main course, from cocktails to the wedding cake, our award-winning chefs will help you create a one-of-a-kind culinary celebration. (Please see the section "Romantic Receptions–Menu Packages" for more information on reception menus.)

• We will also help you estimate your expenses and plan accordingly.

FIGURE 13-13 THE HOTEL DEL CORONADO'S WEDDING RECEPTION PLAN.
(Courtesy of The Hotel Del Coronado, Coronado, California.)

The concept of traveling to a destination for both the wedding cere-mony and the reception is becoming increasingly popular. As a result, hotels and catering companies are being asked to expand their services to include ceremonies as well as reception details. The Flamingo Hilton in Las Vegas, Nevada, has created a series of packages designed to both pamper and entertain the bride and groom, as seen in Figure 13-14. From spa treatments to floral decorations to wedding night entertainment and dinner, these pack-ages are designed to include as many services as possible. By including these costs in one package, the hotels guarantee themselves all of the surrounding revenue associated with the wedding, thereby eliminating outside vendors and services from taking away potential profitable service ventures from the

FIGURE 13-14   THE FLAMINGO HILTON'S SERIES OF WEDDING PACKAGES.
(Courtesy of The Flamingo Hilton, Las Vegas, Nevada.)

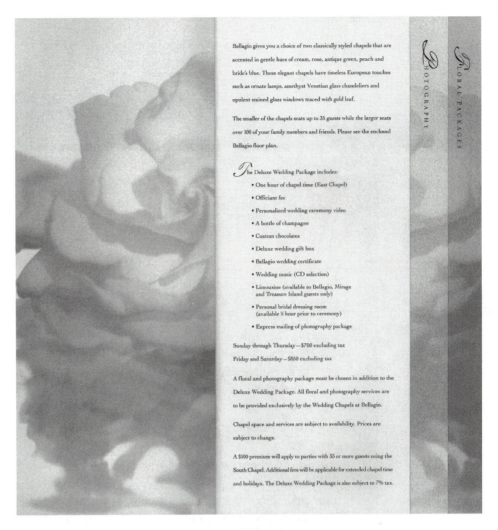

FIGURE 13-15   THE BELLAGIO HOTEL'S WEDDING CEREMONY PLAN,
BELLAGIO HOTEL, LAS VEGAS, NEVADA.
(Courtesy of Mirage Resorts, Incorporated.)

hotel. Figure 13-15 is the wedding ceremony plan from the Bellagio Hotel in Las Vegas.

To create package prices it is necessary to identify the per person costs for each service in order to identify all of the potential costs as well as revenue possibilities. For example, a basic wedding service package plan might include reception flowers, the photographer, a four- to five-piece band, and limousine service in addition to the food and beverage. The service package can be priced in the following way:

Optional service costs are calculated in this example for a reception for 200 guests. The flowers include two centerpieces for the bridal table ($150) and table centerpieces for each table ($350), for a total of $500.

$$\$500/200 = \$2.50 \text{ per person}$$

Photography services are included after the bride and groom have selected one of the package options offered by the participating studio. In this example the photography package included in the reception package price is $3000.

$$\$3000/200 = \$15.00 \text{ per person}$$

A five-piece band for a four-hour reception might be priced at $1000.

$$\$1000/200 = \$5.00 \text{ per person}$$

Limousine service for the bride from her home might be priced at $200.

$$\$200/200 = \$1.00 \text{ per person}$$

The per person cost for optional services is:

Flowers:	$ 2.50
Photographer:	$ 15.00
Five-piece band:	$ 5.00
Limousine service:	$ 1.00
Total per person:	$ 23.50
Wedding reception:	$110.00
Total per person price:	$133.50

This is added to the per person reception costs in Figure 13-11, giving a total reception package price of $133.50. The participating services have lowered their prices in order to guarantee the volume of business created by referrals from the catering service. The catering service adds on a percentage of the cost to cover its efforts in securing the optional services. In the preceding example, the catering service adds a 15 percent service charge to the optional service charge. For $23 per person this amounts to $3 per person, times a total of 200 guests, or:

$$\$3 \times 200 = \$600 \text{ extra revenue}$$

for this function.

This "one-stop shop" marketing strategy takes advantage of the customers need for time-saving convenience that simultaneously assures the quality of the optional services, creating a feeling of quality assurance for the customer.

Marketing catering service packaging requires print materials that relay the full range of service to the customer and establish a perceived value for the catering services. Figure 13-16 shows the wedding chapel package brochure layout from the Bellagio Hotel. This multipage format identifies each area of service offered by the wedding chapel.

Equipment and tents, though initially costly to stock, can be profitable for catering services who specialize in off-premise catering. Creative catering firms can also use subcontractors to gain the flexibility necessary to provide a wide range of theme parties and special events.

FIGURE 13-16 THE BELLAGIO HOTEL'S WEDDING CHAPEL PACKAGE BROCHURE LAYOUT, BELLAGIO HOTEL, LAS VEGAS, NEVADA.

(Courtesy of Mirage Resorts, Incorporated.)

Measuring Customer Satisfaction

The level of customer satisfaction of guests attending catering functions is difficult to evaluate. As discussed in the section Measure Success, the client who booked the function is the principal source of comments. A customer comment form that elicits the information that will be most useful to improving operations and assessing quality service and production levels is shown in Figure 13-17. This format outlines questions for function area conditions,

---

CATERING CUSTOMER COMMENT FORM

Customer Name: _____

Date of Function: _____

Type of Function: _____

To help us to better serve you in the future, please indicate your satisfaction with the following activities surrounding your function.

Location:
     Was it adequately accessible to your guests:_____

     Was it clean and attractive: _____
Services:
     Bar and Beverage Services:_____

     _____

     Reception or cocktail service:_____

     _____

     Main Meal Service:_____

     _____

     Quality of Food Service:_____

     Courtesy of wait staff:_____

     Audio Visual Equipment:_____

     Entertainment:_____
Function arrangements:_____

     _____

Billing:_____

Comments:_____

_____
Thank you for your comments. We welcome your calls to discuss any aspects of your function as well as suggestions that you might have to help us better meet your future needs.

FIGURE 13-17   CUSTOMER COMMENT FORM.

service activities, food and beverage products, and billing. In order for comment information to be as useful as possible, the form should be included with the thank-you letter sent immediately after the function.

Summary

The objectives of marketing—identifying customer needs, developing product/services with appropriate pricing strategies, and effectively promoting such—are activities critical to the ongoing success of catering businesses. Catering services must possess the flexibility to respond to a wide variety of customer needs. Marketing opportunities are created by customer needs that are identified for product and/or service development.

Entertainment and concept packaging provides dynamic and profitable ways to expand catering services. Decorations, entertainment, and cuisine themes combine to create festive settings for business and social functions.

Package pricing of food, beverages, and services responds to customer needs for time-saving services in the catering function planning process.

Endnote

1. American Marketing Association, 1985.

Bibliography

American Heritage. *The American Heritage Cookbook and Illustrated History of American Eating and Drinking*. New York: American Heritage Publishing Company, 1964.

Apicius, *Cookery and Dining in Imperial Rome*. Edited by Joseph Dommers Vehling, New York: Dover Publications Inc., 1977.

Boone, Louis E. and David L. Kurtz. Contemporary Marketing Wired, 9th ed. New York: Harcourt Brace Publishers, 1998.

Booth, Letha. *The Williamsburg Cookbook*. Williamsburg, VA: The Colonial Williamsburg Foundation, 1975.

Brillat-Savarin, Jean Anthelme. *The Physiology of Taste*. Edited by M. F. K. Fisher. San Francisco: North Point Press, 1986.

Cannon, Poppy and Patricia Brooks. *The President's Cookbook*. U.S.A.: Funk & Wagnalls, 1968.

Carter, Rob, Ben Day, and Philip Meggs. *Typographic Design: Form and Communication,* 2nd ed. New York: John Wiley & Sons, 1993.

Carter, Susannah. *The Frugal Colonial Housewife*. Edited by Jean McKibbin. Garden City, NY: Dolphin Books, 1976.

Chefs of ARA Dining. *A Taste for All Seasons*. Boston: The Harvard Common Press, 1990.

Delfakis, Helen, Nancy L. Scanlon, and Janis B. VanBuren. *Food Service Management*. Cincinnati: South-Western, 1991.

Glissen, Wayne. *Professional Cooking,* 4th ed. New York: John Wiley & Sons, 1999.

Glasse, Hanna. *The Art of Cookery Made Plain and Easy.* London, England: Prospect Books, 1983.

Goldblatt, Joe. *Special Events,* 2nd ed. New York: John Wiley & Sons, 1997.

Greenstein, Lou. *A la Carte: A Tour of Dining History.* Glen Cove, NY: PBC International, Inc., 1992.

Hale, William Harlan. *The Horizon Cookbook and Illustrated History of Eating and Drinking through the Ages.* New York: American Heritage Publishing Company, 1964.

Hansen, Bill. *Off-Premise Catering Management.* New York: John Wiley & Sons, 1995.

Harris, Margaret A. *Banquets.* Nashville, TN: Broadman Press, 1937.

Harrison, Molly. *The Kitchen in History.* New York: Charles Scribner's Sons, 1972.

Janson, H. W. *History of Art,* 5th ed. New York: Times Mirror Company, 1995.

Kimball, Marie. *Thomas Jefferson's Cookbook.* Richmond, VA: The University Press of Virginia, 1976.

Klapthor, Margaret Brown. *The First Ladies Cookbook.* New York: Parent's Magazine Press, 1966.

Kotschevar, Lendal H. *Management by Menu,* 3rd ed. Chicago: National Restaurant Association Educational Foundation, 1994.

———. *Quantity Food Purchasing,* 3rd ed. New York: John Wiley & Sons, 1986.

Life Saving Training for Alcohol Serving Professionals. New York: Insurance Information Institute, April 1988.

Lincoln, Anne H. *The Kennedy White House Parties.* New York: The Viking Press, 1967.

McLaughlin, Jack. *Jefferson and Monticello.* New York: Henry Holt & Co., 1988.

McPhee, John. *Oranges.* New York: Farrar, Straus & Giroux, 1996.

Miller, Jack E., Mary Porter, and Karen Eich Drummond. *Supervision in the Hospitality Industry,* 3rd ed. New York: John Wiley & Sons, 1998.

Montagne, Prosper. *The New Larousse Gastronomique.* New York: Crown Publishers Inc. 1961.

Nykiel, Ronald A. *Marketing in the Hospitality Industry.* New York: Van Nostrand Reinhold, 1983.

Old Mr. Boston Deluxe Official Bartenders Guide. Boston: Mr. Boston Distiller Corporation, 1974.

Pauli, Philip. *Classical Cooking the Modern Way,* 3rd ed. New York: John Wiley & Sons, 1999.

Powers, Tom and Clayton W. Barrows, *Introduction to Management in the Hospitality Industry,* 6th ed. New York: John Wiley & Sons, 1999.

Roberts, Laura. "Dining at the John Brown House." *Rhode Island Historical Society: Information for Tour Guides.* Providence, RI: Rhode Island Historical Society, 1980.

Root, Waverly and Richard de Rouchemont. *Eating in America.* New York: William Morrow & Co., 1976.

Rysavy, Francois and Francis Leighton. *A Treasury of White House Cooking.* New York: G. P. Putnam's Sons, 1972.

Sass, Lorna J. *To the King's Taste*. New York: Metropolitan Museum of Art, 1975.

Scanlon, Nancy A. *Quality Restaurant Service Guaranteed*. New York: John Wiley & Sons, 1998.

————. *Marketing by Menu,* 3rd ed. New York: John Wiley & Sons, 1999.

————. *Restaurant Management*. New York: John Wiley & Sons, 1993.

Scully, Terence. *The Art of Cookery in the Middle Ages*. Rochester, NY: The Boydell Press, 1995.

Sherry, John. *Legal Aspects of Foodservice Management*. Chicago: National Restaurant Association Educational Foundation, 1994.

Showman, Richard K. et al., eds. *The Papers of General Nathanael Greene,* Volume III, October 1778 to May 1779. Chapel Hill: University of North Carolina Press, 1983.

Simmons, Amelia. *American Cookery*. Grand Rapids, MI: William B. Eerdmans Publishing Company, 1965.

Szathmary, Louis. *American Gastronomy*. Chicago: Henry Regnery Co., 1974.

Tannahill, Reay. *Food in History*. New York: Stein & Day, 1973.

Toulouse-Lautrec, H. and Maurice Joyant. *The Art of Cuisine*. New York: Holt, Reinhart & Winston, 1966.

Wigger, Eugene G. *Themes, Dreams, and Schemes*. New York: John Wiley & Sons, 1997.

Zeimann, Hugo and F. L. Gillette. *The White House Cookbook*. New York: The Saalfield Publishing Co., 1906.

Index